D DAY TO VE DAY, 1944–45

uncovered editions

Series editor: Tim Coates

Other titles in the series

uncovered editions

D DAY TO VE DAY, 1944–45

GENERAL EISENHOWER'S REPORT

ON THE INVASION OF EUROPE

∞◦◊◦∞

London: The Stationery Office

Applications for reproduction should be made in writing to
The Stationery Office Limited, St Crispins, Duke Street,
Norwich NR3 1PD

ISBN 0 11 702451 1

First published by HMSO as *Report by the Supreme Commander
to the Combined Chiefs of Staff on the Operations in Europe of the
Allied Expeditionary Force* (1946).
© Crown copyright

A CIP catalogue record for this book is available from the
British Library.

Cover photograph © Popperfoto: D-Day landings, 6 June 1944.
US troops wade waist-deep through the water on to the
beaches of northern France.

Typeset by J&L Composition Ltd, Filey, North Yorkshire.

Printed in the United Kingdom for The Stationery Office by
Biddles Limited, Guildford, Surrey.
TJ978   C30   09/00

Uncovered Editions are historic official papers which have not previously been available in a popular form. The series has been created directly from the archive of The Stationery Office in London, and the books have been chosen for the quality of their story-telling. Some subjects are familiar, but others are less well known. Each is a moment of history.

Series editor: Tim Coates

Tim Coates studied at University College, Oxford and at the University of Stirling. After working in the theatre for a number of years, he took up bookselling and became managing director, firstly of Sherratt and Hughes bookshops, and then of Waterstone's. He is known for his support for foreign literature, particularly from the Czech Republic. The idea for 'Uncovered Editions' came while searching through the bookshelves of his late father-in-law, Air Commodore Patrick Cave OBE. He is married to Bridget Cave, has two sons, and lives in London.

Tim Coates welcomes views and ideas on the Uncovered Editions series. He can be e-mailed at timcoatesbooks@yahoo.com

The clear reporting of war by military leaders to Parliament is a tradition that seems to have ended since this report was prepared by General Eisenhower for the US Senate and the British Parliament.

There is a fashionable view that the decisive battle to finish the Second World War took place in a few days of hard fighting on the French coast and some difficult encounters on the Dutch-German border. General Eisenhower's account of the invasion of Europe in 1944 presents the story of a far more arduous struggle against forces whose tenacity he admired and whose skills he feared. It is a tactical account of his understanding of enemy manoeuvres, and his attempts to counter their actions.

The formality of the document is coloured by many personal touches, and the reader senses Eisenhower's growing determination to complete the task. Hindsight would have had the general take more notice of Russian activity, but that this was not obvious to him is one of the fascinations of such a contemporary document.

General Eisenhower went on to become President of the United States from 1953 to 1961, during one of the most difficult periods of the Cold War. In this edition we have retained his American spelling and reproduced the maps as they were presented in the original report.

DIRECTIVE TO SUPREME COMMANDER ALLIED EXPEDITIONARY FORCE
(*Issued* 12 *February* 1944)

1. You are hereby designated as Supreme Allied Commander of the forces placed under your orders for operations for liberation of Europe from Germans. Your title will be Supreme Commander Allied Expeditionary Force.

CHAIN OF COMMAND

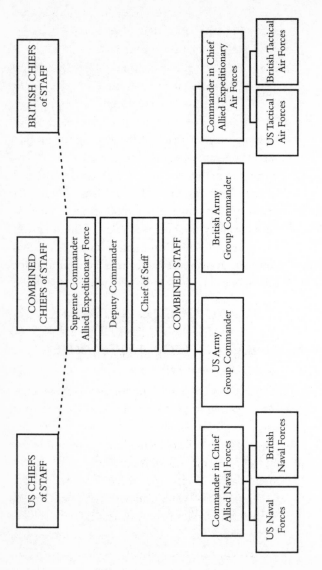

2. *Task* You will enter the continent of Europe and, in conjunction with the other United Nations, undertake operations aimed at the heart of Germany and the destruction of her armed forces. The date for entering the Continent is the month of May 1944. After adequate channel ports have been secured, exploitation will be directed towards securing an area that will facilitate both ground and air operations against the enemy.

3. Notwithstanding the target date above you will be prepared at any time to take immediate advantage of favorable circumstances, such as withdrawal by the enemy on your front, to effect a re-entry into the Continent with such forces as you have available at the time; a general plan for this operation when approved will be furnished for your assistance.

4. *Command* You are responsible to the Combined Chiefs of Staff and will exercise command generally in accordance with the diagram given. Direct communication with the United States and British Chiefs of Staff is authorized in the interest of facilitating your operations and for arranging necessary logistic support.

5. *Logistics* In the United Kingdom the responsibility for logistics organization, concentration, movement, and supply of forces to meet the requirements of your plan will rest with British Service Ministries so far as British Forces are concerned. So far as United States Forces are concerned, this responsibility will rest with the

United States War and Navy Departments. You will be responsible for the coordination of logistical arrangements on the Continent. You will also be responsible for coordinating the requirements of British and United States forces under your command.

6. *Coordination of operations of other forces and agencies*
In preparation for your assault on enemy-occupied Europe, sea and air forces, agencies of sabotage, subversion, and propaganda, acting under a variety of authorities, are now in action. You may recommend any variation in these activities which may seem to you desirable.

7. *Relationship to United Nations forces in other areas*
Responsibility will rest with the Combined Chiefs of Staff for supplying information relating to operations of the forces of the USSR for your guidance in timing your operations. It is understood that the Soviet Forces will launch an offensive at about the same time as Overlord with the object of preventing the German forces from transferring from the Eastern to the Western front. The Allied Commander in Chief, Mediterranean Theater, will conduct operations designed to assist your operation, including the launching of an attack against the south of France at about the same time as Overlord. The scope and timing of his operations will be decided by the Combined Chiefs of Staff. You will establish contact with him and submit to the Combined Chiefs of Staff your views and recommendations regarding operations

from the Mediterranean in support of your attack from the United Kingdom. The Combined Chiefs of Staff will place under your command the forces operating in southern France as soon as you are in a position to assume such command. You will submit timely recommendations compatible with this regard.

8. *Relationship with Allied Governments—the re-establishment of Civil Governments and Liberated Allied Territories and the administration of enemy territories* Further instructions will be issued to you on these subjects at a later date.

SUMMARY OF OPERATIONS IN NORTHWEST EUROPE

The broad strategy behind our main effort against the German war machine included as a highly desirable preliminary the successful conclusion of operations in North Africa and their extension across Sicily to the Italian mainland. With these accomplished, with the Mediterranean "flank" freed for Allied shipping, and with the necessary special equipment built or in sight, we were at last in a position to prepare for the final cross-Channel assault which had been agreed upon since April 1942 as our main operation against Germany. It was correctly believed that only on the historic battlefields of France and the Low Countries could Germany's armies in the west be decisively engaged and defeated.

America and England—the Western Allies—could not be sufficiently strong to undertake the assault against France until June 1944, but the broad tactical plans for the operation were completed and approved by the Combined Chiefs of Staff in August 1943, prior to my assumption of command of the European Theater in February 1944.

As part of our basic strategy, and in accordance with the task given to the Strategic Air Force under the Casablanca Directive in January 1943, the bombing of Germany, begun early in the war by the British Bomber Command, was intensified in May 1943 and continued with mounting strength to the end of the campaign. Neither the contemplated invasion of Europe nor the direct attack on the German industrial and economic system would be feasible until we had achieved supremacy over the German Air Force. This struggle for air supremacy, which had been going on throughout the war, was given added impetus by a new directive (known as Pointblank) in January 1943 which aimed at subjugating the enemy air force by the spring of 1944. In the event, German air might was thoroughly dominated by D Day and we were free to apply the immense strength of the Allied air forces in the manner we wished and to launch the invasion confident that our plans could not be seriously upset by the German Air Force. In addition, air bombardment had disrupted the German communications system, immeasurably aiding our ground forces by impeding enemy movements.

Our main strategy in the conduct of the ground campaign was to land amphibious and airborne forces on the Normandy coast between Le Havre and the Cotentin Peninsula and, with the successful establishment of a beachhead with adequate ports, to drive along the lines of the Loire and the Seine Rivers into the heart of France, destroying the German strength and freeing France. We anticipated that the enemy would resist strongly on the line of the Seine and later on the Somme, but once our forces had broken through the relatively static lines of the beachhead at St-Lô and inflicted on him the heavy casualties in the Falaise pocket, his ability to resist in France was negligible. Thereafter our armies swept east and north in an unimpeded advance which brought them to the German frontier and the defenses of the Siegfried Line.

Here enemy resistance stiffened, due primarily to the fact that he had fallen back on long-prepared defenses. At the same time our own offensive capabilities were lessened because our forces had, in their extremely rapid advance, outdistanced supply lines which had been maintained only by herculean efforts. By mid-September our armies in the north and center were committed to relatively static warfare and faced the threat of stabilization. This was true also on our southern flank, where forces landed from the Mediterranean against the south of France in mid-August had swept north through the Rhône Valley to link with the Central Group of Armies and close the Belfort Gap.

At this time we planned to attack quickly on the northern front in an effort to establish a bridgehead over the lower Rhine while the German armies were still reeling from our blows, but the airborne operation launched at Arnhem was not altogether successful in this respect, although considerable ground was gained and our positions in this area improved. Coincidentally with approving the Arnhem operation, it was directed that operations be undertaken to clear Antwerp as a supply port on the north, essential to our continued offensive action. This was accomplished in November.

While our forces moved slowly in attacks launched at selected points on the front to close to the Rhine, the enemy on 16 December launched a desperate and last counter-attack designed to throw our campaign into disorder and to delay our planned advance deep into Germany. The attack was not without its immediate effect upon us, but the sturdy defense by our forces followed by our rapid and continuous counter-attacks brought home clearly to Germany's military leaders that this last effort had failed completely and that the Nazi war machine faced inevitable disaster.

My plan was to destroy the German forces west of the Rhine along the entire length of the front in a series of heavy blows beginning in the north, and it was my expectation that the enemy would, as he had done in Normandy, stand without giving ground in a futile attempt to "fight it out" west of the Rhine. Moreover, the air forces were used intensively to destroy his mobility. By March, when our forces crossed the river north of the Ruhr, at Remagen, and at various points to the south, resistance on the eastern bank was again reduced to resemble that in France following the breakthrough, particularly because the enemy, mistaking our intentions, crowded a great part of his remaining forces into the Ruhr area.

Our attack to isolate the Ruhr had been planned so that the main effort would take place on the front of the Northern Group of Armies with a secondary effort on the Central Group of Armies' front. This secondary effort was to be exploited to the full if success seemed imminent. Clearing the left bank of the Rhine throughout its length released the means required to strengthen this secondary effort. With the capture of the Remagen bridgehead and the destruction of enemy forces west of the Rhine, the anticipated opportunity became almost a certainty.

Our forces were now able to bridge the Rhine in all sectors and they fanned out in great mobile spearheads through western Germany, disrupting communications, isolating one unit from another, and in the area of the Ruhr completing perhaps the largest double envelopment in history, rendering that great industrial area useless to support what was left of the Nazi armies.

As our forces moved rapidly eastward with the main effort in the center, to establish contact with the advancing Russian armies at the Elbe, and in turn to swing swiftly north and south to cut off any remaining refuge, the German High Command reluctantly recognized defeat and belatedly initiated negotiations which terminated with unconditional surrender on 7 May 1945.

In these campaigns the United States of America and Great Britain worked as one nation, pooling their resources of men and material. To the Combined Chiefs of Staff, through whom the directives of the two governments were expressed, we constantly accorded our admiration for their well-devised system of command by which they applied the concerted national efforts. Their political leaders, the President of the United States and the Prime Minister, also contributed immeasurably to the success of our armies in the field; once they had committed themselves to a course of action they never failed to give us unstinted support.

References in this document to the operations of Allied and enemy units are based upon contemporary reports received at SHAEF [Supreme Headquarters Allied Expeditionary Force]. Often these reports were not clear or were fragmentary. The narration of our operations in full and accurate detail will be more adequately performed by historians, who, aided by the complete records, will be able to present in their true perspective the magnificent achievements of each of the manifold units which composed the Allied Expeditionary Force.

PLANNING AND PREPARATION

THE COSSAC PLAN

In June 1942, I was ordered to England with instructions to begin preparations for United States participation in a cross–Channel attack against Fortress Europe which had been agreed upon by the American and British governments in April of that year as the Allied principal effort in the defeat of Germany. Some planning, in cooperation with

Admiral Sir Bertram H. Ramsay, General Sir Bernard C. T. Paget, and Air Chief Marshal Sir Sholto Douglas, all of the British forces, was undertaken immediately following my arrival, but this had not proceeded beyond the informal, conversational stage when I received orders to take command of the Allied attack in Northwest Africa, decided upon on 26 July. As a result of these conversations it seemed clear that the Normandy region offered the greatest chance of success in an invasion of Europe, although some individuals favored a more direct attack against the Calais area.

The successful conclusion of the campaign in North Africa was necessary before the attention of the Allies could be devoted to a full-scale attack upon Europe, but at the Casablanca Conference, in January 1943, the Combined Chiefs of Staff felt that the time had come at least to evolve the outline tactical plans for cross-Channel operations. They directed that preparations be undertaken for an emergency return to the Continent in the event that Germany suddenly should weaken sufficiently to permit our landing in the face of light or negligible resistance. While preparations for such a hoped-for contingency were necessary, the chief problem was the planning for the full-scale assault to be launched against the Continent as early as possible in 1944. Some consideration was given to the possibility that a return to the Continent in force might take place late in 1943, but a review of the build-up figures of United States forces in the United Kingdom indicated that this would be impossible and that no large-scale attack could be undertaken until 1944.

Accordingly, in preparation for the day when a Supreme Commander should be appointed to command the Allied forces, the Combined Chiefs of Staff named Lieut. Gen. Sir F. E. Morgan to the post of Chief of Staff to the Supreme Allied Commander (designate). Using the initials of this title, the organization was called Cossac, and, with a staff composed of both United States and British personnel, work began upon the creation of the assault plan against Fortress Europe. By July 1943 the Outline Plan for Overlord, as the operation was called, was ready for presentation to the Combined Chiefs of Staff. In August of the same year the Combined Chiefs, with the concurrence of President Roosevelt and Prime Minister Churchill, approved the plan at the Quebec Conference and ordered the completion of its details insofar as this was possible prior to the arrival of a Supreme Commander.

In the creation of the plan, Cossac had been instructed on 25 May, through a supplementary directive from the Combined Chiefs of Staff, that the target date for the operation was to be 1 May 1944, and that simultaneous landing-craft lift for the assault forces would be limited to craft sufficient to load five divisions. A total of 29 divisions in all was to be available for the assault and immediate build-up. Of these, five infantry divisions were to be simultaneously loaded in the landing craft, three to assault initially with two in the immediate follow-up. In addition, two airborne divisions were to be employed and two other infantry divisions were to follow as quickly as turn-around shipping became available. In all, then, nine divisions were to be initially employed in the assault and immediate follow-up period. The remaining 20 divisions were to be available for movement to the lodgement area as quickly as the build-up could be achieved.

The fact that simultaneous landing-craft lift for only five divisions had been allotted made mandatory a definite concentration of effort. The basic factor in determining where the initial assault was to be made lay in the requirement that the lodgement area should contain sufficient port facilities to maintain a force of some 26 to 30 divisions and enable that force to be augmented by follow-up shipments from the United States or elsewhere of additional divisions and supporting units at the rate of three to five divisions per month.

For such purposes, the Pas-de-Calais region offered advantages in that its proximity to England would facilitate air support and a quick turn-around for shipping. On the other hand, its beaches, while favorable to the actual landing, lacked good exits to the hinterland. Also the area was the most formidably defended on the whole French coast and was a focal point of the enemy fighter air forces disposed for defense. Moreover, the area did not offer good opportunities for expansion of the lodgement zone, and it would have been necessary to develop the beachhead to include either the Belgian ports as far as Antwerp or the Channel ports westward to include Le Havre and Rouen.

A second area considered was the Cotentin Peninsula where it was recognized that the assaulting forces would initially have a reasonable chance of success and would additionally gain the valuable port of Cherbourg. This area, however, lacked suitable airfields, and might have become a trap for the assault troops, since the enemy could, with relatively light forces, defend the neck of the peninsula, bottling Allied troops within the beachhead and denying them any expansion into the interior of France.

In the Caen sector the defenses were relatively light and the beaches were of high capacity and sheltered from the prevailing winds. The terrain, moreover, was suitable for airfield development and for the consolidation and subsequent expansion of the beachhead. Air support to the initial area at such a distance from the English coast presented the chief difficulty. From a beachhead in the Caen sector it was believed that it would be possible to seize the Brittany ports between Cherbourg and Nantes, and through them to build up sufficient forces for the subsequent advance eastward.

In view of these considerations, it was decided that the initial landing on the Continent should be effected in the Caen area with the subsequent seizure of a lodgement area comprising the Cherbourg–Brittany ports.

The assault itself, according to the Cossac plan, was to be launched with a short air bombardment of the beach defenses, after which three assault divisions would be landed on the Caen beaches, followed by the equivalent of two tank brigades and a regimental combat team. At the same time, airborne forces were earmarked for the capture of the town of Caen, while subsidiary operations were to be undertaken by commandos and airborne units to neutralize certain coast defenses and to seize important river crossings. The object of the assault forces was to occupy the general line Grandcamp–Bayeux–Caen.

Action subsequent to the assault and early build-up was to take the form, under this initial plan, of a strong thrust southward and southwestward with a view to destroying enemy forces, acquiring sites for airfields, and gaining depth for a turning movement into the Cotentin Peninsula directed on Cherbourg. When sufficient depth had been gained, a force was to advance into the Cotentin and seize Cherbourg. At the same time a thrust was to be made to deepen the beachhead southeastward to cover the establishment of additional airfields in the area southeast of Caen. It was estimated that within 14 days of the initial assault Cherbourg would be taken and the beachhead extended to include the general line Trouville–Alençon–Mont-St-Michel. By that time it should have been possible to land some 18 divisions and to have in use about 14 airfields from which 28 to 33 fighter-type squadrons could operate.

Later operations based upon this plan were necessarily to be dictated to a large extent by enemy reactions. If he proved sufficiently weak, an immediate advance might be undertaken to seize Le Havre and Rouen. More probably, however, it was felt that it would be necessary to take and bring into use the Brittany ports first in order to build up forces sufficient to breach the line of the Seine upon which it was expected the enemy would make a stand with the bulk of his forces. For this purpose a thrust southward would be made to seize Nantes and St-Nazaire, followed by Brest and the smaller Brittany ports. The beachhead would be consolidated on the left flank along the Eure River from Dreux to Rouen and thence along the Seine to the sea, while Chartres, Orléans, and Tours were occupied. As soon as lines of communications in this area were developed and sufficient air forces established, operations would be instituted against Paris and the Seine ports, with subsidiary operations to clear the Biscay ports for the reception of additional United States troops and supplies.

In broad outline, this was the plan proposed for the assault upon Nazi Europe. Following approval by the Combined Chiefs of Staff and in accordance with their instructions, the Cossac organization proceeded with more detailed planning, and by 29 November sufficient progress had been made to permit of directives being issued to 21 Army Group and to the United States First Army.

DEVELOPMENT OF PLAN OVERLORD

During the period of this staff planning for Overlord, I was personally occupied with the Mediterranean campaigns and was not in close touch with the plans evolved for the campaign in Northwest Europe, nor did I during this period know that I would ultimately be connected with the operation. In December, however, I was notified by the Combined Chiefs of Staff that I had been appointed Supreme Commander of the Allied Expeditionary Force and that prior to assuming command in England early in January I was to return briefly to Washington for conferences with General Marshall and the Combined Chiefs.

Prior to leaving my Headquarters in North Africa, I was able early in December 1943 to see a copy of the Outline Plan of Overlord and to discuss it with Field Marshal (then General) Sir Bernard L. Montgomery, who was to command 21 Army Group, and with my Chief of Staff, Lieut. Gen. (then Maj. Gen.) Walter B. Smith. I instructed them to consider the plan in detail upon their arrival in England because, while agreeing with the broad scope of the operation and the selection of the assault area, I nevertheless felt that the initial assaulting forces were being planned in insufficient strength and committed on too narrow a front. This they did, and shortly after my arrival in London on 15 January, I was able, with them and my other commanders, to reach an agreement which altered the Overlord operation in this respect.

While my appointment as Supreme Commander did not become official until the receipt of a directive★ from the Combined Chiefs of Staff on 14

★ The text of the directive is reproduced at the beginning of this report, along with the organization chart. It should be noted that the US Strategic Air Forces in Europe and the RAF Bomber Command remained under the control of the Combined Chiefs of Staff.

February, and while the status of my Headquarters—to be known as SHAEF—was not recognized until the following day, the basic work of planning continued during this transitional period. The staff brought into being as Cossac came under my control was greatly expanded as the pressure of time and the vast scope of our work required.

I patterned my Headquarters upon the closely integrated Allied establishment which it had been my policy to maintain at AFHQ in the Mediterranean, and in this respect I was fortunate in obtaining for my staff men whose proved ability had already been demonstrated in previous campaigns—Air Chief Marshal Sir Arthur W. Tedder as my Deputy Supreme Commander, General Walter B. Smith as my Chief of Staff, and Lieut. Gen. Sir Humfrey M. Gale as Chief Administrative Officer. General Morgan remained as Deputy Chief of Staff, his detailed knowledge of tactical plans making him absolutely indispensable.

Relationship between SHAEF and the Headquarters of my Commanders-in-Chief for the Navy, Army, and Air Forces was established on the operational planning level through a Joint Planning Staff which closely integrated the work of all. The Headquarters of Cossac had been located at Norfolk House, St James' Square, with an annex at 80, Pall Mall, and it was here initially that my own Headquarters came into being. However, I was convinced by past experience that a Headquarters located in the heart of a great city would not be as unified as one located elsewhere. Accordingly SHAEF was moved in March to Bushy Park, near Kingston-on-Thames. Here we studied the operation in detail and ironed out all the numerous and frequently vexing problems relating to so vast an undertaking.

The chief changes which we were to make in the assault plan were considered at the first meeting which I held with my Commanders-in-Chief at Norfolk House on 21 January. Field Marshal Montgomery (Commanding General, 21 Army Group), Admiral Sir Bertram H. Ramsay (Commander of the Allied Naval Expeditionary Force), and Air Chief Marshal Sir Trafford Leigh-Mallory (Commander of the Allied Expeditionary Air Force) reviewed operation Overlord as a whole with me and were in agreement upon certain amendments to the plan.

The Cossac plan called for an initial assaulting force of three divisions. I had felt when I originally read the Overlord plan that our experiences in the Sicilian campaign were being misinterpreted, for, while that operation was in most respects successful, it was my conviction that had a larger assault force been employed against the island beachheads our troops would have been in a position to overrun the defenses more quickly. Against the better prepared defenses of France I felt that a three-division assault was in insufficient strength, and that to attain success in this critical operation a minimum of five divisions should assault in the initial wave. Field Marshal Montgomery was in emphatic agreement with me on this matter, as were also Admiral Ramsay and Air

Chief Marshal Leigh-Mallory, even though a larger assault force raised great new problems from both the naval and air points of view.

In addition to increasing the assault force from three to five divisions, I felt that the beach area to be attacked should be on a wider front than that originally envisaged. Particularly, it was considered that an attack directly against the Cotentin Peninsula should be included in the plan, with a view to the speedy conquest of Cherbourg. In the event that our troops were able to attain a high degree of surprise in the attack, they would be in a better position to overwhelm the strung-out defenses before the enemy could regroup or mass for a counter-attack. Conversely, in the event of strong resistance, we would be more advantageously situated, on a wider front and in greater force, to find "soft spots" in the defense.

The original Cossac plan included the beachhead areas from Courseulles in the east to Grandcamp in the west. We decided to extend this area eastward to include the Ouistreham beaches, feeling that this would facilitate the seizure—by rapidly securing the eastern flank—of the important focal point of Caen and the vital airfields in the vicinity. Westward, we decided that the assault front should be widened to include the Varreville beaches on the eastern side of the Cotentin Peninsula itself. A strong foothold on the peninsula and a rapid operation to cut its neck would greatly speed up the capture of the port of Cherbourg.

For the operation against the neck of the Cotentin to be successful, it was believed that two airborne divisions should be employed in support of the troops assaulting the Varreville beaches, still leaving one airborne division to hold vital bridges in the Orne–Dives Rivers area to the northeast of Caen. Field Marshal Montgomery and Admiral Ramsay were in agreement on this point, but Air Chief Marshal Leigh-Mallory saw technical difficulties which it was necessary to consider closely.

It was his feeling, both then and subsequently, that the employment of airborne divisions against the South Cotentin would result in landing losses to aircraft and personnel as high as 75–80%. In the face of this estimate, however, I was still convinced of the absolute necessity of quickly overrunning the peninsula and attaining the port of Cherbourg, vital to the support and maintenance of our land forces. Without the airborne divisions an assault against the Varreville beaches would have been most hazardous, since our attack here could only be on a one-division front. Behind the landing beach was a lagoon, traversed only by a few causeways; the exits of these had to be captured from the rear, or else the strip of beach would quickly become a death trap. In addition, this beach was separated from the other four beaches to be assaulted by an estuary and marsh lands which would have effectively prevented the junction and link-up of the forces for several days, permitting the enemy in this sector more easily to dislodge us and threaten our right flank. Support by the airborne troops was essential, and I ultimately took upon myself the heavy responsibility of deciding that the airborne operation against the Cotentin be carried out. The decision, once taken, was loyally and efficiently executed by the airborne forces, and it is to them that immeasurable credit for the subsequent success of the western operation belongs. The airborne landing losses proved only a fraction of what had been feared, amounting in fact to less than 10%.

Our decisions to strengthen the forces employed in the initial assault, to widen the area of attack, and to employ the airborne forces in the Cotentin rather than at Caen, were communicated to the Combined Chiefs of Staff on 23 January, and at the same time I brought up the subject of the target date for the operation.

In the original plan, the target date for the D-Day assault had been 1 May. A new factor, however, which made me doubt that the date could be adhered to was our deficiency in assault craft for the larger five-division attack. In the Cossac plan, three divisions in the assault and two immediate follow-up divisions, a total of five, were to be preloaded in assault craft. Sufficient craft for five divisions had been planned. The new plan, calling for five divisions in the assault, still retained the two follow-up divisions, requiring therefore sufficient craft to preload seven divisions. There was considerable doubt that the additional craft could be made available by 1 May, and I informed the Combined Chiefs of Staff that, rather than risk failure with reduced forces on that date, postponement of the target date for a month would be preferable if I could be assured of then obtaining the strength required. My planners had advised me that a month's additional production of assault craft in both Great Britain and the United States would go far toward supplying the deficiency they then foresaw for the earlier date.

From the air point of view, the extension of the target date would afford a longer opportunity for the strategic bombing of Germany and the wearing down of German air strength. In addition, the tactical bombing of railheads and transportation centers, the preliminary softening of fortifications on the Channel coast, and the diversionary heavy air attacks in the Pas-de-Calais could be undertaken with greater thoroughness. The training of the invasion forces, and particularly the troop-carrier crews for the airborne operations, could also be carried on more thoroughly.

The Navy, moreover, desired additional time for the training of the assault craft crews and for the delivery and assembly of the extra vessels needed in the enlarged attack. From the naval viewpoint a postponement of the target date to the first of June was preferable to any briefer postponement, say of two weeks, since an early June date guaranteed the favorable tides necessary for the beach operations as well as a full moon.

From the strategic point of view the postponement seemed desirable, since weather conditions at the end of May would be likely to be more favorable for the mounting of a large-scale Russian offensive to assist the Overlord operation. Additionally, the situation in the Mediterranean might be sufficiently resolved by that time to preclude the necessity of an operation against the south of France closely coordinated with our western assault. The German forces in that theater might be so heavily engaged by our armies that a diversionary and containing assault would not be required in direct and immediate assistance to Overlord.

The Combined Chiefs of Staff agreed on 1 February that Overlord would be mounted with a target date not later than 31 May. We indicated that the exact date of the assault should be left open and subject to weather conditions prevailing during the first week of June. Later, on 17 May, I set 5 June as the "final" date for the assault, subject, of course, to last-minute revision if the weather should prove unfavorable. The selection of this date was based primarily on tidal and light conditions. It was necessary that the tide be sufficiently low to enable the initial assault elements to land and prepare lanes through the heavy obstacles which were above water only at or near a low tide. Also, this tidal condition had to coincide with a period of sufficient light to permit visual bombing by aircraft of the beach defenses and bombardment by the naval vessels. The dates of 5, 6, and 7 June were all acceptable on this basis, but any postponement beyond these dates would have necessitated waiting until 19 June for a similar favorable tidal period. This later date would have necessitated the acceptance of moonless conditions.

Strategically, the postponement of the target date proved to be a sound measure. By 1 May, the original date, our forces in Italy were still encountering heavy resistance south of Rome along the Gustav Line, while Russian forces were occupied in the Crimea and still forming for a western attack. By the first week in June, however, Rome had fallen, Kesselring's forces were in retreat, the Crimea had been cleared, and Germany was nervously predicting an all-out Russian offensive. Furthermore, the enemy had been keyed up to a 1 May Allied offensive from the United Kingdom, to judge from his "invasion any day now" feelers. The month's delay served perhaps to lull him into believing that we would now not attack until some time in July. The month's postponement also guaranteed, as events proved, the availability of assault craft and shipping to move the staggering number of men and vehicles required for the D-Day assault.

It should be noted here, however, that had it been possible to adhere to the initial date, the weather would have been much superior for the invasion than was the weather encountered during the first week of June. During the first week of May, in the full-moon period, the Channel was consistently calm and the skies cloudless, ideal both for naval and air operations. The weather was strikingly similar to that which favored England during the disastrous days of Dunkirk. In the first week of June, on the other hand, the Channel was choppy at best, with heavy seas running most of the time. The skies were overcast, and days of rain hampered air operations. The full extent to which this unfavorable weather influenced our operations will be considered later in this report.

With the settlement of the basic problems essential to firm planning—the size of the assault and the target date—the Army, Navy, and Air Forces were in a position to develop their final plans for the attack against the Normandy beaches. The best method of controlling the effort of the Strategic Air Forces was still under discussion and will be referred to later in the section on "Preparatory Operations." Immediately under my command in the pre-D-Day period were the Commanders-in-Chief already mentioned, Field Marshal Montgomery, Admiral Ramsay, and Air Chief Marshal Leigh-Mallory.

Within 21 Army Group, Field Marshal Montgomery had under his command the Canadian First Army (2 Corps) under Lieut. Gen. H. D. G. Crerar; the British Second Army (1, 8, 12, and 30 Corps) under Lieut. Gen. (then Maj. Gen.) Sir M. C. Dempsey; the British airborne troops (1 and 6 Divisions) under Lieut. Gen. F. A. M. Browning; and the United States First Army (V, VII, VIII, and XIX Corps, with the attached airborne troops of the 82nd and 101st Divisions) under General (then Lieut. Gen.) Omar N. Bradley. While plans called for eventual organization of American and British ground forces each under their own commander, directly responsible to me, the initial assault was foreseen as a single battle, closely interrelated in all its parts, and requiring the supervision of a single battle-line commander. All agreed on this necessity.

The army plans for the assault and subsequent build-up period were prepared, pursuant to periodical directives from Supreme Headquarters, by the planning staffs of the American and British Army Headquarters, coordinated by 21 Army Group Headquarters, and subsequently reviewed by the G-3 Division of my staff under Maj. Gen. H. R. Bull and his deputy, Maj. Gen. J. F. M. Whiteley. Constant revision of the plans was necessary throughout the early months of 1944, due primarily to the continuing uncertainty as to the exact number of assault craft to be made available for the loading of the troops. Even with the extra month's production of craft in both the United States and the United Kingdom, it seemed that sufficient lift would not be forthcoming, and it became necessary during this period to consider drawing craft from either the Mediterranean or the Pacific to round out the figure needed. This entailed a constant exchange of views between theaters and between my Headquarters and the Combined Chiefs of Staff until the problem was finally settled—as late as 24 March. Since the problem also was related to the mounting of operation Anvil, the assault against southern France from the Mediterranean, reference will be made to the matter again in this report. Suffice it to say here, however, that before firm planning can be undertaken on any major amphibious operation, involving, as such an operation does, the forces of both the Army and the Navy, the primary factor of assault craft must be definitely determined. This decision should be made as early as humanly possible, for it is a matter of the first priority.

Based upon the Cossac plan for the assault, together with the revisions as to date and size of attack which have been mentioned, the final plan produced by 21 Army Group and approved by Supreme Headquarters thus came into being.

Broadly, the army plan of attack involved a D-Day assault on a five-divisional front on the beaches between Ouistreham and Varreville with the immediate purpose of establishing beachheads to accommodate follow-up troops. The initial objectives of the attack included the capture of Caen, Bayeux, Isigny, and Carentan, with the airfields in their vicinity, and the essential port of Cherbourg. Thereafter our forces were to advance on Brittany with the object of capturing the ports southward to Nantes. Our next main aim was to drive east on the line of the Loire in the general direction of Paris and north across the Seine, with the purpose of destroying as many as possible of the German forces in this area of the west.

Because it was ultimately intended to supply the United States forces engaged in Europe directly from American ports, American troops were assigned the right flank in the operations. They were to take Cherbourg and the Brittany ports as supply bases, while the British, driving east and north along the coast, were to seize the Channel ports, as far north as Antwerp, through which they were to be supplied directly from England.

On the right, American forces of General Bradley's First Army were to assault the Varreville (Utah) beach and the St-Laurent (Omaha) beach. Lieut. Gen. (then Maj. Gen.) J. Lawton Collin's VII Corps was to land with the 4th Infantry Division in the assault on Utah beach just north of the Vire Estuary. During the early morning hours of D Day the 82nd and 101st Airborne Divisions were to drop in the area southeast and west of Ste-Mère-Eglise where their mission was to capture the crossings of the Merderet River, secure the line of the Douve River as a barrier, and assist the landing of the 4th Infantry Division at the beach. By the end of D Day, we anticipated that VII Corps, with the airborne divisions under command, would control the area east of the Merderet from just south of Montebourg to the Douve.

Lieut. Gen. (then Maj. Gen.) Leonard T. Gerow's V Corps planned its attack on a 7,000-yard stretch of beach known as Omaha, on the northern coast of Calvados near St-Laurent. One combat team of the 29th Infantry Division on the right and one combat team of the 1st Infantry Division on the left, both under the command of the 1st Infantry Division, were to assault in the initial wave.

The primary objective of VII Corps, supported by the airborne divisions, was to cut the Cotentin Peninsula against attack from the south, and, driving northward, to seize the port of Cherbourg—we hoped by D plus 8. While Cherbourg was being taken, troops of V Corps and follow-up forces were to drive south towards St-Lô, seizing the city by D plus 9. With the reduction of the Cotentin Peninsula, the forces engaged there and follow-up forces subsequently landed were also to turn south, join with the forces landed over Omaha, and drive to a line Avranches–Domfront by approximately D plus 20.

Forces of General (then Lieut. Gen.) George S. Patton's Third Army were, during this period, to be landed across the American beaches and initially come under the operational control of First Army, passing to the control of Third Army when its headquarters moved to the Continent at about D plus 30. While First Army was to make an initial turning movement into the Brittany Peninsula in the direction of St-Malo, it was planned that Third Army, with its growing forces, would take over the reduction of the peninsula and the Brittany ports from First Army on this same date. First Army, then, freed of the responsibility for Brittany, was to turn its forces south and east along the Loire, reaching a line beyond Angers–Le Mans on the Sarthe River by D plus 40.

British and Canadian forces, landing on the Ouistreham (Sword), Courseulles (Juno), and Asnelles (Gold) beaches were in the meantime to protect the left flank of the Allied forces against what was expected to be the main German counter-attack from the east. An additional important task was to gain the ground south and southwest of Caen, favorable for the development of airfields and for the use of our armor. The first assault was to be made by three divisions of General Dempsey's British Second Army;

the 3 Canadian and 3 British Infantry Divisions of 1 Corps, and the 50 Infantry Division of 30 Corps. British 6 Airborne Division was to be dropped behind the beach defenses to secure the vital bridges over the Caen Canal and the Orne River between Caen and the sea, together with certain other objectives in that locality. These forces with follow-up troops, advancing southward, were to occupy territory inland to a line Vire–Falaise, including the Caen road center, by about D plus 20.

After occupation of this area, the British forces were to continue expansion along the general line of the Seine, advancing on the left of the American divisions until, by D plus 90, the general Allied front was to stand on the Seine from Le Havre to Paris on the north, and along the Loire from Nantes to Orléans, Fontainebleau and Paris on the south and east. In the west the Brittany Peninsula was to be fully occupied. By D plus 90 the armies were to be ready to take Paris, force the crossing of the Seine in strength in an advance northward to the Somme, and continue east along the Marne in a drive toward the German frontier.

Early in May 1944 after I had approved Field Marshal Montgomery's plans for establishing our forces on the Continent, and for placing them in position prepared for eruption from the lodgement area, the planning staff presented their visualization of the several lines of action which might be followed for the continuance of the campaign, up to and including the final period, for a drive into the heart of Germany. The favored line of action was sketched on a map of the Continent. It contemplated an advance on a broad front with the main effort constantly on the left (north) flank and with another thrust toward Metz, passing north and south of Paris in the event the Germans determined to hold it as a fortress, joining up with General Devers' forces coming from the south to cut off southwest France; penetration of the Siegfried Line, still with the main effort in the north; elimination of the German forces west of the Rhine either by decisive defeat or by pressure which would force their withdrawal, with particular emphasis on the area from Cologne–Bonn to the sea; a power crossing of the Rhine north of the Ruhr, coupled with a secondary effort via the Frankfurt Corridor, the two thrusts to join in the general area of Kassel, encircling the Ruhr. Thereafter it was anticipated that the destruction of remaining German strength would be easy.

This estimate made at this early date is particularly interesting since the proposed scheme of maneuver was practically identical with that which was followed during the campaign.

Later in this report is described the supporting air plan, success in which was vital to the attainment of the ambitious objectives prescribed for the land forces. Also necessary to an understanding of the whole battle is a knowledge of the information we possessed, prior to the assault, regarding the enemy dispositions, a summary of which is also included in a subsequent section.

In the initial phases of Overlord, Field Marshal Montgomery, whom I had designated as tactical commander of the early land battles, was to have operational control of all land forces, including the United States First Army, until the growing build-up of the American forces made desirable the establishment of an independent Army Group. When sufficient forces had disembarked on the Continent, a United States Army Group was to come into being, equal both operationally and administratively to the British 21 Army Group, which latter was to continue under Field Marshal Montgomery's command. Although no definite time was set for this, it was estimated that it would take place when Third Army had become fully operational; the date was also dependent, of course, upon the progress of the initial land battles beyond the beachhead area where, as already pointed out, simplicity of command in a narrow space was desirable.

In the matter of command, it can be said here that all relationships between American and British forces were smooth and effective. Because of certain fundamental national differences in methods of military supply and administration, it was early agreed that no unit lower than a corps of one nationality would be placed under command of the other nationality except where unavoidable military necessity made this imperative.

To carry out the mission of invading Western Europe, there were to be available, by D Day, in the United Kingdom 37 divisions: 23 Infantry, 10 armored, and 4 airborne. These were to be employed in the assault and subsequent build-up period in France. As the campaign progressed, the flow of divisions to the Continent was to be maintained at a rate of three to five divisions per month, and this flow was to be augmented by the divisions entering the European Theater with the assault against southern France from the Mediterranean. Ultimately, at the time of the German surrender, I had under command a total of 90 divisions: 61 American, 13 British, 5 Canadian, 10 French, and 1 Polish. These divisions, with anti-aircraft, anti-tank, and tank units habitually attached, averaged about 17,000 in combat strength, well over twice the strength of Russian divisions. In addition there were three French divisions which were not completely equipped, and lesser units of Czech, Belgian, and Dutch forces on the Continent, as well as the units of the French Forces of the Interior. Our Headquarters estimated that, at times, the value of these latter French forces to the campaign amounted in manpower to the equivalent of 15 divisions, and their great assistance in facilitating the rapidity of our advance across France bore this out.

The initial success of the land forces in the assault against Northwest Europe was dependent upon the operations of the Allied Naval Expeditionary Force under the command of Admiral Ramsay. In his operational orders issued on 10 April, he clearly defined the Navy's mission to those under his command: "The object of the Naval Commander-in-Chief is the safe and timely arrival of the assault forces at their beaches, the cover of their landings, and subsequently the support and maintenance and the rapid build-up of our forces ashore." To accomplish this mission successfully months of detailed planning and training, closely coordinated with the ground and air forces, were necessary.

Reports on the North African and Sicilian Campaigns have made mention of the magnitude of the naval forces involved, but the sea power displayed there was to fade by comparison with the forces to be employed in this great amphibious assault. The extent of the problem of berthing, loading, and moving the forces involved may be realized with the knowledge that over 5,000 ships and 4,000 additional "ship-to-shore" craft were to be engaged in the Channel operations during the assault and build-up period. That everything went according to plan is a remarkable tribute to the hard work, coordinated effort, and foresight of the thousands engaged in the initial planning and training and, as Admiral Ramsay stated in his report, to the "courage of the tens of thousands in the Allied navies and merchant fleets who carried out their orders in accordance with the very highest traditions of the sea."

With the expansion of the assault from a three-divisional to a five-divisional attacking force, increased naval forces were necessary both to protect the invasion fleet *en route* and to bring added fire power to bear on the beaches. These were allotted by the Combined Chiefs of Staff on 15 April 1944. The chief units in the final naval forces included 6 battleships, 2 monitors, 22 cruisers, and 93 destroyers.

Under the naval plan the assault area for the naval forces was bounded on the north by the parallel of 49° 40′ N, and on the west, south and east by the shores of the Bay of the Seine. This area was subdivided into two Task Force Areas, American and British, the boundary between them running from the root of the Port-en-Bessin western breakwater in an 025° direction to the meridian of 0° 40′ W, and thence northward along this meridian to latitude 49° 40′ N. Within these defined areas, the Western Task Force, operating in the American zone, was under the command of Rear Adm. A.G. Kirk, and the Eastern Task Force, operating in the British zone, under the command of Rear Adm. Sir P. L. Vian. The Western and Eastern Task Forces were again subdivided to include, altogether, five assault forces, each responsible for the landing of an assault division upon one of the five beach areas, and two follow-up forces. The assault forces were known for the American zone as Force "U" and Force "O" (Utah and Omaha) and were under the command respectively of Rear Adm. D. P. Moon and Vice Adm. (then Rear Adm.) J. L. Hall, Jr. For the British zone the assault forces were similarly known as Force "S," Force "J," and Force "G" (Sword, Juno, and Gold), and were commanded by Rear Adm. A. G. Talbot, Commodore G. N. Oliver, and Rear Adm. C. Douglas-Pennant.

In order to ensure the safe arrival of the assault troops on the beaches, the Navy was to provide adequate covering forces to protect the flanks of the routes of our assault and was, with mine-sweeping vessels, to clear the Channel ahead of the assault craft. For this latter purpose 12 mine-sweeping flotillas were to be employed. Once within range of the beachhead area, the heavy naval guns were to neutralize the enemy coastal batteries, supplementing the work of the air forces, and then, as the landing craft drove inshore, there was to be an intense bombardment of the beach defenses by every gun that could be brought to bear.

Some consideration had initially been given to the possibility of assaulting at night in order to obtain the maximum surprise, but it was decided that the lessons of the Pacific should be adhered to, and that, possessing superiority in air and naval forces, the assault against strong defenses should take place by day. This was palpably advantageous to the Navy in the coordinated movement of a vast fleet in relatively narrow waters. H Hour varied for most of the five assault forces, due to varying beach conditions such as the necessity for higher tide to cover certain rock obstacles and the length of time needed to remove enemy obstructions. Force "U" was to touch down at 0630 hours while Force "J" was not to land until 35 minutes later.

With the success of the assault determined, the naval forces were to maintain swept channels between France and England through which supplies and reinforcements could be shuttled to the Continent. In view of the initial limited port facilities and the fact that we did not anticipate seizing the Brittany ports for some time after the assault, the Navy was also charged with providing for the establishment off the French coast of five artificial anchorages (Gooseberries). Two of these were subsequently to be expanded into major artificial harbors (Mulberries); through these the bulk of our stores were to be unloaded during the early stages of the campaign. To provide oil and gasoline in bulk, the Navy was also to set up tanker discharge points off the French coast and to establish cross-Channel submarine pipe lines.

By 26 April, the five naval assault forces were assembled in the following areas: Force "U," Plymouth; Force "O," Portland; Force "S," Portsmouth; Force "G," Southampton; and Force "J," Isle of Wight. The two follow-up forces, Force "B" and Force "L," were assembled in the Falmouth–Plymouth and Nore areas. In addition to the berthing problems inherent in the assembly of these seven forces, other space had to be found for the many ships and craft which were assigned the tasks of supply, maintenance, repair, and reinforcement. The berthing problem was one of major proportions, but it was solved, as Admiral Ramsay reported, by making use of every available berth from Milford Haven to Harwich. Many units had, additionally, to be berthed in the Humber, at Belfast, and in the Clyde.

The concentration of ships in southern ports was bound, we felt, to be detected by the enemy and would thus give him some indication that our assault was about to be launched. In order to confuse him in this respect, arrangements were made with the British Admiralty to have the large number of commercial ships destined for the Thames and also the ships to be used in later supply convoys to our forces on the Continent held in Scottish ports until the operation was under way. The concentration of shipping thus spread itself automatically throughout the whole British Isles and was not confined to a single area. As was the case against Sicily, we did not believe that the growing preparations and the size of our forces could be entirely concealed from the enemy. We hoped, though, to be able to confuse him as to the time of the assault and the exact beachhead area of attack. In this we were to be successful for a variety of reasons which I shall consider later.

The air plan in support of the amphibious operation consisted of two parts, the preparatory phase and the assault phase, and was brought into being under the direction of Air Chief Marshal Leigh-Mallory, commanding the Tactical Air Forces. These forces, composed of the British Second Tactical Air Force and the US Ninth Air Force, were to operate in direct support of the land armies. The Strategic Air Forces also would be given definite tactical responsibilities during critical periods, although their principal mission would be to continue their attacks on the industrial potential of Germany, with emphasis now placed on the facilities for aircraft production.

Until January 1944, the view had been held that the heavy bombers of the Strategic Air Forces could make sufficient direct contribution to the assault in a period of about a fortnight before D Day. Further consideration, however, indicated the need to employ them for a much longer period—about three months—and a plan was finally adopted which aimed at the crippling of the French and Belgian railway systems and the consequent restriction of the enemy's mobility. The plan had a wider conception than the dislocation of the enemy's lines of communication in the zone in which the land forces were to be deployed. It was looked upon as the first of a series of attacks, which as they spread eastward, would ultimately affect the whole German war effort. The adoption of this plan entailed a major effort by the Strategic Air Forces.

In the preparatory phase, the striking power of the Tactical Air Forces was to be directed against rail targets, bridges, airfields in the vicinity of the assault area, coastal batteries, radar stations, and other naval and military targets. In addition to reserve aircraft, these forces had operationally available 2,434 fighters and fighter-bombers, and 700 light and medium bombers.

The program of attack on rail centers and bridges was designed to deprive the enemy of the means for the rapid concentration of men and material and to hinder his efforts to maintain an adequate flow of reinforcements and supplies, forcing him to move by road with resultant delay, increased wastage in road transport and fuel, and increased vulnerability to air attack. Blows against the railroad centers were to be started about D minus 60 and were to cover a wide area so as to give the enemy no clue to our proposed assault beaches. Shortly before D Day, however, the attacks would be intensified and focused on key points more directly related to the assault area but still so controlled as not to indicate to the enemy the area itself.

Attacks against coastal batteries, airfields, bridges, and other targets in the preparatory period were planned in such a manner that only one-third of the effort expended would be devoted to the targets threatening the success of our assault. The preliminary attacks upon the bridges in northwestern France were scheduled to begin on D minus 46 and to be intensified in tempo as D Day approached. The ultimate purpose of these attacks was to isolate the battle area from the rest of France by cutting the bridges over the Seine and the Loire below Paris and Orléans, respectively. The attacks upon the airfields had a similar purpose. Within a 130-mile radius of the battle area, all enemy airfields and air installations were to be attacked beginning not later than D minus 21. By neutralizing the fields, we were certain to limit the maneuvrability of German fighter forces, compelling them to enter the battle from fields situated a considerable distance from the Normandy beaches.

This preparatory bombing program was placed in effect as scheduled and, as D Day approached, the intensity of our attacks increased and the preparatory phase gave way to the assault phase. In the assault itself, the air forces were assigned the tasks, in conjunction with the navies, of protecting the cross-Channel movement of our forces from enemy air and naval attack. They were also to prepare the way for the assault by destroying the enemy's radar installations and by neutralizing coastal batteries and beach defenses between Ouistreham and Varreville, the area of our attack. Additionally, the air forces were to provide protective cover over the landing beaches and, by attacking the enemy, reduce his ability to reinforce and counter-attack. Subsequent to the establishment of the beachhead, the Tactical Air Forces were to support the land troops in their advance inland from the assault beaches.

During the assault it was planned to maintain a sustained density of ten fighter squadrons to cover the beach area, five over the British sector and five over the American. An additional six squadrons were to be maintained in readiness to support the beach cover if necessary. Over the main naval approach channels we agreed upon a sustained density of five squadrons centered at 60 miles and three at 80 miles from the south coast of England. Additionally, a striking force of 33 fighter squadrons was to be held in reserve for use as the air situation might require, subsequent to its initial employment as escort to the airborne formations.

The total fighter aircraft which we allocated for the D-Day assault was as follows:

Beach Cover	54	squadrons
Shipping Cover	15	squadrons
Direct Air Support	36	squadrons
Offensive Fighter Operations and Bomber Escort	33	squadrons
Striking Force	33	squadrons
Total	171	squadrons

The photographic reconnaissance units of the Allied Air Forces were the first to begin active and direct preparations for the invasion of Europe from the west. For more than a year, much vital information was accumulated which contributed very greatly to the ultimate success of the assault. The variety, complexity, and the detailed accuracy of the information gathered was of great importance in the preparatory phase of the operation. One of the most remarkable tasks accomplished was the series of sorties flown to obtain low-level obliques of underwater beach defenses.

LOGISTICAL PROBLEMS

In support of operation Overlord it had been proposed at the Casablanca Conference that an assault against southern France be mounted from the Mediterranean to coincide closely with the timing of the assault against northwest France. I had been engaged in the planning phase of this operation, known initially as Anvil and subsequently as Dragoon, prior to leaving my command in the Mediterranean, and felt then that its contribution to the downfall of the enemy would be considerable. I continued to recognize its importance after leaving the Mediterranean Theater, fully conscious not only of the psychological effect upon the enemy and upon Europe as a whole of the double assault, but of the great military value the southern blow would have in splitting all enemy forces in France and of thus assisting Overlord.

Initially we had hoped that the Anvil assault could be mounted with three divisions or, at the worst, with two divisions, building up to a strength of ten divisions in the follow-up. However, on 23 January 1944, it became necessary to recommend to the Combined Chiefs of Staff that some consideration be given to reducing the Anvil assault to one division, maintaining it as a threat until enemy weakness justified its employment. This recommendation was necessary because of our shortage of assault craft for the enlarged Overlord operation. We hoped that craft in the Mediterranean, originally allocated for Anvil, would thus be freed for our use.

The Combined Chiefs of Staff did not agree with this proposal and on the basis of planning data available to them stated that sufficient craft would be on hand to mount an Overlord assault of seven divisions (including the two follow-up divisions) and an Anvil of two divisions. These figures did not coincide with those of my own planners and the discrepancy was explained to the planners at Washington by my Chief of Staff. It was pointed out that the divisions involved in the assault each actually represented a division plus a regimental combat team and included the armor attached to it. Additionally, a number of subsidiary assaults by Commandos and Rangers necessitated craft for 5,000 personnel. Beyond this, the nature of the terrain, the heavy beach defenses, and the large rise and fall of tide in the Channel demanded the use of a very much larger number of engineer personnel and personnel for work on the beaches than would have otherwise been necessary. The scale of the problem may be understood more readily, perhaps, by the fact that we intended on D Day and D plus 1 to land 20,111 vehicles and 176,475 personnel. The vehicles included 1,500 tanks, 5,000 other tracked fighting vehicles, 3,000 guns of all types, and 10,500 other vehicles from jeeps to bulldozers.

This explanation helped to clarify our needs, and the Combined Chiefs of Staff recognizing the situation, met it by suggesting that the Anvil assault be postponed rather than mounted simultaneously with Overlord. Field Marshal (then General) Sir Maitland Wilson, as Supreme Commander in the Mediterranean Theater, and the British Chiefs of Staff in London, had at one time suggested that the Anvil operation be cancelled, chiefly because of weakness in the initial assault and the length of time required to build up sufficient forces. However, this was held to be inadvisable from the strategic point of view and contrary to the decisions reached at Teheran. The military advantages to be gained through a force of an additional ten or more divisions operating on our right flank after clearing Southern France would, I believed, be of extraordinary value later in the campaign. Accordingly, on 24 March, Anvil was postponed from a target date of 31 May to one of 10 July, some four weeks after the Overlord assault, and the craft necessary to round out our full needs were in part drawn from Mediterranean resources and allocated to our use. Although the question of Anvil was to reappear and the target date to be again postponed to 15 August, our problem in the mounting of Overlord had been settled and the priority of our needs in the larger operation established.

While the problem of assault craft was being resolved, the build-up of American troops and supplies in the United Kingdom continued under the direction of Lieut. Gen. John C. H. Lee. Planning for Bolero, the name by which this logistical program was known, had begun in the United Kingdom as early as April 1942. The small original staff was divided for the North African (Torch) operation, but expanded in 1943 and 1944 as the Overlord task became larger until, by D Day, the Communications Zone establishment contained 31,500 officers and 350,000 enlisted personnel. By July 1943 some 750,000 tons of supplies were pouring through English ports each month and this amount was steadily increased until in June 1944 1,900,000 tons were received from the United States. Much of this material was used to supply the troops already arrived in England, and other amounts were stored for use as Overlord progressed, but the stock pile earmarked for the American forces, over and above basic loads and equipment, was a full 2,500,000 tons for the invasion alone. By 1 June also, the number of US Army troops in the United Kingdom had risen from 241,839 at the end of 1942 to 1,562,000.

The operation of transporting supplies from the United States to the United Kingdom was facilitated by the fact that cargoes were discharged through established ports and over established rail lines.

Additionally, large quantities of materials for the invasion were made directly available from British resources within the United Kingdom itself. These conditions could not, of course, exist on the Continent and plans were accordingly made to overcome the difficulties envisaged. It was recognized that the major tonnage reception on the Continent would be over the Normandy beaches during the first two months, with the port of Cherbourg being developed at an early date. Successively, it was anticipated that port development would proceed in Brittany, the major effort in that area to be an artificial port at Quiberon Bay with complementary development of the existing ports of Brest, Lorient, St-Nazaire, and Nantes. While these were being brought into use the flow of supplies over the beaches was to be aided by the two artificial harbors (Mulberry "A" and Mulberry "B"). As the campaign progressed, it was anticipated that the bulk of American supplies would flow directly from the United States through the Brittany ports, while the Channel ports to the north, including Ostend and Antwerp, would be developed for the British armies. These expectations, however, did not materialize, due primarily to enemy strategy and the vicissitudes of the campaign. That both the American and British supply systems were able, in spite of this, to support the armies to the extent they did is a remarkable tribute to the flexibility of their organizations and to their perseverance in a single purpose.

The importance of the steady supply of our forces, once landed, may be gauged by reference to

German strategy. This was intended to ensure that our supplies should never be permitted to begin flowing into the beachheads. The German philosophy was: "Deny the Allies the use of ports and they will be unable to support their armies ashore." For this reason the chain of Atlantic and Channel ports from Bordeaux to Antwerp was under orders from Hitler himself to fight to the last man and the last round of ammunition. The Germans fully expected us to be able to make a landing at some point on the Channel coast, but they were nevertheless certain that they could dislodge us before supplies could be brought ashore to maintain the troops. They had no knowledge of our artificial harbors, a secret as closely guarded as the time and place of our assault. The impossible was accomplished and supplies came ashore, not afterwards to support a force beleaguered on the beachheads, but actually with the troops as they landed. The Germans were, by virtue of our initial supply, denied the opportunity of dislodging us and were subsequently, throughout the campaign, under sustained attack as the result of the feats of maintenance performed by our administrative organizations.

A captured enemy document, written by a division commander, perhaps pays as great a tribute to all the forces responsible for supply of the front-line troops as could be found. He wrote:

> I cannot understand these Americans. Each night we
> know that we have cut them to pieces, inflicted
> heavy casualties, mowed down their transport. We

know, in some cases, we have almost decimated entire battalions. But—in the morning, we are suddenly faced with fresh battalions, with complete replacements of men, machines, food, tools, and weapons. This happens day after day. If I did not see it with my own eyes, I would say it is impossible to give this kind of support to frontline troops so far from their bases.

GERMAN MISCALCULATIONS

While our plans developed and the build-up of supplies and men in readiness for the operation continued with regularity, we had been studying the possible action which the enemy might take in the expectation of an assault against him mounted from the United Kingdom. In any operation as large as Overlord it was palpably impossible to keep from the enemy the fact that we intended, during 1944, to launch an attack against Europe. Where, when, and in what strength the attack would be launched was another matter, and I was not without hope that he would not necessarily appreciate that our target was the Normandy beaches. Indeed we had some reason to believe that the enemy expected numerous attacks from many quarters and was continually uncertain as to the strength of any of them, unable in his own mind to determine or distinguish between a threat which we had no intention of launching, a diversion in strength, or an all-out main assault. In consequence he was stretched to the utmost in every theater.

We thought that to the German High Command an assault upon the Pas-de-Calais would be the obvious operation for the Allies to undertake. Not only was this the shortest sea journey where the maximum air cover would be available, but a lodgement in the Pas-de-Calais would lead the Allies by the shortest road directly to the Ruhr and the heart of Germany. Such an operation would have to be mounted mainly from southeast England and the Thames area. Concentrated in the Pas-de-Calais was the German Fifteenth Army, which had the capability both of shifting its forces to Normandy prior to the assault if the intended area of the attack were to become known and also of quickly reinforcing the divisions in Normandy, after the assault.

Acting on the assumption that this would be the German estimate we did everything possible to confirm him in his belief. Without departing from the principle that the efficient mounting of the operation remained at all times the first consideration, we took every opportunity of concentrating units destined ultimately for the Normandy beachhead in the east and southeast rather than in the southwest. In this way it was hoped that the enemy, by his observations based on aerial reconnaissance and radio interception, would conclude that the main assault would take place farther to the east than was in fact intended. As a result of these measures, we also felt that had an enemy agent been able to penetrate our formidable security barrier, his observations would have pointed to the same conclusion.

Shipping arrangements were made with the same end in view. Surplus shipping was directed to the Thames Estuary where an enormous concentration was already assembled in preparation for the invasion; while landing craft were moored at Dover, in the Thames, and at certain East Anglian ports.

Further support was afforded by the aerial bombing program. The distribution of bombing effort was so adjusted as to indicate a special interest in the Pas-de-Calais. It was also hoped that the bombing of the V-1 sites would be misinterpreted in our favor. Finally the large and very visible components of the artificial harbors, which were subsequently set up on the Normandy beaches, were anchored in Selsey Bay immediately before the invasion, a point farther east than originally proposed.

After the assault had gone in on 6 June we continued to maintain, for as long as possible, our concentrations in the southeast and our displays of real and dummy shipping, in the hope that the enemy would estimate that the Normandy beachhead was a diversionary assault and that the main and positive blow would fall on the Pas-de-Calais when the diversion had fulfilled its purpose.

The German Fifteenth Army remained immobile in the Pas-de-Calais, contained until the latter part of July by what we now know from high-level interrogation was the threat of attack by our forces in the southeast of England. Not until 25 July did the first division of the Fifteenth Army advance westward in a belated and fruitless attempt to reinforce the crumbling Normandy front.

Every precaution was taken against leakage of our true operational intentions against Normandy. The highest degree of secrecy was maintained throughout all military establishments, both British and American, but additional broader measures affecting the general public were necessary as D Day approached.

On 9 February, all civilian travel between Britain and Ireland was suspended to prevent the leakage of information through Dublin, where German agents continued officially to represent their government. On 1 April, also as a result of a request made by me, the British Government imposed a visitors' ban on the coastal areas where our assault was being mounted and extending inland to a depth of ten miles.

Because even the most friendly diplomats might unintentionally disclose vital information which would ultimately come to the ears of the enemy, the British Government took the further unprecedented step of restricting diplomatic privileges. On 17 April it banned the movement of diplomats or their couriers into and out of the United Kingdom and subjected hitherto immune correspondence to censorship. At my request this ban was maintained until 19 June.

Lastly, it was considered expedient on 25 May to impose an artificial delay of ten days on the forwarding of all American mail to the United States and elsewhere and to deny to American personnel trans-Atlantic telephone, radio, and cable facilities. The mail of all British military personnel due to take part in the Normandy operation had been, even within England itself, subject to strict censorship since April.

PREPARATORY OPERATIONS

Preparatory operations incident to the assault were already under way. These were the special concern of the Air Forces and the Navy, and consisted, apart from the Tactical Air Forces' operations already considered, primarily of the strategic bombing of Germany and the Channel exercises designed to afford training to the assault forces.

By a decision taken by the Combined Chiefs of Staff, prior to my arrival in the theater, command of the strategic bombing forces—the RAF Bomber Command and the United States Strategic Air Forces (composed of the Fifteenth Air Force in the Mediterranean Theater and the Eighth Air Force in the European Theater)—ultimately rested with the Combined Chiefs themselves. This decision had been taken with the purpose of coordinating strategic bombing against Germany from all sides. Within the European Theater overall command of the United States Strategic Air Forces rested with General (then Lieut.-General) Carl A. Spaatz and command of the RAF Bomber Command with Air Chief Marshal Sir Arthur Harris. The Strategic Air Forces were thus not under my direct orders, their commanders being instead responsible directly to the Combined Chiefs in Washington. While understanding the long-range motives which brought this decision into being, I was nevertheless dissatisfied with the arrangement, feeling that, since responsibility for the principal effort against Germany fell upon my Headquarters, all the forces to be employed within the theater—by land, sea, and air—should be responsible to me and under my direction, at least during the critical periods preceding and succeeding the assault.

I stated these views to the Combined Chiefs of Staff. At the same time I set forth the necessity for concentrated bombing of the rail network of Northwest Europe and particularly France, to which there was considerable opposition, the reasons for which will be considered shortly. I felt strongly about both these matters.

In a review of the matter, the Combined Chiefs of Staff, who were aware of my problems, gave me operational control of the air forces from 14 April. The Strategic Air Forces after this date were to attack German military, industrial, and economic targets in an order of priority established within the Theater and approved by the Combined Chiefs. Additionally, they were to be available to me upon call for direct support of land and naval operations when needed. This was a role for which they had not previously been normally used, but the Salerno campaign had afforded convincing evidence of their effectiveness for the purpose.

In the final command set-up of the air forces, then, the commanders of the Strategic Air Forces (RAF Bomber Command and the United States

Strategic Air Forces) reported to Supreme Headquarters independently as did also Air Chief Marshal Leigh-Mallory, commanding the tactical forces which comprised the Allied Expeditionary Air Force. The effort of the three separate commands was coordinated, under my direction, through the Deputy Supreme Commander, Air Chief Marshal Tedder.

Prior to my arrival in the theater, the Combined Chiefs of Staff had approved a combined bomber offensive plan against Germany which included the strategic bombing of critical industrial and military targets in the Reich. It had been determined that Germany's vulnerability lay primarily in six industrial systems indispensable to the German war effort: submarines, aircraft, ball bearings, oil, rubber, and communications. Of these six targets, aircraft, oil, and communications became the three which were to occupy the continuing attention of the Strategic Air Forces throughout the war. The bombing attacks upon these targets were to assist materially in weakening the enemy's potentiality to resist our offensives and immeasurably to aid our ground forces in their advance.

An indispensable condition to the success of our Normandy assault was, at the very least, sufficient control of the air to ensure the build-up in England and subsequently on the beachhead of our invasion forces and supplies. In anticipation of D Day, therefore, the Allied forces were first concerned with weakening the German Air Force through attacks upon its installations and resources on the ground and on the force itself in the air. Quite apart from the direct assistance these attacks lent to the success of our landings, they were essential also as a preliminary to the intensive bombing of German industry.

We were aware that the Germans had planned, as far back as July 1942, to develop an air force equal to the task of smashing any invasion. Their aircraft expansion program had as its ultimate goal the production of some 3,000 combat aircraft per month. It was also estimated that the enemy planned to have a first-line strength of 10,000 aircraft, adequately supplied by reserves in depth and a steady flow of replacements. Considerable progress had been made with this program before the growth of Allied aircraft strength in this Theater permitted the intensive scale of air fighting which began in May 1943. Commencing with that date, our attacks upon German aircraft production centers checked the projected increase of manufacture, but the German Air Force was able, nevertheless, to survive 1943 with its front-line strength little changed. In December 1943 the Germans planned to produce 3,000 single-engine fighters per month, thus indicating that their production program was influenced as much by the necessity for countering the allied bombing offensive as for stopping a possible ground invasion.

Beginning in January 1944, however, the assaults upon aircraft production centers were intensified and the effect of these attacks was such that the German Air Force had been robbed by mid-summer of most of its production capacity and also deprived of the adequate reserves necessary to maintain its front-line strength. These conditions resulted not only from damage to production centers but also from such other factors as attrition of aircraft and crews in air battles, shortage of aviation gasoline for training purposes, and disruption of communications. As the invasion date approached, a clear sign of our superiority in the air was the obvious unwillingness of the enemy to accept the challenge to combat which we initiated with large-scale fighter sweeps over his territory. Our D-Day experience was to convince us that the carefully laid plans of the German High Command to oppose Overlord with an efficient air force in great strength were completely frustrated by the strategic bombing operations. Without the overwhelming mastery of the air which we attained by that time our assault against the Continent would have been a most hazardous, if not impossible, undertaking.

This mastery of the air was maintained throughout 1944 and 1945 by continuing attacks against production centers. But the enemy was able, through factory reconstruction and dispersal, together with the development of jet aircraft, to maintain into 1945 a fighter force of a theoretical strength by no means negligible. Nevertheless, it still was not qualitatively good and proved incompetent to perform successfully for any substantial period any of the normal missions of an air force.

By D Day the Strategic Air Forces together with the Tactical Air Forces had so successfully performed their mission of disrupting enemy communications that there was a chronic shortage of locomotives and cars, repair facilities were inadequate, coal stocks were reduced to a six days' supply, and 74 bridges and tunnels leading to the battle area were impassable. The communications chaos thus produced had fatal effects upon the enemy's attempts at reinforcement of the threatened areas after our landings.

The initial attacks upon the communications system in France were undertaken as the result of an extremely difficult decision for which I assumed the full responsibility. I was aware that the attacks upon the marshalling yards and rail centers, by both the Strategic and Tactical Air Forces, would prove costly in French lives. In addition, a very important part of the French economy would for a considerable period be rendered useless. On separate occasions both Prime Minister Churchill and General Koenig, Commander of the French Forces of the Interior, asked that I reconsider my decision to bomb these particular targets. General Koenig requested once that he be permitted to participate as a member of a review board to determine the relative necessity of bombing centers of population; with regard to the loss of French lives, however, he took a stern and soldierly attitude, remarking: "It is war." I was aware of all the implications inherent in my decision, even of the heartrending possibility that our French Allies might be alienated from us. Nevertheless, for purely military reasons, I considered that the communications system of France had to be disrupted. The fate of a Continent depended upon the ability of our forces to seize a foothold and to maintain that foothold against everything we expected the enemy to throw against us. No single factor contributing to the success of our efforts in Normandy could be overlooked or disregarded. Military events, I believe, justified the decision taken, and the French people, far from being alienated, accepted the hardships and suffering with a realism worthy of a far-sighted nation.

With mastery of the air achieved in the spring of 1944, it became more readily possible for the Allied Strategic Air Forces to concentrate their power overwhelmingly against the declining oil reserves of Germany. The attack against the German oil industry commenced in April and continued until the termination of operations. Within the first month of attack German production fell to 80% of its previous normal capacity, and by December 1944 it had fallen to a mere 30%. This 30% itself was only produced as the result of herculean efforts which diverted manpower and labor hours from other equally essential industries, such as, for example, the production of the new and ingenious weapons of war with which Germany hoped to decide the issue of the conflict.

The subsequent shortage of oil brought on by our operations contributed to the complete collapse of the German bomber force and must have had its effect upon the decline of the U-boat★ menace. Immobility from oil shortage caused the capture of

★ German submarine.

tens of thousands of German soldiers and the destruction of their vehicles. Lack of oil and communications shattered by air bombardment retarded divisions arriving to reinforce the Normandy front in June. By December, when von Rundstedt's forces attacked in the Battle of the Ardennes, many units had to set out with extremely limited supplies of fuel, hoping desperately to overrun our positions so quickly that captured stocks would support their further advance. Within Germany the oil situation was so desperate that the recovery and repair program for the shattered industry was given the highest priority in the national war effort, above aircraft and submarine production and all other activities.

In addition to the strategic bombing of oil, aircraft, and communications targets, we were, during the campaign, to call upon the Strategic Air Forces for tactical support. At the time of the breakthrough in Normandy and several times later, including the Battle of the Ardennes, strategic bombers were employed in strength to attack enemy positions, supply bases immediately supporting the enemy front, and strongpoints and communication centers within the battle area. In these instances of tactical assistance, the Strategic Air Forces aided immeasurably in turning the decision of battle in our favor.

While the preparatory air operations of both the Strategic and Tactical Air Forces were growing in intensity as D Day approached, the naval and assault forces were engaged in Channel exercises designed not only to afford final training to the troops and

crews but also to test enemy reaction to our mounting preparations. During the assembly of the five
assault forces in the areas of Plymouth, Portland,
Portsmouth, Southampton, and the Isle of Wight,
which was completed on 26 April, considerable
enemy E-boat★ activity was noted which was primarily reconnaissance rather than offensive in nature. On
26 April the first full-scale exercise, Tiger, involving
Force "U" under the command of Admiral Moon,
took place from the Plymouth area. Owing to the fact
that one of the escorting destroyers was damaged in a
collision during the night of 26/27 April and was not
on hand when the assault convoy was attacked by E-
boats, there was an unfortunate loss of life in the
sinking of two LSTs.[†] In other respects the exercises
were successful and valuable lessons were learned,
relating not only to the movement and handling of
the task force ships, but also to the assault against
beaches. Areas such as Slapton Sands in southwest
England, similar to those which the troops would
encounter in France, were used for practice purposes.

Subsequent to Exercise Tiger, further Channel
exercises involving the other task forces were undertaken during the first week of May. Considerable
enemy reaction had been anticipated, but the exercises proceeded without any undue interference or
even attention from the enemy. In certain cases it
seemed apparent that he lacked information as to the

★ Small German torpedo boat.
[†] Tank landing ships.

extent and nature of the exercises. Our air superiority had driven his reconnaissance planes from the skies, the watch kept by our naval forces was unceasing, and the security precautions taken effectively neutralized the efforts of any agents whom he may have employed. Following the E-boat attack upon Force "U," the German radio had, for example, simply announced that ships of a Channel convoy had been torpedoed and sunk, indicating that the German command was unaware that the ships were assault craft and not the usual merchant ships in convoy. We also knew that the enemy was aware in other instances of our purposes, but preferred to reserve his forces for use on D Day itself rather than to expend them against local exercises.

ENEMY CAPABILITIES

In our planning for the assault, it was necessary—and increasingly so as D Day approached—to take into consideration the normal enemy capabilities which he might employ against our attack. We assumed that the enemy, once aware that a full-scale invasion was under way, would throw everything he possessed on the land, sea, and in the air against the assault. We accordingly made preparations to counter his reaction. Mention has already been made of the enemy's capability in the air and the overall disruption of his plans as the result of strategic bombing of the German Air Force production resources and of the tactical bombing of air-fields in the vicinity of the assault area. In spite of his losses, nevertheless, it was anticipated that he might, by carefully husbanding the fighters and bombers remaining to him, attack the invasion forces with furious—if brief—air effort. Against this, our covering squadrons of fighters were allocated as already outlined in the air plan for the assault.

In addition to air attack, the ruthless and even reckless employment of all enemy naval forces was also expected. We estimated that the enemy was capable of employing within the first few days of the assault the following forces: 5 destroyers, 9–11 torpedo boats, 50–60 E-boats, 50–60 R-boats, 25–30 "M" class mine sweepers, and 60 miscellaneous local craft. In addition to the surface craft available, the enemy was also in a position to use 130 U-boats forthwith and to reinforce these by D plus 14 to a total of 200. Against the anticipated attacks from these craft, the Navy was to undertake preliminary minelaying outside the channels of our approach. Aircraft of RAF Coastal Command also were to maintain a constant patrol in sufficient density and over such an extended stretch of the Channel that no U-boat would be capable of reaching the battle area without first surfacing and becoming vulnerable to attack. In the event that any enemy vessels proved capable, in spite of these measures, of reaching the task forces and assault convoys, the Navy's protective screen of ships, together with the considerable air umbrella supporting the task forces, was felt to be in sufficient strength to neutralize any serious threat.

The enemy had, as early as February, disposed of 53 divisions in the west under the Supreme Command of Field Marshal von Rundstedt. By 3 June his strength in France, Belgium, and Holland had been increased to 60 divisions, including 10 panzer type and 50 infantry divisions. Of these, 36 infantry and 6 panzer divisions were located in the general coastal area opposite England, from Holland to Lorient in Western France. In the immediate area of our Normandy assault the Germans had concentrated nine infantry divisions and one panzer division, while their greatest strength—the Fifteenth Army—remained in the Pas-de-Calais. The bombing of the Seine bridges and other communications served to isolate the battle zone from immediate reinforcement and the diversionary plans were responsible for holding strategic reserves away from the Normandy beaches. Thus, although disposing of 60 divisions, the enemy's immediate capabilities for their employment were considerably reduced.

Apart from the estimates of normal enemy capabilities, one unusual danger hung as a threat over Overlord from July 1943 through D Day. The Germans were emplacing what appeared to be rocket or pilotless aircraft sites on the Channel coast, and while the weapons appeared to be largely oriented on London, there was the possibility that our concentration of shipping in the ports of southern England would prove an attractive target and that the mounting of the operation would meet with interference from the new menace. The staff consequently gave some consideration to changing the areas where the amphibious forces were to be mounted, but, because other places did not have adequate facilities and the whole naval plan would have had to be altered, we adhered to our original plans. Defensive and offensive countermeasures against the threat were taken, and the Pas-de-Calais area, where the majority of the sites were located, was subjected to severe and continual bombing which served to delay the employment of the "V" weapons until after our assault had been launched.

With our land forces assembled in the area where the assault was to be mounted and with the Channel exercises under way, I felt that the final decision as to the launching of the assault should be made from a forward command post located near the invasion bases on the Channel coast and, accordingly, my tactical headquarters were set up in the vicinity of Portsmouth. As 1 June approached I had visited the greater part of the divisions to be engaged in the operations as well as air force installations and several of the larger naval ships. Without exception, the morale of the men was extraordinarily high, and they looked forward to the immediate task confronting them with sober confidence. This same confidence, born of the long hours of arduous preparatory toil, existed within all echelons of the services and was noticeably present when the final plans of all the commanders were formally presented at St Paul's School, 21 Army Group Headquarters in London, on 15 May.

With the planning and preparatory period completed, it now became necessary to make the supreme decision for which I was responsible—the designation of the exact day for the assault against the Continent of Europe.

THE ASSAULT

June 1944 saw the highest winds and roughest seas experienced in the English Channel in June for 20 years.

From 1 June onward, my commanders and I met daily to correlate our last-minute preparations and to receive the weather forecasts upon which we had to base our final decision as to the date of launching the assault. The provisional D Day was 5 June, but the meteorological predictions which came in on the 3rd

The Assault

Legend:
- Infantry Division
- Armoured Division
- 82 United States Airborne Div
- 101 United States Airborne Div.
- 6 British Airborne Division

UTAH
9 US
90 US
4 US

OMAHA
2 US
29 US
1 US

GOLD
49 BR
7 BR
50 BR

JUNO
51 BR
3 CDN

SWORD
3 BR

CHERBOURG
MONTEBOURG
ST MÈRE ÉGLISE
CARENTAN
ST JÉAN DATE

LAURENT SUR MER
VIERVILLE
COLLEVILLE SUR MER
ST LAURENT INTÉRIEUR
BAYEUX
TREVIÈRES
ARROMANCHES
ASNELLES SUR MER
MEUVAINES
COURSEULLES SUR MER
DOUVRES
CAEN

R. Aure
R. Odon

0 5 10 15 20 Miles

were so unfavorable that at our meeting on the morning of the 4th I decided that a postponement of at least 24 hours would be necessary. By that time part of the American assault force had already put out into the Channel, but so heavy were the seas that the craft were compelled to turn about and seek shelter.

By the morning of 5 June conditions in the Channel showed little improvement, but the forecast for the following day contained a gleam of hope. An interval of fair conditions was anticipated, beginning late on the 5th and lasting until the next morning, with a drop in the wind and with broken clouds not lower than 3,000 feet. Toward evening on the 6th, however, a return to high winds and rough seas was predicted, and these conditions were then likely to continue for an indefinite period.

The latest possible date for the invasion on the present tides was 7 June, but a further 24-hour postponement until then was impracticable as the naval bombardment forces which had already sailed from their northern bases on the 3rd would have had to put back into port to refuel and the whole schedule of the operation would thus have been upset. I was, therefore, faced with the alternatives of taking the risks involved in an assault during what was likely to be only a partial and temporary break in the bad weather, or of putting off the operation for several weeks until tide and moon should again be favorable. Such a postponement, however, would have been most harmful to the morale of our troops, apart from the likelihood of our losing the benefits of tactical surprise. At 0400 hours on 5 June I took the final and irrevocable decision: the invasion of France would take place on the following day.

On D Day the wind had, as forecast, moderated and the cloud was well broken, with a base generally above 4,000 feet. This afforded conditions which would permit of our airborne operations, and during the hour preceding the landings from the sea large areas of temporarily clear sky gave opportunities for the visual bombing of the shore defenses. The sea was still rough, and large numbers of our men were sick during the crossing. The waves also caused some of the major landing craft to lag astern, while other elements were forced to turn back.

As events proved, the decision to launch the assault at a time when the weather was so unsettled was largely responsible for the surprise which we achieved. The enemy had concluded that any cross-Channel expedition was impossible while the seas ran so high and, with his radar installations rendered ineffective as a result of our air attacks, his consequent unpreparedness for our arrival more than offset the difficulties which we experienced.

The weather was not the only circumstance surrounding the Allied landings which was contrary to the enemy's expectations. Apparently he had assumed that we should make our attempt only when there was a new moon and on a high tide, and that in choosing the place of main assault we should pick the immediate neighborhood of a good harbor and avoid cliffs and shallow, dangerous waters. In point of fact, we assaulted shortly after low tide, when the moon was full; we landed away from large harbors and at some points below sheer cliffs; and the waters through which we approached the shore were so strewn with reefs and subjected to strong currents that the German naval experts had earlier declared them to be impassable for landing craft.

While our assault forces were tossing on the dark waters of the Channel en route for France, the night bombers which were to herald our approach passed overhead. Shortly after midnight the bombing commenced, and by dawn 1,136 aircraft of RAF Bomber Command had dropped 5,853 tons of bombs on ten selected coastal batteries lining the Bay of the Seine between Cherbourg and Le Havre. As the day broke, the bombers of the US Eighth Air Force took up the attacks, 1,083 aircraft dropping 1,763 tons on the shore defenses during the half-hour preceding the touchdown. Then medium, light, and fighter-bombers of the Allied Expeditionary Air Force (AEAF) swarmed in to attack individual targets along the shores and artillery positions farther inland. The seaborne forces bore witness to the inspiring morale effect produced by this spectacle of Allied air might and its results as they drew in toward the beaches.

During the remainder of the day, the heavy bombers concentrated their attacks upon the key centers of communication behind the enemy's lines, through which he would have to bring up his reinforcements. Fighters and fighter-bombers of the AEAF roamed over the entire battle area, attacking the German defensive positions, shooting up build-ings known to house headquarters, strafing troop concentrations, and destroying transport. During the 24 hours of 6 June, the Strategic Air Forces flew 5,309 sorties to drop 10,395 tons of bombs, while aircraft of the tactical forces flew a further 5,276 sorties.

The lightness of the losses which we sustained on all these operations is eloquent of the feeble enemy air reactions and testifies to the effectiveness of our diversionary operations. Such reconnaissance and defense patrols as were flown by the Germans were mainly over the Pas-de-Calais area while over the assault beaches and their approaches only some 50 half-hearted sorties were attempted. Our heavy bombers were permitted to carry out their allotted tasks without any interference from enemy fighters. One result of this absence of opposition was that our own fighter-bombers were able to operate in small units of one or two squadrons, thus permitting their all-important harassing attacks to be more continu-ously maintained and their activities to cover a wider field. Not until two days after the initial landings did the enemy reinforce his air strength over the invasion zone to any appreciable extent.

As the night bombers were finishing their work in the early hours of 6 June, the Allied sea armada drew in toward the coast of France. The crossing had, as Admiral Ramsay reported, an air of unreality about it, so completely absent was any sign that the enemy was aware of what was happening. No U-boats were encountered, the bad weather had driven the enemy surface patrol craft into port, the German radar system was upset as a result of our air attack and scientific countermeasures, and no reconnaissance aircraft put in an appearance. Not until after the naval escort fleets had taken up their positions and commenced their bombardment of the shore defenses was there any enemy activity, and then, taken unprepared as the Germans were, it was mainly ineffective. We achieved a degree of tactical surprise for which we had hardly dared to hope. The naval operations were carried out almost entirely according to plan. The damage to his communications by the Allied bombing caused the enemy to remain in the dark as to the extent and significance of the airborne landings which had already been carried out. He was still uncertain as to whether he had to deal with invasion or merely a large-scale raid while our first assault wave was plunging shoreward to discover the truth about the vaunted Atlantic Wall.

The layout of the defenses which the Allied armies had to breach in order to establish their beach-heads on French soil had been largely determined by the Germans' experience at the time of the Dieppe raid in 1942. This raid convinced the enemy that any attempt at invasion could, and should, be destroyed on the beaches themselves, and the defense system subsequently constructed on this principle was lacking in depth.

Appreciating that one of our chief initial objectives would be the capture of a port, the enemy had developed heavy frontal defenses during 1943 at all the principal harbors from Den Helder to Brest. As the invasion threat grew, Cherbourg and Le Havre were further strengthened, while heavy guns were installed to block the entrance to the Bay of the Seine. Between the ports stretched a line of concrete defense positions, and coastal and flak batteries, each self-contained, heavily protected against air bombing and lavishly equipped. These positions were usually designed for all-round defense, their frontal approaches were mined, and where possible artificial flooding was used to guard the rear approaches. Fixed heavy and medium guns, intended to bombard approaching shipping, were sited well forward at the rear of the beaches, while divisional artillery of light and medium guns, which were to lay down a barrage on the beaches themselves, were located some two to three miles inland. Behind these defenses, however, there was no secondary defense line to check our invading armies if they should succeed in penetrating beyond the beach areas. The enemy was so confident in the strength of his "wall" that when our landings came upon him he had not the mobile reserves necessary to stem our advance and prevent our establishment of a lodgement area. Therein lay the main factor behind our successes following the disembarkations.

The assumption of command in France by Field Marshal Erwin Rommel during the winter of 1943–1944 was marked by a vigorous extension and intensification of the defensive work already in progress, and this continued up to the very day on which our landings took place. While the coastal guns were casemated and the defense posts strengthened with thicker concreting against the threat of air attack, a program was commenced in February 1944 of setting up continuous belts of underwater obstacles against landing craft along the entire length of all possible invasion beaches. It was intended by this means to delay our forces at the vital moment of touchdown, when they were most vulnerable, and thus to put them at the mercy of devastating fire from the enemy positions at the rear of the beaches. These obstacles—including steel "hedgehogs", tetrahedrons, timber stakes, steel "Element C" curved rails and ramps—were developed to cover high and lowtide contingencies, and most of them had affixed mines or improvised explosive charges. The program was not completed by 6 June, and the obstacles which our men encountered, though presenting considerable difficulties, nevertheless fell short of current German theory. Few mines were laid on the actual beaches, while the minefields at their exits were often marked and proved less troublesome to our troops than we had feared might be the case.

Despite the massive air and naval bombardments with which we prefaced our attack, the coastal defenses in general were not destroyed prior to the time when our men came ashore. Naval gunfire proved effective in neutralizing the heavier batteries, but failed to put them permanently out of action, thanks to the enormous thickness of the concrete casemates. Air bombing proved equally unable to penetrate the concrete, and after the action no instances were found of damage done by bombs perforating the covering shields. Such of the guns as were silenced had been so reduced by shellfire through the ports. The pre-D-Day bombing had, nevertheless, delayed the completion of the defense works, and the unfinished state of some of the gun emplacements rendered them considerably less formidable than anticipated.

The defenses on the beaches themselves were also not destroyed prior to H Hour as completely as had been hoped. The beach-drenching air attacks, just before the landing, attained their greatest success on Utah beach, where the Ninth Air Force bombed visually below cloud level. But elsewhere patches of cloud forced the aircraft to take extra safety precautions to avoid hitting our own troops, with the result that their bombs sometimes fell too far inland, especially at Omaha beach.

Nevertheless, the air and naval bombardments combined did afford invaluable assistance in ensuring the success of our landings, as the enemy himself bore witness. Although the strongly protected fixed coastal batteries were able to withstand the rain of high explosives, the field works behind the beaches were largely destroyed, wire entanglements were broken down, and some of the minefields were set off. Smoke shells also blinded the defenders and rendered useless many guns which had escaped damage. The enemy's communications network and his radar system were thrown into complete confusion, and during the critical period of the landings the higher command remained in a state of utter ignorance as to the true extent, scope, and objectives of the assault. The German gun crews were driven into their bomb-proof shelters until our forces were close inshore, and the sight which then confronted them was well calculated to cause panic. The terrible drum-fire of the heavy naval guns especially impressed the defenders, and the morale effect of this bombardment following a night of hell from the air was perhaps of greater value than its material results. Such return fire as was made from the heavy batteries was directed mainly against the bombarding ships, not the assault forces, and it was generally inaccurate. The close-support fire from destroyers, armed landing craft, rocket craft, and craft carrying self-propelled artillery, which blasted the beaches as the infantry came close to shore, was particularly effective.

The men who manned the static beach defenses were found to be a very mixed bag. A large proportion of them were Russians and other non-Germans, but with a Teutonic stiffening, and under German officers. Of the German troops, many companies were found to be composed of men either under 20 or over 45 years of age, and a large proportion were of low medical categories. Their morale was not of the best: the lavishness of the defenses and the concrete protection to their underground living quarters had produced a "Maginot Line complex," and, having gone below when the bombing began, they were not prepared for so prompt a landing when the bombs stopped falling. The field troops who manned the mobile artillery and many of the works between the heavy batteries, on the other hand, were of a different caliber and offered a stout resistance to our landings. By themselves, however, they were powerless to prevent our gaining a foothold.

The high seas added enormously to our difficulties in getting ashore. Awkward as these waters would have been at any time, navigation under such conditions as we experienced called for qualities of superlative seamanship. Landing craft were hurled on to the beaches by the waves, and many of the smaller ones were swamped before they could touch down. Others were flung upon and holed by the mined underwater obstacles. Numbers of the troops were swept off their feet while wading through the breakers and were drowned, and those who reached the dry land were often near exhaustion. It was, moreover, not possible on every beach to swim in the amphibious DD tanks upon which we relied to provide fire support for the infantry clearing the beach exits. These were launched at Sword, Utah, and Omaha beaches, and, although late, reached land at the two former; at Omaha, however, all but two or three foundered in the heavy seas. At the remaining beaches the tanks had to be unloaded direct to the shore by the LCTs, which were forced, at considerable risk, to dry out for the purpose. Fortunately the beaches were sufficiently flat and firm to obviate damage to the craft.

Despite these difficulties, the landings proceeded, and on all but one sector the process of securing the beachheads went according to plan. Meanwhile, four and a half hours before the first seaborne troops set foot upon the shore of France at 0630 hours, the air transport commands had commenced dropping the airborne assault forces on either flank of the invasion zone. In this operation, the biggest of its kind ever to date attempted, 1,662 aircraft and 512 gliders of the US IX Troop Carrier Command and 733 aircraft and 355 gliders of 38 and 46 Groups, RAF, participated.

In the British sector, the very accurate work of the Pathfinder force enabled the RAF groups to overcome the difficulties arising from the use of different types of aircraft, carrying various loads at various speeds, and the 6 Airborne Division troops were dropped precisely in the appointed areas east of the Orne River. Thanks to this good start, all the main military tasks were carried out, and at a lower cost than would have been paid in using any other arm of the service. The party charged with the mission of securing the Bénouville bridges over the Orne and the Caen Canal was particularly successful. Landing exactly as planned, in a compact area of just over one square kilometer, the troops went into action immediately and secured the bridges intact, as required, by 0850 hours. The tactical surprise achieved, coupled with the confusion created by the dropping of explosive dummy parachutists elsewhere, caused the enemy to be slow to react, and it was not until midday that elements of 21st Panzer Division counter-attacked. By that time our men had consolidated their positions and the enemy's efforts to dislodge them were in vain. During the day reinforcements were safely landed by gliders, against which the German pole obstructions proved ineffective; the operation went off like an exercise, no opposition was encountered, and by nightfall the division had been fully resupplied and was in possession of all its heavy equipment. This formation continued to hold the flank firmly until our lodgement area had been consolidated and the breakout eastward across France relieved it of its responsibility.

On the western flank, at the base of the Cotentin Peninsula, the American airborne forces of the 82nd and 101st Divisions were faced with greater initial difficulties. Owing to the cloud and atmospheric conditions, the Pathfinders failed to locate the exact areas fixed for the parachute drops, and the inexperience of some of the pilots led to wide dispersal of troops and supplies. The 6,600 parachute elements of 101st Division were scattered over an area 25 miles by 15 miles in extent, and 60% of their equipment was lost in consequence. Nevertheless, the operation represented an improvement upon those undertaken in Sicily, and the great gallantry with which the troops fought enabled them in general to accomplish their mission successfully. Gliders flown in during the day suffered considerable casualties, but reinforcements were introduced during the night of 6/7 June. While 101st Division held the exits to Utah beach and struck southward toward Carentan, the 82nd Division, despite heavy shelling in the Ste-Mère-

Eglise area, also established contact with the troops pushing inland from Utah beach early on 7 June. The element of surprise was as effective in the western as in the eastern sector, and the enemy himself bore witness to the confusion created by the American troops in cutting communications and disorganizing the German defense. The success of the Utah assault could not have been achieved so conspicuously without the work of the airborne forces.

The seaborne assault on the British–Canadian sector was carried out according to plan, and despite the rough approach, substantial beachheads were established on D Day. In the 1 Corps area, on the left flank, British 3 Division assaulted Sword beach, west of Ouistreham. The initial opposition ashore was only moderate, although light batteries shelled the landing craft as they came in to beach. The obstacles were forced, the DD tanks swam ashore to give fire support, and by 1050 hours the powerful coast defense battery in this sector was taken and elements of the assault force had advanced to Colleville-sur-Orne. By evening a considerable penetration inland had been made and reinforcements were coming in over the beaches. To the west, Canadian 3 Division landed on Juno beach, in the region of Courseulles-sur-Mer and Bèrnières-sur-Mer. Though met by considerable shelling and mortar fire, the troops succeeded in clearing the beaches by 1000 hours and pushed inland towards Caen.

In the 30 Corps sector, British 50 Division landed on Gold beach, near Asnelles-sur-Mer. Although strongpoints on the left flank caused some trouble, the enemy opposition as a whole was found to be less than anticipated, and the defenses at the rear of the beaches were successfully overcome. During the day Arromanches, Meuvaines, and Ryes were occupied and a firm footing was obtained inland.

It was in the St-Laurent-sur-Mer sector, on Omaha beach, where the American V Corps assault was launched, that the greatest difficulties were experienced. Not only were the surf conditions worse than elsewhere, causing heavy losses to amphibious tanks and landing craft among the mined obstacles, but the leading formations—the 116th Infantry of the 29th Division at Vierville-sur-Mer and the 16th Infantry of the 1st Division at Colleville-sur-Mer— had the misfortune to encounter at the beach the additional strength of a German division, the 352nd Infantry, which had recently reinforced the coastal garrison. Against the defense offered in this sector, where the air bombing had been largely ineffective, the naval guns were hampered by the configuration of the ground which made observation difficult and were able to make little impression. Exhausted and disorganized at the edge of the pounding breakers, the Americans were at first pinned to the beaches but, despite a murderous fire from the German field guns along the cliffs, with extreme gallantry, they worked their way through the enemy positions. The cost was heavy; before the beaches were cleared some 800 men of the 116th had fallen and a third of the 16th were lost, but by their unflinching courage they turned what might well have been a catastrophe into a glorious victory.

The American 4th Division (VII Corps) assault on the Utah beaches just west of the Vire Estuary, met with the least opposition of any of our landings. Moreover, an error in navigation turned out to be an asset, since the obstacles were fewer where the troops actually went ashore than on the sector where they had been intended to beach. The enemy had apparently relied upon the flooding of the rear areas here to check any force which might attempt a landing, and the beaches themselves were only lightly held. Complete surprise was achieved and a foothold was obtained with minimum casualties, although it was here that we had expected our greatest losses. The airborne troops having seized the causeways through the inundated hinterland and prevented the enemy from bringing up reinforcements, the 4th Division struck northwest toward Montebourg, on the road to Cherbourg.

Apart from the factor of tactical surprise, the comparatively light casualties which we sustained on all the beaches except Omaha were in large measure due to the success of the novel mechanical contrivances which we employed and to the staggering morale and material effect of the mass of armor landed in the leading waves of the assault. The use of large numbers of amphibious tanks to afford fire support in the initial stages of the operation had been an essential feature of our plans, and, despite the losses they suffered on account of the heavy seas, on the beaches where they were used they proved conspicuously effective. It is doubtful if the assault forces could have firmly established themselves without the assistance of these weapons. Other valuable novelties included the British AVRE (Armoured Vehicle Royal Engineers) and the "flail" tank which did excellent work in clearing paths through the minefields at the beach exits.

The enemy's confusion in the face of our assault was very clearly shown in the telephone journal of the German Seventh Army Headquarters which subsequently fell into our hands. Although Field Marshal von Rundstedt claimed on 20 June that the Germans were not taken by surprise, the evidence of this document told a very different story. Convinced that the main Allied assault would be delivered in the Pas-de-Calais, the Army HQ was at first of the opinion that the Normandy operations were of a diversionary nature and unlikely to include seaborne landings, even after the airborne operations had been followed by the opening of the naval bombardment. When, on 8 June, an operation order of the US VII Corps fell into the Germans' hands, they concluded that while this unit was in charge of all the Contentin operations, the V Corps mentioned in the order must embrace all the Anglo-American forces assaulting the Calvados area from the Vire to the Seine. The enemy assumed, in view of the anticipated further landings in the Pas-de-Calais, that the Allies could not afford to employ more than two corps elsewhere.

On D Day, because of the chaos in communications produced by our bombing, the Seventh Army

HQ did not hear of the Calvados landings until 0900 hours, and then the information was both meager and inaccurate. It was not until 1640 hours that the Army learned of the Utah seaborne assault, having previously received reassuring reports as to the progress being made against the airborne forces dropped in that area. Meanwhile at noon, the German LXXXIV Corps had optimistically, but prematurely, announced that the attempted landings by the V Corps troops at St-Laurent had been completely smashed. Thanks to such misinformation and to a faulty estimate of the situation, Seventh Army decided by the evening of D Day that the landings near the Orne constituted the chief danger in the area so far invaded, and took steps to commit its strongest and most readily available reserves in that sector. Little was known of the strength or objectives of the American landings, and the operations in the Cotentin continued to be regarded simply as a diversionary effort which could easily be dealt with. This estimate of the situation dominated the enemy's policy, with fatal results, during the ensuing days.

On 7 June I toured the assault area by destroyer, in company with Admiral Ramsay, and talked with Field Marshal Montgomery, General Bradley, and the Naval Force Commanders. All were disappointed in the unfavorable landing conditions and longed for an improvement in the weather that would enable our troops to exploit to the full their initial successes. After noon on this day the weather did show some signs of moderating, and a chance was offered for us to catch up in part with our delayed unloading schedule. On Omaha beach, which continued to cause us most anxiety, General Bradley reported some improvement, but in view of the check received here I decided to alter the immediate tactical plan to the extent of having both V and VII Corps concentrate upon effecting a link-up through Carentan, after which the original plan of operations would be pursued. Of the morale of the men whom I saw on every sector during the day I cannot speak too highly. Their enthusiasm, energy, and fitness for battle were an inspiration to behold.

During the next five days our forces worked to join up the beachheads into one uninterrupted lodgement area and to introduce into this area the supplies of men and material necessary to consolidate and expand our foothold.

In the British–Canadian sector, chief interest centered in the thrust by the British 3 and Canadian 3 Divisions toward Caen. Exploiting the success achieved on D Day, they pushed southward, and, despite heavy casualties, succeeded on 7 June in reaching points some two or three miles north and northwest of the city. However, the enemy fully appreciated the danger in this sector and, employing the tanks of 21st Panzer and 12th SS Panzer Divisions, counter-attacked successfully in ideal tank country. This counter-attack penetrated nearly to the coast, and drove a wedge between the two Allied divisions, preventing a combined attack upon Caen for the time being. Subsequent events showed that the retention of the city was the key to the main enemy strategy, and during the struggles of the following weeks the Germans fought furiously to deny us possession and to prevent our breaking out across the Orne toward the Seine. Further west Bayeux was taken on 8 June and the beachhead expanded inland.

Meanwhile the Allies had their first experience of the enemy's skill and determination in holding out in fortified strongpoints behind our lines. Although German claims of the effect of these strongpoints in delaying the development of our operations were greatly exaggerated, it was undeniably difficult to eliminate the suicide squads by whom they were held. The biggest of these points was at Douvres in the Canadian sector, where the underground installations extended to 300 feet below the surface. It was not until 17 June that the garrison here was compelled to surrender.

In the American sector the V Corps assault forces, having overcome their initial difficulties, reached the line of the Bayeux–Carentan road by midday on 7 June, and on the next day established contact with the British 50 Division on their left flank. On 9 June, reinforced by the 2nd Infantry Division, V Corps advanced rapidly to the south and west, reaching the line Caumont–Cerisy Forêt–Isigny by 11 June. Reinforcements then stiffened the German defenses, particularly in the hills protecting St-Lô. At the other end of the American zone, the enemy rushed forces to bar the Cherbourg road at Montebourg. In the center there was a stern struggle to link the two beachheads across the marshlands of the Vire Estuary. The prevention of this junction was regarded by the enemy as second in importance only to the defense of Caen, but on 10 June patrols of the two American corps made contact, and on the 12th Carentan fell. The Germans made desperate but fruitless efforts to recover the town and re-establish the wedge between our forces. Our initial lodgement area was now consolidated, and we held an unbroken stretch of the French coast from Quinéville to the east bank of the Orne.

Meanwhile, on and off the beaches, the naval, mercantile marine, and land force supply services personnel were performing prodigies of achievement under conditions which could hardly have been worse. Enormous as was the burden imposed upon these services even under the best of conditions, the actual circumstances of our landings increased the difficulties of their task very considerably. The problems of unloading vast numbers of men and vehicles and thousands of tons of stores over bare beaches, strewn with mines and obstacles, were complicated by the heavy seas which would not permit the full use of the special landing devices, such as the "Rhino" ferries, which had been designed to facilitate unloading at this stage of operations. The beaches and their exits had to be cleared and the beach organizations set up while the fighting was still in progress close by, and on either flank the unloading had to be carried on under fire from German heavy artillery. Off shore, enemy aircraft, although absent by day, laid mines each night, requiring unceasing activity by our mine sweepers. By 11 June, despite these complications, the machinery of supply over the beaches was functioning satisfactorily. Initial discharges of stores and vehicles were about 50% behind the planned schedule, but against this we could set the fact that consumption had been less than anticipated. Reserves were being accumulated and the supply position as a whole gave us no cause for concern. The artificial harbor units were arriving and the inner anchorages were already in location. During the first six days of the operation, 326,547 men, 54,186 vehicles and 104,428 tons of stores were brought ashore over the beaches. These figures gave the measure of the way in which all concerned, by their untiring energy and courage, triumphed over the difficulties which confronted them.

On 11 June, with the linking up of the beachheads, the stage was set for the battles of the ensuing two months during which the fate of France was to be decided. The enemy never succeeded fully in recovering from the confusion into which he was plunged by the surprise of our attack and the effects of our air and naval bombardment. During the first five days of the campaign all the symptoms developed which were to characterize the Germans' resistance in the subsequent battles. Desperate attempts to repair the shattered communications system met with little success while the Allied air forces continued their onslaught against the enemy lines and far to the rear. At some critical moments the Army lost touch with

corps, corps with divisions, and divisions were ignorant of the fate of their regiments. Already the panzer
divisions were reporting that they were halted
through lack of fuel, reinforcements were unable to
reach the battle area for the same reason, and by 13
June the Seventh Army had no fuel dump nearer
than Nantes from which issues could be made.
Ammunition was also scarce, and the fall of Carentan
was explained as due to the fact that the defending
forces lacked shells. These things were lacking, not
because the Germans did not possess the means to
wage war, but because the movement of supplies to
the fighting zone was practically impossible when the
Allied domination of the skies was so complete. All
this explains the enemy's failure to regain the initiative following his loss of it when our forces broke
through the Atlantic Wall defenses upon which
Rommel had, with such fatal misjudgment, pinned
his faith.

From 11 June onward the enemy strove desperately but vainly to contain the beachheads which he
had been unable to prevent us from securing. The
orders of 7 June that the Allies were to be driven back
into the sea were already obsolete; the aim now was
to save Cherbourg, to attempt to re-establish the
wedge between the Cotentin and Calvados at
Carentan, and to hold fast on the eastern flank by
denying us possession of the city of Caen. The next
six weeks were to see the failure of all three of these
aims before the moral and material superiority of the
Allied armies.

ESTABLISHMENT OF THE
LODGEMENT AREA

After the success of the assault operations had gained
us a foothold on French soil, there followed six weeks
of gruelling struggle to secure a lodgement area of sufficient depth in which to build up a striking force of
such magnitude as to enable us to make full use of our
potential material superiority. The process took longer
than we had expected, largely owing to the adverse
weather conditions which repeatedly interrupted the

Establishment of the lodgement area

flow of men and stores across the Channel. The enemy fought tenaciously to contain our beachheads, though he was at no time able to collect the strength to constitute a serious offensive threat. Consequently our operations fell somewhat behind the planned schedule, but we were able to build up our armies to a power which made it possible, when the breakthrough came, not only to regain the time lost but to outstrip the anticipated rate of advance.

Our immediate need was to expand our shallow beachhead inland to a depth sufficient to secure the beaches from enemy gunfire in order that the build-up might proceed without interruption. We also had to capture the port of Cherbourg, which was essential to permit of the rapid inflow of the vast stocks of war material required for future operations.

Then, as our strength grew, we needed space in which to maneuver and so dispose our forces that the best use could be made of our material assets and a decisive blow be delivered at the enemy. To this end we had to secure Caen and establish bridgeheads across the Orne and Odon Rivers, to eliminate the possibility of the enemy's driving a wedge between the Allied sectors east and west of the Vire River, and to extend our hold upon the southern part of the Cotentin Peninsula.

Meanwhile, the enemy found himself in a dilemma. He had pinned his faith on Rommel's policy of concentrating upon the beach defenses, and when they failed to prevent the establishment of the Allied beachheads, he lacked any alternative means of combatting the threat offered. Rommel's confidence in his mines and concrete was indeed to have disastrous results for the German Army. There being no system of defense in depth, when the beaches were forced the enemy lost the initiative and never subsequently succeeded in regaining it. The hand of von Rundstedt, endeavoring to remedy the errors of his lieutenant, became apparent after the first two or three weeks of the campaign, when desperate attempts were made to form a mobile armored striking force in reserve; but it was too late. The enemy had been forced, by reason of his shortage of infantry, to use his armor in purely defensive roles. Once this armor was so committed, our constant pressure made it impossible for the enemy to withdraw his mobile forces for more appropriate employment until early in August, when the breakthrough of the US forces on the west flank had already sealed the fate of the German Seventh Army.

Lack of infantry was the most important cause of the enemy's defeat in Normandy, and his failure to remedy this weakness was due primarily to the success of the Allied threats levelled against the Pas-de-Calais. This threat, which had already proved of so much value in misleading the enemy as to the true objectives of our invasion preparations, was maintained after 6 June, and it served most effectively to pin down the German Fifteenth Army east of the Seine while we built up our strength in the lodgement area to the west. I cannot overemphasize the decisive value of this most successful threat, which paid enormous dividends, both at the time of the assault and during the operations of the two succeeding months. The German Fifteenth Army, which, if committed to battle in June or July, might possibly have defeated us by sheer weight of numbers, remained inoperative throughout the critical period of the campaign, and only when the breakthrough had been achieved were its infantry divisions brought west across the Seine—too late to have any effect upon the course of victory.

A certain amount of reinforcement of the Normandy front from other parts of France and from elsewhere in Europe did take place, but it was fatally slow. The rate of the enemy's build-up in the battle area during the first six weeks of the campaign averaged only about half a division per day. By 16 June he had committed his four nearest panzer divisions to battle, and his six nearest infantry divisions were brought in by 19 June. But it was not until the beginning of July, when the scale of the Allied effort was no longer in any doubt, that reinforcements began to arrive from more distant locations.

This process of reinforcement was rendered hazardous and slow by the combined efforts of the Allied air forces and the French patriots. Despite the comparative speed with which tracks could be repaired, our prolonged bombing campaign against rail centers and marshalling yards had effected a marked reduction in the operating efficiency of the rail systems of northeast France and Belgium, and by D Day 27% of the locomotive servicing facilities, 13% of the locomotives themselves, and 8% of the other rolling stock had been destroyed. All but two of the Seine bridges below Paris were cut by Allied bombers before D Day, and during the subsequent weeks these surviving ones were also demolished, together with the principal road and rail bridges across the Loire. Thus the battle area in Normandy was virtually isolated except for the routes which led into it through the Paris–Orléans "gap" between the two rivers; there the roads and railroads inevitably became congested and afforded rich opportunities for sabotage and bombing. The Tactical Air Forces also, by a series of concentrated attacks against junctions on the edge of the tactical area during the first few days following the assault, drew a line beyond which all enemy rail movement was impossible by day. This line of interdiction originally ran through Pontaubault, Fougères, Mayenne, Alençon, Dreux, and Evreux, but was subsequently adjusted as the ground situation developed.

The consequence of these attacks upon enemy communications was that the Germans were compelled to detrain their reinforcement troops in eastern France, after a circuitous approach over a disorganized railway system, and then to move them up to the front by road. Road movement, however, was difficult by reason of the critical oil shortage, apart from the exposure of the columns to Allied bombing and strafing. During the first six months of 1944 the German oil production was reduced by at least 40% as a result of the bombing of the plants by the Strategic Air Forces, and the outcome was seen in the trials of the enemy reinforcements and supply columns as they struggled toward Normandy. Whole divisions were moved on seized bicycles, with much of their impedimenta on horse transport, while the heavy equipment had to follow as best it could by rail, usually arriving some time after the men. The 275th Infantry Division, for instance, took a week to move 150 miles from Fougères. It began the journey by train but was halted by bombing, then the French seized the horses which had been collected to move the division by road, and the destination was eventually reached on foot, movement being possible only at night because of the perils of air strafing by day. The 9th and 10th SS Panzer Divisions took as long to travel from eastern France to Normandy as from Poland (where they had been stationed) to the French frontier; while the men of the 16th GAF Division, having left the Hague by train on 18 June, were forced to make a grand tour of Holland, Belgium, the Rhineland, and eastern France before they eventually reached the front on 3 July. Travelling under such conditions, the reinforcements arrived in Normandy in a piecemeal fashion, and were promptly thrown into battle while still exhausted and unorganized. By mid-July, units had been milked from Brittany, the southwest and west of France, Holland, Poland, and Norway; only the Fifteenth Army in the Pas-de-Calais, waiting for a new invasion which never came, was still untouched.

Meanwhile the Allied air forces enjoyed absolute supremacy over the battle area, as indeed over the whole of Nazi-occupied Western Europe. During fine weather, a normal total of over 1,000 US heavy bombers by day and over 1,000 RAF heavy bombers by night was dispatched on strategic missions. Their top-priority targets were the German oil refineries, synthetic oil production plants, and dumps, but they were also available for use, at my request, against tactical targets connected with the Normandy front. Unfortunately the prevalent bad weather prevented our full use of the air weapon, operations being repeatedly reduced or cancelled for this cause.

The weather, however, failed to stop the AEAF (Allied Expeditionary Air Force) from constantly hammering its tactical targets. While in fine weather as many as 4,000 sorties a day were flown by aircraft of this command, the attacks were continued on the maximum scale possible even under the most adverse conditions. During the first week of the campaign the Tactical Air Forces flew some 35,000 sorties in direct support of ground troops, and by their persistent blows in subsequent weeks against their targets behind the enemy lines—transport, communications, strongpoints, airfields, fuel dumps, and troop concentrations—they caused a degree of confusion and dislocation that was essential to the success of our breakthrough in late July. So complete was our air mastery that in fine weather all enemy movement was brought to a standstill by day, while at night the attacks were continued with the aid of flares. Von Rundstedt himself reported that the Allied tactical aircraft controlled not only the main battlefield areas but also the approach routes to a depth of over 100 miles. Even a single soldier, he claimed, was not immune from attack.

An important factor in ensuring the success of our close-support air operations lay in the establishment of landing strips on French soil, from which our fighter planes could operate. Work began on the preparation of these strips as soon as we obtained a footing on shore, and, thanks to the brilliant work of our engineer services, I was able to announce on the morning of 9 June that for the first time since 1940 Allied air forces were operating from France. Within three weeks of D Day, 31 Allied squadrons were operating from the beachhead bases.

All this extremely effective use of our great air superiority was possible despite the very considerable diversion of our striking power against the enemy's preparations to attack the United Kingdom by means of flying bombs and heavier rocket projectiles. The first flying bombs fell on England during the night of 12–13 June, and the regular attacks commenced three days later. Attacks upon the V-1 sites were difficult by reason of their smallness, the effective nature of their camouflage, their comparative mobility and the ease with which they could be repaired. For this reason it was considered more profitable to attack the supply dumps, transport facilities and services. Blows designed to delay progress on the larger, massive concrete structures, of the exact purpose of which we were at the time still uncertain, also required the attentions of large formations of heavy planes, dropping the biggest types of bombs.

In contrast to the intensity of the Allied air effort, the activities of the German Air Force (GAF) apart from sporadic fighter-bomber attacks by flights of 20 to 30 aircraft on the assault area, were limited to cautious patrolling by day and sea-mining by a small number of heavy bombers at night. We were now to reap the fruits of the long struggle for air supremacy which had cost the Allied air forces so much effort since the start of the war. Following the enemy's failure to take effective action against our forces during the initial stages of the assault, he remained on the defensive, being chiefly concerned with the protection of his bases, stores, and lines of communication. Aggressive support of his ground forces was noticeably lacking, and even defense of their positions against our fighter-bomber attacks was weak and desultory. The enemy was, in fact, in an awkward predicament. To take the offensive when his numerical strength was so inferior to that of the Allies was to court disaster; yet to remain always on the defensive would mean slow attrition and a decline in ground force morale because of the absence of the air cover which had played so large a part in the victories of 1940.

The number of GAF planes available for employment in the invasion area had been built up during the six weeks prior to the assault, but this increase in strength was neutralized by our air forces, and post-D-Day reinforcement proved less than expected. The GAF fighter bases, from Bordeaux to Belgium, were subjected to attacks of such scope that the enemy was unable to concentrate his fighter resources over the battle zone, and his planes were thus denied effective employment. Normally the Luftwaffe fighter activities were limited to defensive patrolling behind the Germans' own lines, an average of 300–350 sorties per day being flown in fine weather with a maximum of about 450. There was also some enemy activity against the beaches, and bombing and torpedo attacks against shipping. It was a reflection of this enemy weakness that on 14 June RAF Bomber Command was able to send some 350 heavy bombers against Le Havre and Boulogne in daylight, the first daylight operation in force by the Command since early in the war, and lost only one aircraft on the operation.

When the enemy planes did come up, they showed a marked tendency to avoid combat. Only on 12 June did they react in any considerable strength when a mass onslaught was made on French airfields by 1,448 Fortresses and Liberators of the US Eighth Air Force—the largest force of heavy bombers hitherto airborne on a single mission. On this occasion the enemy suffered severely at the hands of the Allied fighters and failed to reach the bombers. The reluctance normally shown to engage our planes was doubtless in part dictated by the need to conserve a depleted strength; but there was also noticeable a lack of organization and experience on the part of the German pilots. The persistent RAF night bombing attacks of the past had led the German command to concentrate on the training and development of night fighters, with the result that day fighter pilots were generally of a poorer standard and rarely a match for their Allied opponents. As a consequence of this weakness, our forces—both on operations over the battle area and on long-range strategic daylight missions—frequently encountered no air opposition whatsoever, and the overall weekly Allied losses averaged only about 1% of the aircraft employed.

The quality of the German ground forces with whom our armies came in contact varied considerably. At the top of the scale came the troops of SS panzer and parachute units, considerably better than those of the ordinary infantry divisions. Their morale, backed by a blind confidence in ultimate Nazi victory, was extremely good, and whether in attack or defense they fought to a man with a fanatical courage. But in the infantry divisions we found opponents inferior, both physically and morally, to those against whom we had fought in North Africa. The lack of air and artillery support, the breakdown of ration supplies, the non-arrival of mail, the unsoldierly behaviour of some of the officers, the bombing of home towns—all tended to lower the men's spirits. Perhaps two-thirds of them were under 19 or over 30 years of age, and many were obviously tired of the war. Nevertheless they had not yet reached the dangerous state of indifference. Their inborn Teutonic discipline and their native courage enabled them to fight on stubbornly, and it was only toward the end of the campaign in France that their morale broke momentarily. Many who were so-called non-Nazis saw no hope for Germany other than through Hitler, and thought it better to go down fighting than to suffer a repetition of 1918. Moreover, it cannot be doubted that the governmental propaganda on "V" weapons had a considerable effect in strengthening morale in these early stages of the campaign. At the bottom of the scale came the foreigners who had either volunteered for, or been pressed into, the service of Germany. These men were dispersed throughout fixed garrisons and infantry divisions in order that adequate supervision could be exercised over them, but it was from their ranks almost exclusively that deserters came.

The abortive plot of the German military clique to assassinate Hitler, which astonished the world on 20 July, seemed to have little effect upon enemy morale. The details were little publicized by the German authorities, and the majority of the soldiers apparently regarded the facts as presented to them by the Allies as mere propaganda. Nor did the subsequent Himmler purge of non-Nazi elements in the army produce any marked change in the outlook of the enemy rank and file.

The struggle which took place during this period of the establishment of the lodgement area, following the success of our initial assault, took the form of a hard slugging match on the British sector of the front, with the city of Caen as its focal point. Here the enemy concentrated the bulk of his strength, while the men of the US First Army fought their way up the Cherbourg Peninsula to capture the port itself, subsequently regrouping and consolidating their position to the south in preparation for what was to prove the decisive breakthrough at the end of July.

By his anxiety to prevent the capture of Caen and the eastward extension of our beachhead, the enemy to some extent contributed to the accomplishment of our initial plan insofar as the capture of Cherbourg was concerned, and from D plus 6 or 7 the battle developed in general as foreseen. This enemy anxiety in the east was manifested from D plus 1 onwards, following the failure of our attempt to seize the city of Caen in our first rush inland. It was vital for the enemy to deny us the Seine basin: partly as it afforded the last natural barrier defending the V-1 and V-2 sites; partly because he needed the river ferries to bring over supplies and reinforcements to his divisions in Normandy; partly because he feared a thrust on Paris which would cut off all his forces to the west; partly because he foresaw a threat to Le Havre, which was an invaluable base for his naval craft operating against the approaches to the assault area; but perhaps most of all because he wished to avoid the possibility of a link-up between those Allied forces already ashore and those which he expected to land in the Pas-de-Calais.

For these reasons, therefore, he committed all his available armor and a considerable part of his infantry to the battle in the Caen sector, thus rendering easier the task of the Allied troops in the west but denying us access to the good tank and airfield country toward Falaise. His secondary aims, which crystallized as our strategy became clear to him, were to maintain a wedge threatening to divide the US forces in the Cotentin from those in Calvados, to prevent the cutting of the Cherbourg Peninsula and to block the way to Cherbourg itself. He fully appreciated the importance to us of securing this port—indeed, he overestimated the necessity of it, being ignorant of our artificial harbors project and probably underestimating our ability to use the open beaches—but his shortage of infantry and preoccupation with the Caen sector impaired his ability to defend it.

Our strategy, in the light of these German reactions, was to hit hard in the east in order to contain the enemy main strength there while consolidating our position in the west. The resulting struggle around Caen, which seemed to cost so much blood for such small territorial gains, was thus an essential factor in ensuring our ultimate success. The very tenacity of the defense there was sufficient proof of this. As I told the press correspondents at the end of August, every foot of ground the enemy lost at Caen was like losing ten miles anywhere else. At Caen we held him with our left while we delivered the blow toward Cherbourg with our right.

The enemy's tenacity in the east did not mean that the Allied forces in the west enjoyed a walk-over. The terrain through which they fought was overwhelmingly favorable to the defense. In the close "bocage" countryside, dotted with woods and orchards, and with its fields divided by high tree-topped embankments, each in itself a formidable anti-tank obstacle, armor was of little value, and the infantry had to wage a grim struggle from hedgerow to hedgerow and bank to bank, harassed by innumerable snipers and concealed machine-gun posts. For this type of warfare, experience gained by some of our units in their intensive pre-invasion exercises in battle-training areas of southwest England proved valuable, as they had there been taught to fight in country resembling that in which they found themselves at grips with the real enemy.

After the fall of Carentan on 12 June, marking the effective junction of the two American beachheads, the enemy became anxious concerning the drive of the 82nd Airborne and 9th Infantry Divisions which, striking towards St-Sauveur-le-Vicomte, threatened to cut the neck of the peninsula and thus isolate Cherbourg. Although the enemy's 77th Infantry Division had been brought up from Brittany to assist, his available forces were not sufficient to cope with this thrust as well as with the more direct threat to Cherbourg levelled by our 4th and 90th Infantry Divisions which were pushing north on both sides of the Montebourg road. The enemy concentrated, therefore, on counter-attacks from the south in an unsuccessful endeavor to recapture Carentan and re-establish the "wedge," while deploying a considerable mass of artillery to bar the way north at Montebourg. The town eventually fell on 19 June, but meanwhile the enemy weakness in the center led to the evacuation of St-Sauveur on 16 June. Patrols of 82nd Airborne Division entered the town on that day, and on 17 June the 9th Infantry Division reached the west coast at Les–Moitiers–d'Allone and St-Lô-d'Ourville, north and south of Barneville. The enemy had formed two battle groups, one of which was to defend Cherbourg and the other to escape to the south, but when the peninsula was cut, part of the "escape" force was trapped. The forces isolated to the north included the bulk of two infantry divisions, parts of two others, and the naval and garrison personnel employed in Cherbourg itself. Once VII Corps had reached the west coast, the enemy was unable to reopen his corridor to the north.

The Montebourg defense having been broken by 19 June, the advance on Cherbourg continued. Valognes fell on the following day, and three infantry divisions (the 4th on the right, 79th in the center, and 9th on the left) under VII Corps closed in on the city. The German attempt to hold us at Montebourg, as personally ordered by Hitler, proved to be an error of judgment, since, when the line was forced, the units which retreated to Cherbourg were in no state of organization to maintain a protracted defense of the city. Had the withdrawal taken place earlier, Cherbourg might have been able to hold out as long as Brest did subsequently. The lesson had been learned by the time the fighting reached Brittany.

An attack on Cherbourg was launched on the afternoon of 22 June, following an 80-minute bombardment of the outer defenses, but the enemy at first fought back stoutly. By 25 June, however, our men were fighting in the streets while the thunder of the German demolitions in the port area reverberated from the surrounding hills. At 1500 hours on 26 June, the joint commanders, Maj. Gen. von Schlieben (land forces) and Rear Adm. Hennecke (naval forces), despite having previously exacted no-surrender pledges from their men, gave themselves up. The Arsenal held out until next morning, and other fanatical groups which even then continued to resist had to be eliminated one by one. A certain number of the enemy still remained to be rounded up in the northwest corner of the peninsula, but on 1 July their commander, Colonel Keil, was captured with his staff and all resistance in the northern Cotentin came to an end.

It was the judgment of Rommel himself that, with Cherbourg in our hands, elimination of the beachhead was no longer possible. The admission was tantamount to a confession of the failure of his own policy of relying on a concrete "wall" to frustrate an invasion on the very beaches. The next few weeks were to see the enemy making a frantic but unavailing effort, under von Rundstedt's supervision, to create the mobile striking force necessary for a policy of elastic defense. But it was too late now.

This inability of the enemy, after the initial success of our landings, to form an adequate reserve with which to regain the initiative and drive us into the sea became very apparent during the fighting in the British–Canadian sector. While the US V Corps pushed inland from its Calvados beachhead to the south and east of Caumont, a heavy, see-saw battle was fought by the Second Army in the Tilly area, with two panzer divisions initially providing the bulk of the opposition. As our pressure increased, reinforcements were introduced by the enemy from two other armored divisions, but these proved inadequate. On 28 June, the British 8 Corps established a bridgehead some 4,000 yards wide and 1,000 yards deep beyond the Odon River near Mondrainville. The greater part of eight armored divisions was now flung into the battle by the enemy in a fruitless attempt to halt the advance and to cut the Allied corridor north of the river. Despite the bad weather, which deprived us of full air support, the bridgehead was reinforced and stood firm. The cream of the SS panzer troops failed to dislodge us, not because they were lacking in fighting spirit, but because they were put into the battle piecemeal as soon as they could be brought to the scene. In his efforts to prevent a break-through, the enemy found it necessary to employ his forces in small groups of about 200 infantry supported by 15 to 20 tanks, a process which proved both ineffective and expensive. The British forces compelled the enemy to continue these tactics, until by 1 July any chance he may have had of mounting a large-scale blow at any one point had been completely destroyed. By their unceasing pressure they had never allowed the initiative to pass to the enemy and had never given him the respite necessary to withdraw and mass his armored resources.

Nevertheless, in the east we had been unable to break out toward the Seine, and the enemy's concentration of his main power in the Caen sector had prevented us from securing the ground in that area we so badly needed. Our plans were sufficiently flexible that we could take advantage of this enemy reaction by directing that the American forces smash out of the lodgement area in the west while the British and Canadians kept the Germans occupied in the east.

Incessant pressure by the Second Army to contain the enemy's strength was therefore continued by Field Marshal Montgomery during July. Simultaneously, the US forces in the Cotentin proceeded to fight their way southward, alongside those who had landed east of the Vire, to win ground for mounting the attack which was to break through the German defenses at the end of the month. Field Marshal Montgomery's tactical handling of this situation was masterly. By this time, I was in no doubt as to the security of our beachhead from any immediate enemy threat, and the chief need was for elbow room in which to deploy our forces, the build-up of which had proceeded rapidly. We were already approaching the stage when the capacity of Cherbourg, the beaches, and the artificial ports would no longer be adequate to maintain us, and it was imperative that we should open up other ports, particularly those in Brittany, so that we might make our great attack before the enemy was able to obtain substantial equality in infantry, tanks, and artillery. The danger we had to meet was one of a position of stalemate along the whole front, when we might be forced to the defensive with only a slight depth of lodgement area behind us.

The indomitable offensive spirit animating all sections of the Allied forces prevented such a situation from arising; but it was hard going all along the front, and the first half of July was a wearing time for both sides. While the Second Army battled furiously against the enemy's armored strength to the east, the First Army struggled forward on both sides of the Vire.

It had been my intention that General Bradley's forces should strike south as soon as Cherbourg had fallen, but the need to reorganize and regroup prevented a start being made until 3 July. Then the advance was a laborious business owing to the close nature of the country and the atrocious weather. The enemy resisted fiercely along the whole front. In the VIII Corps sector violent fighting raged in the La-Haye-du-Puits area from 4 to 10 July, when the enemy's strongly organized positions were finally broken. VII Corps, attacking in terrain restricted by swampy land, suffered heavy losses for small gains along the Carentan–Périers highway. XIX Corps attacked across the Vire and established a bridgehead at St-Jean-de-Daye, then struck southward. The Germans, for the first time, transferred some armor from the eastern to the western sector, when the 2nd SS Panzer Division had been the only armored unit in action. Panzer Lehr now joined it west of the Vire. On 11 July, Panzer Lehr's counter-attack was smashed by the 9th and 30th Infantry Divisions, and on the same day, the US First Army opened a new drive east of the Vire and directly toward St-Lô. Promising gains were made but the German 2nd Parachute Corps rallied to prevent any breakthrough to St-Lô.

In view of the strength of this opposition to the First Army, which caused the advance to be disappointingly slow although General Bradley attacked unceasingly with everything he could bring into action, Field Marshal Montgomery had decided to redouble the efforts on the eastern flank and, as he said, to "put the wind up the enemy by seizing Caen" in preparation for establishing a bridgehead across the Orne. When this had been done, the Second Army could either drive south with its left flank on the Orne or else take over the Caumont sector in order to free more American troops for the thrust toward Brittany.

In spite of his reinforcement of the western part of the front, it was evident that the enemy continued to regard the defense of Caen as the matter of greatest importance, and 700 of his available 900 tanks were still located in this sector. They were now under command of Panzer Group West, which held the sector east of the Drôme River, facing the British Second Army. Following the establishment of the Odon bridgehead, interest in the Second Army area was focused on a Canadian thrust towards Caen from the west which led to bitter resistance by the Germans at Carpiquet, where a three-day duel (4–6 July) for the possession of the airfield was fought between the Canadian 3 Infantry Division and the 12th SS Panzer Division.

On 8 July, Field Marshal Montgomery mounted his full-scale assault upon Caen. Applying the principles which he had first employed with such success in North Africa, he concentrated a maximum of striking power on one sector to achieve a breakthrough. The attack was preceded by an air bombardment of nearly 500 RAF "heavies," supplemented by effective naval fire from HMS *Rodney, Roberts* and *Belfast*, and by land artillery. Although six hours elapsed between the air bombing and the ground attack, the result was to paralyse the enemy, who broke before our attack. The bombing having cut off their supplies, they ran out of ammunition and rations, and we occupied the whole of the town north and west of the Orne. Our advance was made difficult by the debris and cratering resulting from the bombing, and the enemy still held the Faubourg de Vaucelles across the river.

The entry into Caen was followed by a renewed thrust to extend the Odon bridgehead, and the capture of Maltôt on 10 July threatened to trap the enemy in the triangle between the Orne and the Odon. The threat produced vigorous enemy reaction again, the fighting for possession of Hill 112 being especially bitter. Once more the enemy was forced to bring back into the battle the armored elements which he had been in process of replacing in the line by infantry and withdrawing to form a strong striking force in reserve. A few days later he made another attempt, withdrawing two SS panzer divisions, but the Second Army attack on Evrecy on 16–17 July forced him, not only to bring the armor hurriedly back, but to adopt the dangerous and uneconomical policy of dividing an SS panzer division into two battle groups.

Only the 12th SS Panzer Division, weary from a long period of activity culminating in its defeat before Caen, now remained in reserve, and the big attack south and east of Caen which materialized on 18 July put an end to its relaxation.

This continuing failure by the enemy to form an armored reserve constitutes the outstanding feature of the campaign during June and July: to it we owed the successful establishment of our lodgement area, safe from the threat of counter-attacks which might have driven us back into the sea. Every time an attempt was made to replace armor in the line with a newly arrived infantry division a fresh attack necessitated its hasty recommittal. These continual Allied jabs compelled the enemy to maintain his expensive policy of frantically "plugging the holes" to avert a breakthrough. So long as the pressure continued, and so long as the threat to the Pas-de-Calais proved effective in preventing the move of infantry reinforcements from there across the Seine, the enemy had no alternative but to stand on the defensive and see the Seventh Army and Panzer Group West slowly bleed to death. All that he could do was play for time, denying us ground by fighting hard for every defensive position.

Meanwhile, to the west, the steady pressure of the First Army forced the enemy gradually back through the close countryside, strewn with mines, toward the line of the Lessay–Périers–St-Lô road, where he had decided to make his main stand. His defence was weakest at the western extremity of this line, but in the St-Lô sector he showed a lively anxiety to hold this important road junction, the capture of which was essential to the success of our plan for a break-through. On 18 July, however, St-Lô fell to the 29th Division, and the 9th and 30th Infantry Divisions, west of St-Lô and across the Vire, had reached high ground suitable for launching the breakthrough attempt.

Thus, by 18 July, both the First and Second Armies had taken up the positions from which the breakthrough attacks were to be started. We now had the requisite room to maneuver, and our divisions in the field had been built up to 15 US (including 3 armored) and 15 British and Canadian (including 4 armored), against which the enemy had 27, 8 of which were armored. On account of the losses which we had inflicted, however, the actual strength of the enemy was no more than the equivalent of six panzer or panzer-grenadier and ten full-strength infantry divisions. He had committed 540,000 men to battle and had lost at least 160,000 of them, killed, wounded, and prisoners; of 1,200 tanks committed, 30% had been lost. His reinforcement prospects were not rosy, for only four of his panzer divisions in the west (outside the Pas-de-Calais) had not yet been committed to the battle, and these were not ready for combat. His six divisions in Brittany had already been bled to help hold the line in Normandy, while in the southern half of France there were only 12 divisions left, of which but seven or eight were actually avail-able to guard the coasts, thanks to the action of the

Maquis inland. The southwestern part of the country had been practically evacuated of effective field units. Only the Fifteenth Army in the Pas-de-Calais, 19 divisions strong, was still left substantially intact, waiting for the expected further landings, which the commencement of the flying bomb attacks on 12 June may have made appear more likely than ever to the Germans.

Although the process had taken somewhat longer than we had anticipated, we had undeniably won the first and second rounds. In the first round we had gained our footing in France; in the second we had retained the initiative while expanding and consolidating our lodgement area and building up our strength in men and materials in readiness for the decisive blow to follow.

The enemy never succeeded in remedying the fatal situation into which Rommel's reliance on the Atlantic Wall had led him following the achievement of our landings. It was a coincidence that our old opponent of Africa should be struck down on the eve of the Second Army attack across the Orne, which was to be the precursor of the breakthrough in the west.

THE BREAKTHROUGH

From the beginning of the campaign in Normandy, I agreed with Field Marshal Montgomery and General Bradley that our basic policy should be so to maneuver and attack as to pin down and destroy substantial portions of the enemy in our immediate front in order later to have full freedom of action. The alternative would have been merely a pushing-back, with consequent necessity for slowly battling our way toward the ultimate geographical objectives. By the third week in

The breakthrough

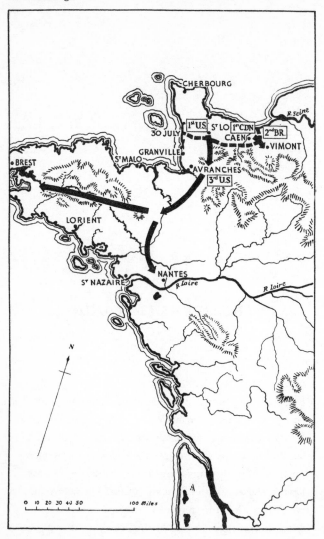

July, our forces were in position to launch the all-out attack, which, in accordance with this strategic idea, was to break through and destroy the enemy divisions then with difficulty attempting to contain us in our lodgement area. By throwing all our weight into an offensive at this stage, I felt confident that we should not only achieve our objectives but that, in the long run, the cost of our victory would be the less.

The enemy's reaction had convinced us that we should strike hard with our left and then follow through promptly with a right-hand blow. In both cases, the whole weight of our air power was to be employed to support the ground attacks. We agreed also that the main attacks were to be supported by aggressive action all along the line to pin down the enemy's local reserves. He had no major reserves immediately available, and we did not fear any serious counter-offensive.

In the Second Army sector, vigorous thrusts in the Évrecy–Esquay area through the Odon bridge-head on 16–17 July were to be in the nature of a feint to distract the enemy's attention and to cause him to withdraw more of his armor westward across the Orne to meet the threat. Then on 18 July, the main British–Canadian thrust was to take the form of a drive across the Orne from Caen toward the south and southeast, exploiting in the direction of the Seine basin and Paris. On the following day, General Bradley would launch his major attack across the Périers–St-Lô. Having achieved a breakthrough, he was to swing his spearheads westward to Coutances, in order to isolate the enemy divisions between St-Lô and the coast, and then strike down through Avranches, creating if possible an open flank. By this means we could then operate into the Brittany Peninsula to open up the much-needed ports, while the German Seventh Army and at least part of Panzer Group West could be encircled and crushed between the US forces to the west and the British and Canadians to the east.

The execution of this plan opened promisingly. The enemy, as we had hoped, was deceived as to our intentions on the Second Army front by the operations in the Évrecy–Esquay area on 16 and 17 July. The reserve which he had been trying to form with two armored divisions was hurriedly broken up and part of one of them was brought westward over the Orne to counter our threat. Consequently our drive to the south and southeast of Caen across the river on 18 July achieved complete tactical surprise.

The attack was preceded at dawn on that day by what was the heaviest and most concentrated air assault hitherto employed in support of ground operations. The operation was a fine example of Anglo-American air cooperation, in which over 2,000 aircraft of RAF Bomber Command and the US Eighth and Ninth Air Forces took part, dropping a total of over 7,000 tons of bombs. While RAF Halifaxes and Lancasters dropped over 5,000 tons of bombs in less than 45 minutes on the area south of the river over which the ground assault was to be made, US planes attacked the enemy concentrations to the rear and on the flanks. In the carpet bombing, fragmentation bombs were used to break the enemy resistance without causing extensive cratering which would have hindered the advance of our tanks. At the same time, a strong naval bombardment was made to supplement the air effort.

Although only temporary in effect, the results of the bombing were decisive so far as the initial ground attack was concerned. Actual casualties to the enemy, in his foxholes, were comparatively few, but he was stunned by the weight of the bombing and a degree of confusion was caused which rendered the opposition to our advance negligible for some hours. At the same time, the spectacle of our mighty air fleets roaring in over their heads to attack had a most heartening effect upon our own men. The attack was led by the 7, 11, and Guards Armoured Divisions under 8 Corps, commanded by Lieut. Gen. O'Connor. These struck across the river at 0745 hours, followed by the infantry of 1 Corps and Canadian 2 Corps on either flank. The enemy at first proved unable to regroup his armor to meet the thrust, while the 21st Panzer and 16th GAF Divisions, which bore the brunt of the attack, were too disorganized by the bombing to offer much resistance. By the afternoon, the 11 Armoured Division had reached the Bourguébus area, the Guards were at Vimont, and the 7 Armoured Division had advanced to the south beyond Démouville. Toward evening, however, enemy resistance stiffened and he was able to counter-attack with 50 tanks south and southeast of

Bourguébus. By nightfall, he succeeded in establishing a strong anti-tank screen with guns which had escaped the bombing, and this effectively halted our advance on the line Emiéville–Cagny–Soliers. On the following days the weather, which had relented to permit the massive air effort of the 18th, broke once more, turning the low-lying country of the battle area into a sea of mud which afforded an effective check to further tank operations.

This break in the weather also delayed the First Army attack which was scheduled for 19 July. Here, as at Caen, General Bradley and I had decided that an overwhelming air bombardment was a necessary prerequisite to the success of our plans. It was not, however, until 25 July that the skies cleared sufficiently to permit this air effort. Meanwhile the men of the First Army were compelled to huddle in their foxholes under the dripping hedgerows in conditions of extreme discomfort, while the enemy, similarly entrenched behind the natural defenses of the country, was alert to every movement. It was not until after six days of waiting, more miserable to the American troops than any others in this campaign, that the opportunity for action came on 25 July.

The plan of the attack was that, following a heavy air bombardment of the enemy positions, the First Army was to advance on a 3-divisional front west of St-Lô, with the general line Marigny–St-Gilles as the primary objective. Three more divisions were then to pass through the first wave, turn westward, and strike for Coutances and Granville, thus cutting off the enemy in the area Périers–Lessay. These first two waves were to be launched by VII Corps, with VIII Corps subsequently taking up the battle in the Lessay sector and advancing along the coast on our right.

As the outcome of the British–Canadian–American joint operations, I envisaged three possibilities. First, given a spell of fine weather, there was good reason to hope for such measure of success by both the First and Second Armies that our forces might encircle the enemy west of Vire and so eliminate his units as practically to create an open flank. In this case, it would be unnecessary to detach any large forces for the conquest of Brittany and the bulk of our strength could be devoted to completing the destruction of the enemy forces in Normandy. As a second possibility, the enemy might succeed in establishing a defensive line running from Caen to Avranches, in which case the task of gaining Brittany would require another large-scale thrust on the right flank. Thirdly, if, as seemed very unlikely, the enemy could manage to block our advance beyond this Caen–Avranches line, we had ready a special amphibious-airborne operation designed to seize Brittany in the enemy's rear. As the situation stood at that time, the conquest of Brittany was still an all-important aim of our policy in order that through its ports we might receive and maintain the additional divisions with which we planned to pursue the battle across France. We could not then envisage the full extent of the defeat which the enemy was to sustain in Normandy.

On the morning of 25 July an area five miles long and one mile wide to the west of St-Lô was blasted by 1,495 heavy bombers of the Eighth Air Force and 388 aircraft of AEAF dropping over 4,700 tons of bombs. At the same time, medium bombers attacked troops and gun concentrations southeast of Caen, and fighter-bombers with bombs and rocket projectiles attacked targets behind the American assault area. The total of AEAF sorties for this day was 4,979. Of all the planes employed in these massive operations, only 6 heavy bombers, 4 light bombers, and 19 fighters were lost. These were chiefly the victims of flak; the enemy fighters offered more combat than usual, but did not succeed in penetrating our fighter screen and reaching the bombers.

As in the case of the bombardment of Caen a week earlier, the air blow preceding the ground attack west of St-Lô did not cause a large number of casualties to the enemy sheltering in their dug-in positions, but it produced great confusion. Communications broke down and supplies from the rear were cut off. During the actual bombing the bewilderment of the enemy was such that some men unwittingly ran toward our lines and four uninjured tanks put up white flags before any ground attack was launched. Again, as at Caen, this stunning effect was only temporary.

The closeness of the air support given in this operation, thanks to our recent experiences, was such as we should never have dared to attempt a year before. We had indeed made enormous strides forward in this respect; and from the two Caen operations we had learned the need for a quicker ground follow-up on the conclusion of the bombing, for the avoidance of cratering, and for attacks upon a wider range of targets to the rear and on the flanks of the main bombardment area. Our technique, however, was still not yet perfected, and some of our bombs fell short, causing casualties to our own men. Unfortunately, perfection in the employment of comparatively new tactics, such as this close-support carpet bombing, is attainable only through the process of trial and error, and these regrettable losses were part of the inevitable price of experience. Among those who lost their lives on this occasion was Lieut. Gen. Lesley J. McNair, who was watching the preparations for the attack from a foxhole in the front line. His death was a heavy blow to the United States Army and a source of keen sorrow to me personally.

At the commencement of the ground battle, VII Corps, in the sector west of St-Lô, had under command the 2nd and 3rd Armored Divisions and the 1st, 4th, 9th, and 30th Infantry Divisions; while VIII Corps, in the Périers–Lessay sector had the 8th, 79th, 83rd, and 90th Infantry Divisions with the 4th Armored Division. The battle began with the advance of VII Corps at midday on 25 July; the 9th Division was on the right flank, 4th Division in the center, and 30th Division on the left, with 1st Division and the armor in the rear. At the same time our VIII, XIX, and V Corps maintained their pressure along the remainder of the army front. South of Caen, the Canadian 2 Corps simultaneously advanced southward astride the Falaise road.

The American advance was met with intense artillery fire, from positions not neutralized by the air bombing, on the left flank, while on the right German parachute units resisted fiercely. The ordinary infantry opposition, provided by elements of three infantry divisions, and of one panzer division, was not so severe. The enemy was still weak in armor in the sector fronting the US armies: although three panzer divisions were there, the bulk of his armored strength was still concentrated under Panzer Group West, with one panzer division west of the Orne, and five east of the river.

The advance at first made slow progress, but by midnight VII Corps had crossed the Périers–St-Lô road, and on 26 July its 1st Infantry and 2nd and 3rd Armored Divisions took up the attack. Lozon, Marigny, and St-Gilles were taken and the St-Lô– Coutances road cut. On the same day VIII Corps attacked across the Périers–St-Lô road to the west of VII Corps. The Germans continued to counter-attack vigorously, and, as the Allied thrust swung westward toward Coutances, it became clear that the enemy intended to retain that town as long as possible in order that he might extricate his troops from the north.

During 27 July the towns of Périers and Lessay were taken, and despite many mines and booby-traps the advance on Coutances was pushed ahead, led by the armored units. Pockets of resistance were by-passed by the tanks and left to be mopped up by the infantry. The enemy meanwhile struggled to withdraw his forces through Coutances, but the infantry elements in the coastal sector had commenced their retreat too late, and our air forces took heavy toll of the vehicles streaming southward along the roads converging on the city. The enemy forces north of Coutances at this time comprised elements of three infantry divisions (77th, 243rd, and 353rd), 2nd SS Panzer and 17th SS Panzer Grenadier Divisions, and battle groups of the 265th, 266th, and 275th Infantry Divisions. The German Command concentrated primarily on evacuating the SS formations, leaving the remainder to their fate.

On 28 July the escape route through Coutances was sealed with the capture of the city by the 4th Armored Division, which, with the 6th Armored Division, formed the spearhead of VIII Corps. These two formations then pressed on southward with gathering speed to the Sienne River, while VII Corps, spearheaded by the 2nd and 3rd Armored Divisions, continued to attack southwestward toward Granville and Avranches. The enemy withdrawal, following the loss of Coutances, began to degenerate into a disorderly retreat, and 4,500 prisoners were taken during the 24 hours of 28 July. Although minefields were laid to slow the pursuit, and German armored units fought a stubborn rearguard action, the advance was not checked. The 5th Parachute Division, Panzer Lehr Division, and 353rd Infantry Division were almost completely accounted for by this time, although, in accordance with German practice, they were reconstituted at a later stage of the campaign.

Meanwhile, on 28 July, XIX Corps, advancing south from St-Lô, reached Tessy-sur-Vire, while V Corps attacked south of the Forêt de Cerisy against stiff resistance by 3rd Parachute Division. Further east, in the British–Canadian sector, Canadian 2 Corps' advance toward Falaise had been halted by a strong defensive belt of anti-tank guns, dug-in tanks and mortars. The Canadians were probing the defenses, with the aid of magnificent support by the RAF 83 Group, and considerable losses were inflicted on the enemy. Our pressure on this sector was not, however, able to prevent the move of 2nd Panzer Division from the east bank of the Orne across to the Tessy area, where it made a stand to cover the general with-drawal from Coutances. Elements of two infantry divisions with a small proportion of the 2nd Parachute Division were also being brought to the battle area from Brittany to bolster up the enemy's front. Prior to the arrival of these reinforcements, the enemy troops opposing the US sector, while nomi-nally consisting of nine infantry, two parachute, one panzer grenadier, and two panzer divisions, had an estimated combat strength of only three and a half infantry, one parachute, and three panzer-type divi-sions. Against the British sector, from Caumont to Cabourg, were nominally eight infantry and five panzer divisions, of a real strength not exceeding that of five and a half infantry and three and a half panzer divisions.

If further reinforcements were to be provided for the Seventh Army, and Panzer Group West, the majority of them would have to be drawn from the Fifteenth Army in the Pas-de-Calais. Of the Seventh Army itself, only the infantry division in the Channel Islands and parts of the two divisions in Brittany remained uncommitted. In the southwest of France, the German First Army had only two limited-employment infantry divisions, three training divisions, and a panzer division (which was engaged against the Maquis). The Nineteenth Army, in the southeast, had already sent three infantry divisions to the battle area, only one of which had been replaced; one field-type infantry division, six limited-employment infantry divisions, and a panzer division remained. The double threat of the Maquis and of Allied landings on the Mediterranean coast made it unlikely that much more would be forthcoming for Normandy from this source, with the possible exception of elements of the panzer division. Holland had contributed three limited-employment divisions to Normandy, and its coast-guarding units were seriously stretched. Replacements from within Germany had begun to arrive in the battle area, but the strength of the divisions opposing the Allies continued to decrease. Many units had been compelled in the recent fighting to use service elements, engineers, and artillery personnel as infantry, and others had been cannibalized to maintain the stronger divisions.

It was at this time that the effectiveness of our threat to the Pas-de-Calais began to decrease as the Germans found themselves faced with a more immediate danger in the shape of the breakthrough in

Normandy. We were anxious to maintain the threat for as long as possible, although its greatest function— that of keeping the Fifteenth Army inactive during the crucial period of the assault and establishment of the lodgement area—had already been completed with such extraordinary success. The first moves from the Fifteenth Army area westward over the Seine coincided with the launching of the US First Army attack on 25 July, when the German 363rd Infantry Division began to cross the river, while others prepared to follow it.

Following the success of our initial breakthrough in the west I considered that, in order fully to exploit our advantages, the time had come for the establishment of the US Third Army. This officially came into existence under General Patton on 1 August, taking over command of VIII, XII, XV, and XX Corps, while V, VII, and XIX Corps remained with First Army. The two armies were placed under command of General Bradley, whose leadership of the First Army had been so brilliantly successful. General (then Lieut. Gen.) C. H. Hodges succeeded him as Commanding General, First Army.

Earlier, on 23 July, the Canadian First Army under General Crerar had also become operational, having under command initially the British 1 Corps, to which was joined the Canadian 2 Corps on 31 July. The army took over the easternmost coastal sector of the entire front. With the British Second Army, under General Dempsey, it now formed 21 Army Group, commanded by Field Marshal Montgomery.

My own operational headquarters was at this time in process of moving to the Continent, and in order to ensure unified control during this critical stage of our operations General Montgomery continued to act as my representative, with authority, under my supervision, over the entire operation as coordinator of activities. This arrangement continued from 1 August until 1 September, when my operations staff and communications were established and I assumed personal direction of the two army groups.

Following the capture of Coutances our plan was for the Third Army to drive south in the western sector, breaking through Avranches into Brittany and seizing the area Rennes–Fougères, thence turning westward to secure St-Malo, the Quiberon Bay area and Brest, and clearing the entire peninsula. Meanwhile the First Army would advance south to seize the area Mortain–Vire.

At the same time the Second Army was to concentrate on a thrust in the Caumont area, side by side with that of the First Army on Vire. The enemy in this part of the front had only some four regiments in the line, reinforced with an occasional dug-in tank, and a great opportunity appeared here for a striking blow which, with General Bradley's offensive in the west, might bring decisive results. Rapidity of action was the vital factor now. We could not afford to wait either for weather or for perfection in the details of our preparations. The enemy was reeling and it was imperative that we should not allow him time to readjust his lines, shift his units, or bring up reserves.

Our policy must be to indulge in an all-out offensive and, if necessary, throw caution to the winds.

Our advance in the west continued. On 29 July VIII Corps' armor crossed the Sienne, south of Coutances; two days later Avranches fell to the 4th Armored Division; and on 31 July the 6th Armored Division reduced the elements resisting at Granville. No effective barrier now lay between us and Brittany, and my expectations of creating an open flank had been realized. The enemy was in a state of complete disorganization and our fighters and fighter-bombers swarmed over the roads, shooting up the jammed columns of German transport to such effect that our own advance was slowed by the masses of knocked-out vehicles. The enemy infantry was in no condition to resist us, and only the weary, badly battered armor put up any considerable fight.

At the same time the British launched their thrust south of Caumont. The enemy was attempting, with two armored divisions, to establish a hinge in the Percy–Tessy area on which to conduct operations designed to prevent a collapse of the entire Normandy front. In this, however, he was defeated by the combined First Army frontal attacks and the Second Army flank drive toward Vire. The British offensive in the Caumont sector was preceded by another smashing air bombardment by nearly 700 RAF heavy bombers, supported by over 500 AEAF light and medium bombers, which, as usual, had a paralysing effect upon the enemy. Prisoners stated that the confusion was so great that effective unit fighting was rendered impossible for at least 12 hours, although the Allies lost some part of this advantage through not launching the ground attack immediately after the cessation of the bombing. Enemy attempts to deny us the high ground west of Mont Pinçon and the valley of the Vire were frustrated; Le Bény-Bocage was captured by the 11 Armored Division (8 Corps) on 1 August and, following heavy fighting, Vire was entered on 2 August only to be temporarily recaptured by two SS panzer divisions on the next day. There was a bitter struggle for some days before the enemy was finally forced back from this sector. Farther to the northeast, Villers-Bocage was taken on 5 August and Évrecy and Esquay, southwest of Caen, on the 4th.

By these combined efforts of the First and Second Armies, the flank of the American salient was safeguarded. The enemy, having finally decided to use his Fifteenth Army resources to reinforce the Normandy front, was now at last replacing, with the newly acquired infantry, the armor which he had hitherto kept massed east of the Orne to prevent any possibility of a breakthrough there toward Paris and the Seine. The armor so freed he proceeded to transfer westward toward the Vire area in support of the Seventh Army troops struggling to prevent a collapse of the front there, and to provide the necessary weight to hurl against the flanks of the Third Army. Resistance accordingly stiffened as four panzer divisions arrived from east of the Orne, followed by a further panzer division and an infantry division from across the Seine.

Following the capture of Granville and Avranches, the Third Army advance continued against negligible resistance into Brittany. The passage of the Selune River was assured by the 4th Armored Division's capture of its dams on 1 August and then this division struck southward to cut the neck of the Brittany Peninsula, while the 6th Armored Division turned westward toward Brest. The airborne operation which we had prepared to assist in "turning the corner" into Brittany was rendered unnecessary by the unimpeded rapidity of the ground force advances. On 2 August the 4th Armored Division was in the suburbs of Rennes, and the 6th Armored Division reached Dinan, by-passing St-Malo. Combat commands of these two divisions, followed by the 8th, 79th, and 83d Infantry Divisions, now proceeded quickly to overrun the peninsula. On 4 August Rennes was in our hands, and while one column drove on from there toward Nantes another secured Fougères and Vitre, continuing southward toward the Loire. By 6 August the line of the Vilaine River was held from Rennes to the sea, thus completing the cutting off of the peninsula, while to the east the 5th Infantry Division reached the Loire River between Nantes and Angers, Nantes itself falling on 10 August. Meanwhile the 6th Armored Division had traversed Brittany to the west and was standing before Brest.

The opposition encountered by General Patton's flying columns in the course of this sweep was negligible, for the enemy's flank had collapsed so completely that there was hardly any resistance offered by organized units above company strength. The Germans, realizing the impossibility of forming any defensive line on which to hold the peninsula, accepted the inevitable and abandoned the interior of Brittany in order to concentrate their available strength to defend Brest, St-Nazaire, St-Malo, and Lorient, the ports which they estimated to be our principal objectives. The forces left to them for this purpose consisted of some 45,000 garrison troops, together with elements of the 2nd Parachute Division and three infantry divisions—in all some 75,000 men. Inland, only small pockets of resistance remained, and these were by-passed by the armored columns and left to be mopped up by the infantry and the local French Forces of the Interior (FFI). By the end of the first week of August the enemy had been forced everywhere to fall back into the ports under siege by the troops of VIII Corps.

Special mention must be made of the great assistance given us by the FFI in the task of reducing Brittany. The overt resistance forces in this area had been built up since June around a core of SAS troops of the French 4th Parachute Battalion to a total strength of some 30,000 men. On the night of 4/5 August the État-Major was dispatched to take charge of their operations. As the Allied columns advanced, these French forces ambushed the retreating enemy, attacked isolated groups and strongpoints, and protected bridges from destruction. When our armor had swept past them they were given the task of clearing up the localities where pockets of Germans remained, and of keeping open the Allied lines of communication. They also provided our troops with invaluable assistance in supplying information of the enemy's dispositions and intentions. Not least in importance, they had, by their ceaseless harassing activities, surrounded the Germans with a terrible atmosphere of danger and hatred which ate into the confidence of the leaders and the courage of the soldiers.

BATTLE OF THE
FALAISE–ARGENTAN POCKET

During the first week of August, the completeness
of the enemy collapse on his western flank was such
that my best hopes were realized and we were presented with the opportunity of operating toward the
rear of his forces in Normandy to effect an encirclement. I felt that the chances of delivering a knockout
blow there were so favorable that, despite our need for
the Brittany ports, I was unwilling to detach for their

Battle of Falaise–Argentan pocket

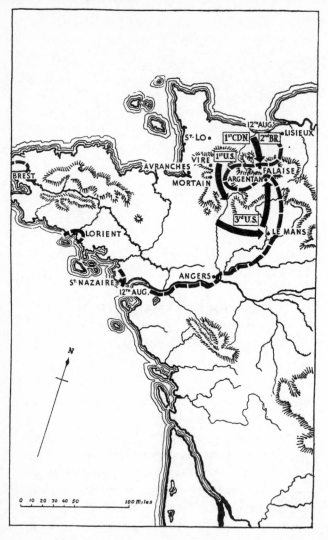

capture major forces from the main armies fighting in Normandy. Into the ranks of the German Seventh Army and Panzer Group West had been drawn the cream of the enemy forces in Western Europe. Our tactics must again be adapted to take advantage of the enemy's reactions. The encirclement and destruction of these armies would afford us complete freedom of action throughout France. Therefore it was decided virtually to turn our backs upon Brittany. The VIII Corps of the Third Army alone would be left with the task of reducing Brittany ports, while the remainder of our troops, supported by the maximum weight of our air effort, could concentrate on the annihilation of the main body of the enemy.

XV Corps of the Third Army, striking south on the left flank of VIII Corps, occupied the towns of Mayenne and Laval on 6 August, and our plan was for this corps to advance thence to the east, supported by XII Corps and XX Corps as these became operational. From Le Mans a spearhead was to turn northward, advancing through Alençon toward Argentan. At the same time the Canadian First Army would continue its thrust on Falaise with a view to an eventual link-up with the Americans at Argentan, thus drawing a net around the bulk of the enemy forces to the west. Meanwhile the British Second Army and US First Army would close in from the north and west respectively.

Our greatest difficulty and danger in the execution of this plan lay in the problem of supply to the Third Army. General Patton's lightning armored thrusts, exploiting the enemy's open flank, had already imposed upon our Services of Supply an immense burden. This was successfully shouldered only by dint of gallant and unceasing efforts by the personnel of the transport columns, the capacity of which was heavily strained. Moreover, because of the enemy's stubborn resistance in the Brittany ports, these supplies had to be brought from the beaches and from Cherbourg all the way down the west side of the Cotentin and through our still narrow corridor at Avranches.

It was the precarious nature of this supply route that now dictated the enemy's strategy, a strategy which, while initially it appeared sound, ultimately helped us to accomplish our object of shattering the two German armies in Normandy. As has been shown, the arrival in the Caen sector of infantry reinforcements from east of the Seine at the end of July enabled the enemy to move armor toward the Vire, to prevent an immediate collapse of his entire front when our breakthrough was achieved west of St-Lô. This armor was now massed in the Mortain area and brought under unified command, with the intention of driving westward through Avranches to the coast and thus cutting off the US Third Army from its supply bases. This was the first occasion since the commencement of the campaign two months earlier that the enemy had been able to assemble his armor into a strong striking force of the traditional panzer type; and it was destined to be his last panzer offensive until von Rundstedt launched his desperate thrust from the Siegfried Line against the First Army on 16 December. The group assembled east of Mortain for the drive on Avranches consisted of the 1st SS, 2nd SS, 2nd and 116th Panzer Divisions, with elements of the 17th SS Panzer Grenadier Division, and supporting infantry: a formidable force. The importance which the enemy attached to the operation was shown by the withdrawal of his long-range bombers from night mine-laying off the beaches (almost their sole employment since 6 June) for use in support of the ground thrust.

The attack was launched on 7 August, while other elements of the Seventh Army counter-attacked at Vire to safeguard the flanks of the armored drive. General Bradley had correctly estimated the enemy intentions, had taken his own dispositions in ample time, and had no concern as to the result. When the blow fell, the 4th, 9th, and 30th Infantry Divisions, the 3rd Armored Division, and part of the 2nd Armored Division were near Mortain. In stern defensive battle these units of VII Corps stemmed the attack. Great assistance in smashing the enemy's spearhead was given by the rocket-firing Typhoon planes of the Second Tactical Air Force. They dived upon the armored columns, and, with their rocket projectiles, destroyed and damaged many tanks in addition to quantities of "soft-skinned" vehicles. The result of the vigorous reaction by ground and air forces was that the enemy attack was effectively brought to a halt, and a threat was turned into a great victory. For once, the weather was on our side, and conditions were ideal for our air operations. If our planes had been grounded, the enemy might have succeeded in reaching Avranches in his first rush, and this would then have forced us to depend for a time on air supply to our troops south and east of the Avranches corridor, necessarily restricting their capacity to maneuver.

Despite this check and the high losses sustained, the enemy persisted for the time being in his efforts to break through to Avranches, and the battle continued during the following days. The fierce attacks of the panzer divisions were met with stubborn resistance by US VII Corps, while our tactical air forces continued to afford magnificent support in bombing and strafing the enemy concentrations. To maintain the weight of his attack, the enemy brought up further armored reinforcements, and the fighting continued heavy and confused around the hills at Mortain. From there the Germans could look westward over the level plain across which they had hoped to drive to Avranches, and perhaps the fact that they thus had their objective within view contributed to the persistence of their efforts.

It was not until 12 August that the first signs became evident that the enemy had resigned himself to the impossibility of attaining his objective and at last was contemplating a withdrawal. As on former occasions, the fanatical tenacity of the Nazi leaders and the ingrained toughness of their men had led the Germans to cling too long to a position from which military wisdom would have dictated an earlier retreat. Already by 10 August it was difficult to see how the enemy's counter-attacks, admitted that they represented a desperate effort to stabilize temporarily a most dangerous general situation, could achieve decisive results.

By 10 August, following a conference at General Bradley's Headquarters, it was decided to seize the opportunity for encirclement offered by the enemy tactics. XV Corps of the Third Army already had pushed eastward to capture Le Mans on 9 August and had thence turned north according to plan to threaten the rear of the armored forces battling at Mortain. At the same time XX Corps drove beyond Châteaubriant toward the Loire and captured Angers on 10 August, thus effectively guarding the southern flank of our encircling movement. On 11 August XV Corps was north of the Sées–Carrouges road, and on the night of 12 August the US 5th Armored Division was in the outskirts of Argentan and the French 2nd Armored Division at Ecouche, with the 79th and 90th Infantry Divisions in support.

Meanwhile the US First Army pushed southwest from Vire against stubborn resistance while the British Second Army forced the enemy from his dominating position on Mont Pinçon (south of Aunay-sur-Odon) and on 13 August occupied Thury-Harcourt. Six days earlier, the Second Army had established a bridgehead across the Orne below Thury-Harcourt at Grimbosq, in the teeth of furious opposition. This salient was created in support of the Canadian First Army thrust down the Caen–Falaise road. Still, as ever, the Caen sector remained the most sensitive part of the front in the north, and the Allied progress was slow and dearly bought against the strongest defenses yet encountered in the campaign. The Fifth Panzer Army, replacing Armored Group West, now defended this sector. On 7 August, over 1,000 heavy bombers of the RAF were employed to soften up enemy concentrations between Caen and Bretteville, and on the following day nearly 500 heavies of the Eighth Air Force laid a carpet in front of a Canadian attack which reached Bretteville itself. The enemy fell back to the line of the Laison River between Potigny and Maizières, where he successfully held the Canadians for several days. Not until 14 August was this line broken, following a further heavy air onslaught, and on 17 August Falaise was finally occupied. From our landings in June until that day, the enemy resistance in this sector had exacted more Allied bloodshed for the ground yielded than in any other part of the campaign. Without the great sacrifices made here by the Anglo-Canadian armies in the series of brutal, slugging battles, first for Caen and then for Falaise, the spectacular advances made elsewhere by the Allied forces could never have come about.

With the Third Army forces at Argentan and the Canadians at Falaise, the stage was set for the "Battle of the Pocket," with the enemy struggling to keep open the gap between the two towns through which to extricate his forces from the west. By 13 August, the withdrawal from Mortain eastward toward Argentan was under way. Infantry reinforcements were being brought hurriedly across the Seine—five divisions crossed during the week preceding 12 August—but it was too late now for them to be able to save the situation. In the pocket, the enemy's strategy was to line the southern lip through Argentan with his armor to defend against the American forces as he extricated what he could through the gap, while a strong defensive barrier against the Canadians was established with the 12th SS Panzer and 21st Panzer Divisions at Falaise. By this means, resisting fiercely, he managed to hold open the jaws of our pincers long enough to enable a portion of his forces to escape. As usual, he concentrated on saving his armor and left the bulk of the infantry to their fate—a subject of bitter comment by prisoners from the latter units who fell into our hands. A considerable part of the 1st SS Panzer, 2nd SS Panzer, 9th SS Panzer, 12th SS Panzer, Panzer Lehr, 2nd Panzer, 9th Panzer, and 116th Panzer Divisions managed thus to get away; but the 326th, 353rd, 363rd, 271st, 276th, 277th, 89th, and part of the 331st Infantry Divisions, with some of the 10th SS Panzer and 21st Panzer Divisions, were trapped. Those armored forces which did escape, however, only did so at the cost of losing a great proportion of their equipment.

Until 17 August, there was a steady seep eastward through the gap, but then came a convulsive surge to get out on the part of all ranks; and the orderliness with which the retreat had hitherto been carried out collapsed suddenly. The 12th SS Panzer Division, aided by the other elements which had managed to escape, counter-attacked from outside the pocket to assist the remainder, but as the gap narrowed they were forced to abandon their efforts and look to their own safety as the advance of the Third Army to the Seine threatened a new trap behind them. All became chaos and confusion as the remaining forces in the pocket struggled to get out through the diminishing corridor by Trun, which was all that remained of the escape route. Road discipline among the columns fleeing toward the Seine became non-existent, and vehicles plunged madly across the open country in an effort to avoid the blocked roads. Our air forces swept down upon the choked masses of transport, and there was no sign of the Luftwaffe to offer any opposition. With the US Third Army on the Seine, the German fighter force had been compelled to retire to airfields in the east of France, too far away for them to be able now to give any assistance to the ground troops in Normandy.

Back inside the pocket, the confusion was still greater, and the destruction assumed immense proportions as our aircraft and artillery combined in pounding the trapped Germans. Allied guns ringed the ever-shrinking "killing-ground," and, while the SS elements as usual fought to annihilation, the ordinary German infantry gave themselves up in ever-increasing numbers. By 20 August the gap was finally closed near Chambois, and by 22 August the pocket was eliminated. The lovely, wooded countryside west of Argentan had become the graveyard of the army which, three months earlier, had confidently waited to smash the Allied invasion on the Normandy beaches. What was left of the Seventh and Fifth Panzer Armies was in headlong flight toward the Seine, and a further stand west of the river was impossible.

THE ADVANCE TO THE SEINE

My decision, following the collapse of the enemy's western flank at the end of July, to concentrate upon the encirclement and destruction of his forces in Normandy, and to use almost the whole of our available strength in order to attain this object, marked a considerable departure from the original Allied plan of campaign. Under this, as already explained, a primary objective had been the capture of the Brittany ports, through which it was intended to introduce the

Advance to the Seine

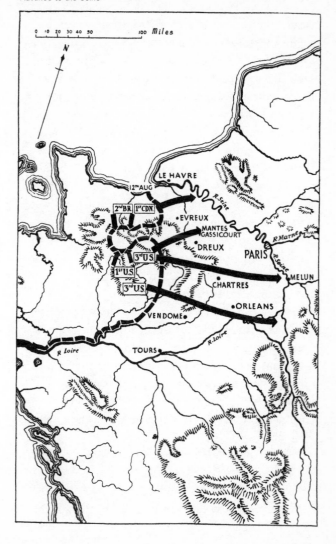

further divisions from the United States necessary to ensure the completion of the German defeat. The capture of these ports had been envisaged as a task for the Third Army as a whole, but in order to accomplish our new plans for the Normandy battle it was necessary to move the bulk of General Patton's forces eastward to carry out the great encircling movement.

The prospect of inflicting a decisive and annihilating defeat upon the Seventh Army and Panzer Group West had been so good that I had no hesitation in making my decision. If their units could be shattered in Normandy, then I knew that there was no further German force in France capable of stopping us, particularly after the Franco-American Dragoon forces landed on the Mediterranean coast on 15 August and proceeded to occupy all the attention of the German Nineteenth Army. In the event that we obtained the victory which I anticipated, the Brittany ports would be isolated without hope of relief, and they would no longer represent a vitally important factor in our build-up considerations, since our rapid advance eastward would be assured and our reinforcements could be introduced through the Channel ports nearer to the front line as these were cleared.

Events demonstrated that the decision to throw the maximum weight into the Normandy struggle rather than detach substantial forces to lay siege to the Brittany ports was fully justified. Even though the battle of the Falaise–Argentan pocket did not accomplish the utter annihilation of the German armies in

Normandy, they were broken as an effective fighting force, and our way across France was opened. While Franco-American armies forced their way up the valley of the Rhône from the south, our forces swept across the north of France and through Belgium without a check by any major delaying action until they stood upon the frontiers of Germany.

The enemy, appreciating our need for the Brittany ports under the terms of our original plan, fortified them and rejected all appeals to surrender. Although the progress of our eastward advance must have made the garrisons realize that the ports they held were no longer necessary to the maintenance of our forces, they continued to hold out in their usual tenacious fashion, no doubt with the intention of proving thorns in our flesh after the manner of the British stand at Tobruk in 1941.

The desperate defense which the enemy was prepared to offer was revealed in the violent and bitter struggle to secure the capitulation of St-Malo, and still more so in the fighting which took place at Brest. By 8 August practically all resistance in the peninsula had ceased outside the ports, and our forces had taken up their positions preparatory to attempting the reduction of these strongholds. At St-Malo, the town was occupied on 14 August, but the garrison held on grimly in the Citadel, which did not capitulate until the 17th. Even after that the enemy batteries on the Ile de Cézembre, commanding the harbor approaches, continued to resist until 2 September despite bombardment by HMS *Malaya* on 31 August.

At Brest the resistance of the garrison of 30,000 men under General Ramcke was more prolonged notwithstanding the air and naval bombardments which we used to supplement the land attacks. Determined to hold on to the great port, which had been his chief Atlantic base for the U-boat campaign against Allied shipping, the enemy had to be driven back in house-to-house fighting before he finally gave in on 18 September. When at last the Allies gained possession, they found the port installations so completely wrecked as to be capable of rehabilitation only to a minor degree, and our plans for the introduction of trans-Atlantic troop convoys to the once magnificent harbor had to be abandoned.

The heavy price which the enemy's resistance had compelled us to pay for this barren prize convinced me that the further employment of large numbers of our troops to secure the reduction of the remaining enemy garrisons in Brittany—at Lorient, St-Nazaire, and Quiberon Bay—was not worth while. At that time our advance to the east had progressed so rapidly that our men were on the threshold of the enemy's homeland, and I wished to employ all the weight we could muster to deliver a knockout blow which might bring Germany to her knees before her exhausted armies could reform and renew the struggle on the Siegfried Line. Already, on 5 September, Third Army had been freed from the embarrassment of commitments in the west, far from the areas where its main forces were operating, by the transfer of VIII Corps to the newly created Ninth

Army, under Lieut. Gen. W. H. Simpson. After the fall of Brest, however, this army also was moved into the line on the German border, leaving the task of containing the remaining enemy in Brittany to the French Forces of the Interior who maintained the siege during the succeeding months, under difficult conditions, with such equipment as it was in our power to provide. Although these troops might not be able to secure the capitulation of the German garrisons, I felt certain that the latter were now in no condition to adopt a policy of aggression.

While VIII Corps was occupied in Brittany, XV Corps of the Third Army pushed eastward and then north to Argentan in the move to encircle the German forces in Normandy. While the enemy was still struggling to escape through the Falaise–Argentan gap, General Patton with XII and XX Corps began his dash eastward across France north of the Loire in another wider encircling movement. As the battle of the pocket drew to a close, XV Corps also joined in this advance, leaving V Corps of the First Army to complete the task of closing the gap north of Argentan. With his main forces trapped and broken in Normandy, the enemy had no means of checking the Third Army drive, the brilliant rapidity of which was perhaps the most spectacular ever seen in modern mobile warfare. The three corps, each spearheaded by an armored division, raced headlong toward Paris and the Seine with an impetus and spirit characteristic of their leader, at once guarding the flank of the armies to the north and seeking fresh objectives of their own.

The primary objective of the Third Army advance was to deny to the enemy the use of the key lines of communication running through the Paris–Orléans gap, between the Seine and Loire Rivers. As has already been seen, the cutting of the bridges over these rivers had compelled the enemy to route part of his supplies and reinforcements from the east to Normandy through this gap, and now it was vital that we should cut it, not only to prevent the German forces in Normandy from receiving their necessary supplies, but also to bar the most convenient line of retreat from their doomed positions. We had prepared an airborne operation designed to accomplish the seizure of this strategic area ahead of the land advances, but, as events proved, General Patton's rapid moves made this unnecessary. By 17 August—two days before the earliest possible date for the airborne operation—Chartres and Dreux were captured, and the routes running to the south of Paris were virtually blocked. On the 19th the process was completed when XV Corps reached the Seine at Mantes-Gassicourt; with this important communications center in Allied hands, the roads to Normandy from Paris itself were severed. Below this point, no bridges across the river remained open, and the enemy, deprived of all hope of supplies from the southeast, had to retreat toward the ferries lower down the river as his only means of escape.

Meanwhile XII Corps, on the southern flank of the Third Army, pushed through Vendôme to reach Orléans on 17 August, by-passing the small groups of the enemy mustered at the Loire crossings upstream from Tours. Advancing parallel with XII Corps, on its left flank, was XX Corps, whose patrols reached Fontainebleau on 20 August. During the following days the tanks swept like a sickle around the southeast of Paris to Melun, driving the enemy back across the Seine. Other elements forced their way past the strongpoints defending the Loing and Yonne Rivers, and by 25 August the spearhead of XII Corps was 40 miles east of Troyes. The pursuit toward Germany continued, so that within one month of the day on which the Third Army became operational in France it had not only broken out of Normandy and through Brittany but had secured the line of the Loire and had advanced 140 miles beyond Paris to within 60 miles of the German border.

Air power again played an important part in making the rapidity of this advance possible. To each of the armored divisions was attached a fighter-bomber group belonging to XIX Tactical Air Command of the US Ninth Air Force, providing the "eyes" of the columns and smashing the enemy's troop concentration, armor, and supply system in advance of the ground forces. The closeness of the air–ground liaison in this work was one of the remarkable features of the advance and produced extraordinarily successful results. The air arm also took over the task of watching the long flank of the Loire and of preventing any dangerous concentration of the enemy there. Strafing and bombing of the small parties of Germans prevented their coalescing into an effective force, and the

Third Army was thus able to pursue its advance untrammeled by the necessity of detaching troops to protect its flank.

The chief difficulty in the drive eastward arose not so much from the armed opposition encountered as from the problems of supply. Already at the beginning of August, when General Patton's men were overrunning the interior of Brittany, the necessity of transporting from Cherbourg and the beaches the gasoline, ammunition, and other supplies needed to maintain the flying armored columns had, as previously mentioned, imposed a severe strain upon our supply organization. Now that the spearheads were far on their way across France to the east, these difficulties were multiplied a hundredfold. With the Brittany ports either wrecked or remaining in German hands, all the materials of war had still to pass through the overworked Normandy bases. As the Third Army neared the Seine, truck transportation became utterly inadequate to cope with the situation, and we were compelled to have recourse to air lift, by troop carrier planes supplemented by heavy bombers, in order to enable the speed of the advance to be maintained. It was at first planned to allot planes for this task sufficient to lift an average of 1,000 tons per day to the Third Army forward bases, but when the capture of Dreux rendered the projected airborne operation in the Paris–Orléans gap unnecessary, this figure was increased to 2,000 tons per day.

Invaluable as this air lift proved, however, the use of the planes for such a purpose was inevitably attended by other drawbacks. The required numbers could only be provided by withdrawing craft from the newly created First Allied Airborne Army. This army had been instructed to prepare for operations, not only to seize the Paris–Orléans gap, but also to assist in crossing the Seine and the Somme should the enemy attempt a stand on the lines of the rivers, and later in breaching the Siegfried Line and in crossing the Rhine. Because of the obligation of making ready for these undertakings, the withdrawing of the planes caused considerable embarrassment to the Airborne Army's commander, Lieut. Gen. L. H. Brereton, whose program of training was thereby interrupted. He justly pointed out that there was a risk that continued cargo carrying would render the troop-carrier commands unfit for a successful airborne operation. Since the procedure and training required for the two functions were in many respects diametrically opposed, combined exercises by airborne troops and the air transport personnel were of the utmost importance. I consider, however, that my decision to use the planes for ground resupply purposes was justified by the fact that thereby the speed of our armies' advances was maintained, and as a consequence of this the projected airborne operations in France were rendered unnecessary.

When our troops had reached the Seine at Melun below and Mantes-Gassicourt above the city, the position of the German garrison in Paris became intolerable. Not only were they faced with a threat of encirclement, but the Allies were at Versailles, threatening a frontal attack. Within the city, the police went on strike and defied the German authorities when the latter laid siege to the Prefecture of Police on the Ile-de-la-Cité on 19 August. The traditional barricades appeared in the streets, the resistance movement came into the open, and for over a week a strange, skirmishing battle was fought through the city. While General von Choltitz, the German commander, made no attempt to destroy the bridges or other installations, a truce to enable the garrison of 10,000 men to withdraw broke down, and the enemy troops retired into the hotels and public buildings which they had turned into strongpoints.

For the honor of being the first Allied troops to re-enter Paris, the French 2nd Armored Division was brought up from the Argentan sector where it had formed part of the Third Army spearhead in the original encircling move resulting in the battle of the pocket. On 24 August the division's tanks were in the outskirts of the city, and on 25 August their commander, General Leclerc, received the surrender of the German commander. During the past four years this division had fought its way from Lake Chad, across the torrid wastes of the Sahara, to play a notable part in the victorious Tunisian campaign, had been brought to England, and had come thence to assist in the liberation of Metropolitan France. For these men to accept in Paris the surrender of the enemy, under whose dominion their country had lain for so long, was a fitting triumph in the odyssey which took them from Central Africa to Berchtesgaden.

Meanwhile, following the XV Corps thrust to the Seine at Mantes-Gassicourt on 19 August, the 79th Infantry Division had established the first bridgehead across the river at the nearby village of Rollebois on 20 August. The remainder of the Corps proceeded to press down the west bank in an endeavor to deny to the enemy the lower crossings and thus to cut off the only remaining escape routes of the elements which had struggled through the jaws of the Falaise–Argentan gap. In this operation our forces encountered stiffening resistance as they advanced, and at Elbeuf the enemy made a desperate stand to guard his last ferries as the remainder of his beaten army streamed across the river.

Following the elimination of the Falaise pocket, the US First Army took over from the Third Army the forces attacking northward toward the mouth of the Seine, while the British and Canadians closed in from the west. Day by day the enemy-held territory west of the river shrank. The Canadians having overcome fierce resistance in Cabourg and other coastal strongpoints, the enemy attempted a delaying action on the line of the Touques River. But that barrier was forced on 24 August, and, supported by the naval guns off-shore, the eastward advance continued. Evreux had fallen on the preceding day, and now Lisieux was cleared. On 25 August Elbeuf was captured, and by the 30th the last remaining pockets had been eliminated; apart from the beleaguered garrisons in Brittany, no German soldier remained west of the Seine who was not in Allied hands. Our bridgeheads were linked up along the whole length of the river, and our forces were pouring over in continued pursuit. The enemy's disorganization was such that any attempt to make a stand on the eastern bank was out of the question, particularly with the Third Army providing yet a further threat to his line of retreat. Once again, therefore, the accomplishments of our ground forces had rendered unnecessary a projected airborne operation designed to facilitate the overcoming of a potentially difficult obstacle. The battle of western France was over, and the liberation of the entire country had been assured. On 31 August General Hans Eberbach, commander of the ill-fated German Seventh Army, was captured with his staff while at breakfast at Amiens.

That the enemy was able to extricate a considerable portion of his forces via the few crossings left to him following our advance to Elbeuf was due to the skill with which he organized his system of ferries and pontoons. These had been established earlier, following our bombing of the bridges, as a means of transporting supplies and reinforcements to Normandy, and now they were to prove invaluable as a means of escape. Some of the pontoons were cunningly hidden under camouflage against the banks by day to avoid detection from the air, and then swung across the stream at night. By such means, 27,000 troops were transported over the river at a single crossing in three days.

Nevertheless, the losses sustained by the Germans at the Seine were enormous. The dense concentrations of tanks and vehicles along the roads leading to the crossings afforded ideal targets for strafing and bombing attacks from the air, and whole columns were annihilated thus. On the river itself, during the seven days preceding 23 August when the exodus was at its peak, 166 barges were destroyed, 10 probably destroyed and 116 damaged, and 3 large river steamers were sunk. Over 2,000 sorties a day were flown by aircraft of AEAF on these missions, while hundreds of planes of the Strategic Air Forces added their weight to the attacks. These attacks were not carried out entirely without opposition, for since the beginning of the battle of the Falaise pocket the Luftwaffe had come up in greater strength than for some time past in a desperate effort to assist the German ground forces. The enemy suffered severely in this air effort, however, and the losses sustained—coupled with the effects of the Third Army's thrust eastward which necessitated a rapid withdrawal to more distant bases on the part of the German fighter squadrons—were such as to produce a marked decline in the scale of the air opposition subsequently encountered.

Although the rush crossing of the lower Seine, planned to be made by 21 Army Group and the US First Army in phase with the Third Army advance through the Paris–Orléans gap, had been somewhat delayed by the stubborn nature of the enemy's rearguard actions, the elimination of the last German pocket west of the river nevertheless marked the completion of a great victory. The German Seventh Army and the Fifth Panzer Army had been decisively defeated, and into the debacle had been drawn the bulk of the fighting strength of the First and Fifteenth Armies. Since our landings on 6 June, of the enemy's higher commanders, three field marshals, and one army commander had been dismissed or incapacitated by wounds, and one army commander, three corps commanders, fifteen divisional commanders, and one fortress commander had been killed or captured.

The enemy's losses in men and equipment since the commencement of the campaign had been enormous. Of his panzer divisions, the equivalent of five had been destroyed and a further six severely mauled. The equivalent of twenty infantry divisions had been eliminated and twelve more (including three crack parachute divisions) had been badly cut up. One parachute and two infantry divisions were trapped in Brittany and another infantry division was isolated in the Channel Islands.

By 25 August the enemy had lost, in round numbers, 400,000 killed, wounded, or captured, of which total 200,000 were prisoners of war. One hundred and thirty-five thousand of these prisoners had been taken since the beginning of our breakthrough on 25 July. Thirteen hundred tanks, 20,000 vehicles, 500 assault guns, and 1,500 field guns and heavier artillery pieces had been captured or destroyed, apart from the destruction inflicted upon the Normandy coast defenses.

The German Air Force also had taken a fearful beating. Two thousand three hundred and seventy-eight aircraft had been destroyed in the air and 1,167 on the ground, in addition to 270 probably destroyed and 1,028 probably damaged in the air. These figures are all the more remarkable when one considers the depleted strength of the Luftwaffe and the feebleness of its attempts to counter the Allied operations.

By the end of August the morale of the enemy, as revealed in the prisoners who passed through the Allied cages, was distinctly lower than it had been a month earlier. A lack of determination was particularly noticeable among the infantry, whose outlook, for the most part, was one of bewilderment and helplessness. This state of mind was produced by the rapidity of the Allies' movements, their overwhelming superiority in equipment (both on the ground and in the air), and by the Germans' own losses of arms and transport which had left them without the necessary means of mounting an adequate defense. Our air strafing attacks had especially contributed toward breaking the enemy's spirit. The great majority of the enlisted men from the ordinary infantry divisions stated that they were glad to be out of the war, but the élite of the SS formations still retained something of their former arrogant self-confidence. Many of the senior officers were now prepared to recognize the inevitability of defeat, but the younger ones, in whom the Nazi spirit was strongest, still proclaimed the invincibility of the German cause. The army as a whole, despite its losses, had clearly not yet reached the stage of mass morale collapse, and, as events subsequently showed, the escaping elements were still capable, when given a pause for breath, of renewing the struggle with all their old determination on the threshold of the Fatherland. Of the generals participating in the Normandy campaign, it is interesting to note that all appeared on the list prepared by the Russians of those guilty of atrocities in the east; it was not likely that surrender would be forthcoming from such men. In fact, although we might have reached the military conditions of 1918, the political conditions which produced the German collapse in that year were still remote.

Behind the strategic reasons for our success lay the many factors embodied in the excellence of the Allied teamwork. This, as in the Mediterranean campaigns, again demonstrated its ability, extending through all services, to overcome the most adverse conditions. Despite difficulties due to the enforced separation of commanders and the burden of maintaining signal communications over long distances and in rapidly changing situations, the command system, based upon complete inter-Allied confidence, functioned smoothly throughout the campaign.

In assessing the reasons for victory, one must take into account not only the achievements in the field but the care and foresight which was applied to the preparations before D Day. It was to the meticulous care in planning and preparation by my staff, supported resolutely in all important aspects by the Combined Chiefs of Staff, that we owed such essential factors as the degree of surprise achieved in our landings, the excellence and sufficiency of our amphibious equipment, and the superb organization which lay behind the miraculous achievements of our supply and maintenance services. While it is true that we had hoped that the tactical developments of the first few days would yield us the territory south and southeast of Caen, so suitable for the construction of necessary airfields and for exploitation of our strength in armor, the fact remains that in the broad strategic development we attained our anticipated line of D plus 90 two weeks prior to that date and in substantial accordance with our planned strategic program. Moreover, I am convinced that without the brilliant preparatory work of our joint air forces—a belief in the effectiveness of which was the very cornerstone of the original invasion conception—the venture could never logically have been undertaken.

The greatest factor of all, however, lay in the fighting qualities of the soldiers, sailors, and airmen of the United Nations. Their valor, stamina, and devotion to duty had proved beyond praise, and continued to be so as the Battle of France gave place to the Battle of Germany.

THE BUILD-UP AND THE
ALLIED NAVIES

The landing in Northwest Europe being the largest
amphibious operation ever undertaken, the problem
of supply to the armies on the far shore entailed an
organization of unprecedented magnitude and complexity. I have already indicated the obstacles which
faced my logistical planning staff during the months
of preparatory effort. There was a struggle to acquire
the necessary shipping and landing craft, a struggle to

collect the requisite tugs, a struggle against time to prepare the novel devices, such as the various elements of the artificial harbors upon which we so greatly relied; eventually there was the herculean pre-D-Day task of assembling the vast armada in the ports of southern England in such a manner that it might be loaded and sailed to schedule and yet achieve the seemingly impossible in escaping the attention of the enemy. Events were to show the success with which these and many other difficulties were overcome. I must also acknowledge the work of my Chief Administrative Officer, General Gale, of whose abilities I had received full evidence during the campaign in North Africa and Italy, but whose achievements in that theater were dwarfed by his accomplishments in the invasion and liberation of Northwest Europe.

When the anxieties of D Day were over, the burden of responsibility of those in charge of our logistical services was in no way lightened. Some problems might be solved by experience, but new ones were ever arising. The smooth running of the shuttle service across the Channel, the efficient transfer of supplies to the armies over the beaches and through the ports, the protection of the supply routes, and safeguarding of the packed anchorages as the build-up progressed, remained the responsibility of the Allied Naval Commander, Admiral Ramsay. His untimely death on 2 January 1945 was a great loss to the Allied cause. The handling of the large number of varied craft employed was a most praiseworthy feat on the part of Admiral Ramsay and the Task Force

Commanders responsible for the execution of his orders. Over 5,000 ships and craft were employed in the actual assault, and in addition over 2,000 Allied merchantmen, with an aggregate displacement of some 4,000,000 tons, had to be prepared and fitted into the complex plan of the subsequent build-up. These merchant ships presented a peculiarly delicate problem, as the 70,000 men who sailed them were not under direct naval discipline. Nevertheless, their crews surrendered many of the age-old privileges of the sailor in their willingness to become part of the great invasion machine, and during the months following D Day they served the cause with consistent courage and devotion to duty.

The lightness of our losses at sea and in the anchorages compared with the number of ships involved is the best measure of the success with which the Allied navies kept the seas and held the enemy at bay from the invasion area. Behind this success lay in part the experience gained in the expedition to North Africa in 1942, but off France, operating in much more difficult waters, the problems facing them were often new and always far more complex than those encountered earlier. In this operation we staked our all in many respects upon unknown factors, and to the skill with which the navies met the unexpected our initial victory was largely due. New enemy defense devices and weather of unprecedented foulness even for the capricious English Channel alike failed to overcome this ingenuity and determination. Such adverse factors might prevent our supply from attaining the theoretical maximum, but from D plus 2 onward, except for the great storm later in June, there was never any real danger of our maintenance failing, and the armies never went short of food for men or ammunition for guns. On 1 July the Chief Administrative Officer was able to report that the commanders in the field had complete freedom of action as far as supply arrangements were concerned.

By D plus 5 we had in the main successfully overcome the initial struggle to get the beachheads organized. We had cleared the enemy from all the beaches; the Allies had linked up along the whole of the invasion coastline; the first units of the artificial harbors were in position and the build-up forged ahead steadily. The enemy was still in a position to bring gunfire to bear upon the beaches and anchorages on either flank; his coastal forces were massing at Cherbourg and Le Havre to prey upon the approaches; and his aircraft were nightly engaged in laying mines. It was, moreover, not only with the human antagonist that our navies and mercantile marines had to contend. The weather during June 1944, was the worst experienced for that month during the present century. The gales which had threatened us with disaster on D Day itself continued to hamper our operations throughout subsequent weeks, culminating in the great storm of 19–22 June, the effects of which were so serious as to imperil our very foothold upon the Continent. After the gales came the fogs of July, which once more held up the cross-Channel shuttle services. Through all this the perseverance of the seamen kept the armies in the field.

The principal handicap to the build-up after D Day sprang from the shortage of landing and ferry craft following the serious losses among the mines and obstacles during the assault. Also, apart from the invaluable dukws,* many of the minor landing craft proved too lightly built for continuous service in waters as rough as we experienced, and this was particularly true of the rhino ferries, the serviceability of which rarely rose above 50%. Another major worry arose from the losses we suffered in motor transport ships from mechanical defects and enemy action.

To overcome these difficulties we were compelled to resort to "drying out" LSTs and coasters on the beaches. Such a process had previously been thought too dangerous to attempt, but having been adopted as a desperate expedient on D plus 1, it proved so successful as to be continued as a regular practice. The only drawback was a slower turnaround and consequent tendency for shipping to accumulate off the far shore.

By thus profiting from the lessons of experience, the Allied navies and mercantile marine were able to land over 500,000 men by D plus 9, and the millionth man stepped ashore in France on D plus 28. Apart from the personnel landed, a million tons of stores and nearly 300,000 vehicles were put ashore by D plus 38. At the end of August, when the German

* Amphibious trucks.

armies were in flight eastward beyond the Seine, but while we were still basically dependent for our build-up on the beaches, Cherbourg, and the artificial harbors, the Allied armies under my command exceeded two million men. For them over three million tons of stores had been brought across the Channel, together with over 400,000 vehicles.

Thus, despite the trials of wind and weather and the persistent attacks of an ingenious enemy, the necessary rate of reinforcement to our land forces was maintained. Our build-up outstripped that of the Germans, deceived as they were by our latent threat to the Pas-de-Calais and hampered by our air attacks upon their communications.

A great part of the men and supplies were landed over the beaches by the splendid effort of naval and engineer personnel who handled this difficult operation. Despite the delays occasioned by unfavorable weather, the rate of discharge over the beaches was maintained at a high level. At Omaha beach, for example, the daily average of supplies unloaded from D Day to 30 September was 10,000 tons, the daily rate reaching nearly 12,000 tons for the critical period of July and August. At the smaller Utah beach, the daily average from D Day through September was 5,000 tons, and during this period upward of 750,000 men disembarked at this one point. Since Cherbourg did not begin to function in volume until August, and only approached a 10,000-ton daily average in September, the importance of the beaches to our supply is easy to appreciate.

Another factor of importance was the novel expedient upon which we staked much of our chances of success, the artificial harbors. Although our plan of operations called for the seizure of Cherbourg at an early date, we realized that the Germans might leave the port in such a condition as to preclude its full use for many weeks following its capture. The Mulberry artificial harbors were judged essential to ensure the discharge of cargo, under conditions that would be relatively independent of weather during the crucial early stages of the campaign. When the time came for the execution of the scheme, the Mulberries were subjected to strains of a severity far greater than we had believed likely. Nevertheless, although the American harbor had eventually to be written off as a total loss, the British Mulberry, which suffered less, was repaired and continued to function. It was of tremendous aid to our operations during the summer.

In the months of continued experiment and feverish constructional activity following the Quebec Conference in August 1943, when the outline of the harbor project was approved, the Mulberry scheme occasioned me and my staff many a headache. Some of the prototype units evolved promptly sank when tried out at sea (although their models had behaved excellently in the storms of experimental tanks), labor difficulties caused hold-ups in construction, and securing the necessary tug allocations was in doubt up to the last moment. Confusion, moreover, was occasioned by the division of responsibility between the Admiralty, the War Office, and the British Ministry of Supply. The Minister of Labor performed the miracle of raising the necessary workmen from a labor-exhausted Britain, however, and the construction of the huge concrete caissons in pits beside the rivers, into which on completion they were floated by breaching the retaining banks, was typical of the ingenuity and resource by which difficulties were met and overcome. Not least of our anxieties was the fear that the enemy should learn of our intentions, particularly in view of the large amount of casual labor which had to be employed, but events proved that the secret was well kept, a remarkable achievement considering the thousands of men and women who had a hand in the work of construction. Indeed, so complete was the ignorance of the enemy as to our intentions, and so lacking was he in air reconnaissance when the plans were being put into effect, that it was not until mid-July, when the scheme was practically completed, that he realized the existence and purpose of the Mulberry. Then he failed to appreciate its true significance, assuming it to be an improvised measure forced upon us by the extent of his demolitions at Cherbourg and the ravages of the storms.

Under the final scheme, five sheltered anchorages, known as Gooseberries, where landing craft could operate when an on-shore wind might otherwise hamper their unloading, were to be constructed with sunken blockships, one Gooseberry to each of the five assault beaches. Two of these anchorages were subsequently to be expanded into complete

Mulberry harbors, each the size of Dover and costing some $100,000,000. A Mulberry was to consist of a breakwater of sunken blockships, supplemented with sunken concrete caissons, each 200 feet long, known as a Phoenix. Within the shelter thus provided, LSTs and coasters could discharge their cargoes on to floating Whale piers, so constructed that at low tide they would rest firmly on the rock foreshore. Seven miles of pier with 15 pierheads were planned. Outside the ring of Phoenix caissons and Corncob blockships was to be a further floating breakwater of 200-foot steel Bombardon units, designed to provide a sheltered anchorage for Liberty ships, within which they might transfer their cargoes to ferry craft. The enclosed area at each Mulberry was to extend some two miles in length and one mile in width. In all, 400 units, totalling 1,500,000 tons, had to be towed across the Channel, and 160 tugs were required to make 35 heavy tows daily in order to complete the installation by the target date of D plus 18.

The accurate and successful planting of the Mulberry units represented a triumph of skill for the two navies respectively responsible for the installations off the American and British beaches. The sinking of the Gooseberry blockships began on D plus 1, and by the following day the first Mulberry tows, which had set out on the morning of D Day, had arrived off the French shores. The installation of the harbors in acutely congested waters, under enemy action, during the early stages of our whole gigantic enterprise was a task of extreme complexity, but it was expeditiously and accurately carried out, and in the course of the two weeks following 6 June the ports rapidly took shape. By the morning of D plus 5 the blockship breakwaters in both harbors were completed, and all the Gooseberries were in full use except that at Utah beach, work on which had been hindered by enemy gunfire. By D plus 10 all the Gooseberries were completed and the Mulberries 50% so. The towing of the huge, cumbersome caissons and the sections of piers and pierheads was considerably hampered by the continued bad weather, and nearly a third of the Whale units was lost in transit through this cause. By 19 June, however, lengths of pier were already in use; the Mulberries as a whole were about 90% completed, and over 2,000 tons of stores a day were being handled in the British harbor alone.

On that day, 19 June, broke the great storm which at one time seemed certain to bring all our work to disaster. The weather had been unsettled since D Day, but the on-shore gale which now blew up was the worst known in June for 40 years past. The Mulberries took the full force of the mountainous seas driven by the gale, and the situation was all the worse since the storm had not been expected and no forecasts of it were received. All unloading, except for a few ammunition and fuel cargoes which were taken off by intrepid dukw crews, had to be suspended, and shipping in the congested anchorages was soon in difficulties. The storm continued for four days. During that time, tows caught in passage were lost, and craft and ships off the beaches dragged their anchors and were dashed ashore. To add to our troubles, the enemy's new Oyster mines were activated by the movement of the waters and caused further casualties. By 21 June the Mulberries themselves began to disintegrate, particularly the US installation, which was in an even more exposed position off St-Laurent than the British one at Arromanches. The Bombardons of the outer breakwaters broke adrift and sank; the Phoenix caissons shifted; and the angry seas poured through the gaps, pounding the ferry craft against the piers and smashing them to pieces. Only the blockships saved the situation from becoming one of complete disaster.

During 22 June the fury of the gale gradually abated, but the seas continued to run high and hinder the work of salvage. After the Mulberries had been so near completion and the beach organization had got into its stride, it was appalling to contemplate the damage wrought by the gale. Despite the gallant efforts of the tug crews and other personnel to save the shipping, efforts which cost them heavy loss of life, some 800 craft were stranded on the beaches, and the greater part of these suffered damage. Wreckage was strewn over the sands along the whole invasion coastline. Some 600 craft were eventually refloated on the 8 July spring tides and a further 100 a fortnight later, but the resulting shortage of ferry craft was a serious blow which hampered us throughout the summer.

Of the Mulberries themselves, that at St-Laurent was so shattered as to be irreparable. Due to the scour and sea action, the main Phoenix breakwater at St-Laurent was broken and the blockships had sunk some 10 to 12 feet below their original level. At Arromanches the Phoenix breakwater would be made good, at least temporarily, and the line of blockships had held. The great value of these latter was such that on 23 June, while the seas still ran high, 4,500 tons of much needed supplies were unloaded under the shelter still afforded. The outer Bombardon breakwaters were completely wrecked and had to be abandoned at both anchorages.

On 26 June it was decided that in view of the damage sustained the original plan for the St-Laurent Mulberry would have to be abandoned, although the remaining blockships could be strengthened to provide a shallow anchorage for barges and small craft. The Arromanches Mulberry, having suffered less, could be repaired and completed; moreover, by decking in the caissons and making other modifications, it was thought that it could be made to last until October or possibly longer. Salvaged material from St-Laurent was available to complete the three damaged piers. This scheme for the rehabilitation and winterization of the Arromanches harbor was approved and the work was at once commenced.

In the accomplishment of the work I was given loyal and effective help by the British authorities, although the difficulties facing them were legion. The supply of labor was a particularly serious problem at a time when the repair of V-bombed houses in London drew heavily upon the resources. US general service troops and naval construction personnel were made available to assist in this respect. By great efforts and sacrifices on the part of all concerned, the work was accomplished. Although the winterization modifications had yet to be finished, the harbor was virtually completed and the storm damage repaired by 20 July. At the end of that month nearly 4,000 men, over 400 vehicles, and over 11,000 tons of supplies were disembarked within its shelter during a single period of 24 hours. Throughout the summer and autumn the achievements of the Mulberry exceeded our best hopes, for, although the planned rate of supply discharge was 6,000 tons a day, the actual average, from 20 June to 1 September, was 6,765 tons.

The course of our military fortunes was to make the utmost demands upon the means upon which we were so completely dependent for supply. Although by September we had defeated the enemy decisively in Normandy, he, knowing our necessities, clung obstinately to the western ports of St-Nazaire and Lorient, as well as to the Quiberon Bay area (which we had planned to develop into a major harbor), while demolishing the installations at Cherbourg and Brest so thoroughly that it required many weeks' work before they could be restored to full capacity. Under these circumstances, the open beaches and the Mulberry continued to be the main channels of supply to our armies during the period when their drive eastward across France forced logistical demands to a peak. It was not until Antwerp had been captured and the Scheldt made safe for our shipping that the beach installations and the Mulberry became superfluous. Throughout the summer of 1944 they represented an essential factor in the success of our operations. Without them our armies could not have been adequately maintained in the field, and the men who worked them with so much gallantry and devotion deserve the gratitude of liberated Europe for their share in our victory.

Of the natural ports which fell into our hands before the opening of Antwerp, only Cherbourg, third biggest port of France, had a capacity that would appreciably lighten our supply problems. The small harbors along the Norman coast, such as Ouistreham, Courseulles, and Port-en-Bessin, had their value, particularly during the early days of the campaign, but their capacities were small, and the same was true of Granville, St-Malo, Morlaix, and the other harbors uncovered by our subsequent drive south through the Cotentin and into Brittany. Brest, when it eventually fell to us after stubborn resistance, was so fully destroyed that, in view of its remoteness from the main battle front, it was considered useless to attempt any major rehabilitation.

Cherbourg, however, represented a cardinal factor in our basic logistical plans. The sea and airborne landings in the Cotentin, as has been shown, had been expressly designed to facilitate its early capture so that we might use its valuable harbor as an all-weather base through which to introduce supplies. The enemy, on the other hand, fully appreciated the importance to us of an early seizure of the port, and when his attempt to defend the city failed he undertook the task of rendering the harbor unusable with typical Teutonic thoroughness.

Cherbourg's commander surrendered on 26 June, and the US Port Clearance party began the work of tidying-up on the following day, although nests of resistance among the dockyards were yet unsubdued and the guns of the breakwater forts prevented mine sweeping. While certain major facilities survived, such as the breakwaters enclosing the great anchorage and some of the drydocks, the extent of the enemy demolitions presented a formidable task to the clearance personnel. Seventy-five per cent of the cranes had been destroyed, over a dozen vessels had been sunk to block the dock entrances, and quantities of every kind of mine had been sown. Such equipment as was not destroyed had been immobilized by the removal of vital parts and the skilled labor had been evacuated.

The task of mine sweeping was fraught with difficulties and dangers, even when the forts had been reduced, but by 19 July the port came into use and unloading began. At first the disembarkation of stores was mainly by dukws, but through the summer work on the harbor installations went on at a feverish pace. By the end of August, Cherbourg was handling an average of over 10,000 tons a day, and by the beginning of October, when the work of reconstruction was completed, its capacity was as great as, if not greater than, had been the case before the war.

The cross-Channel supply of fuel for our armies in Operation Overlord constituted a special problem. Although the lines of communication over which the fuel had to be brought, from the United Kingdom to the battle front, were not as long as those to North Africa, the rate of consumption was far higher. During the assault phase we had naturally to rely upon canned gasoline, but by 3 July bulk supply was being introduced by ship-to-shore pipeline from tankers to storage dumps, thus affording a considerable saving of time and tonnage. For the period when the armies had attained the strength to enable them to break out from their lodgement area and sweep across France, however, as well as for the later stages of the campaign against Germany, novel devices were employed, the experimental character of which was second in daring only to the artificial harbors project.

The scheme, developed jointly under naval and military auspices, was known by the name of Pluto. In order to save shipping, to increase the rate of supply, and to prevent interference with the armies' maintenance by bad weather, submarine pipelines were to be laid across the Channel. The pipes were of two types: the Hais and the Hamel, each of which was 3 inches in diameter and expected to discharge 250 tons of gasoline a day. The first lines were planned from the Isle of Wight to the vicinity of Cherbourg—a distance of 56 miles. It was hoped to have ten lines operative by D plus 75, giving 2,500 tons of gasoline daily.

As was to be expected with so experimental a scheme, many obstacles were encountered. The laying of the lines was a hazardous process, and the storms of June and July repeatedly interrupted the work. The first Hais line was completed by 12 August, and a second by the 21st, but leaks and stoppages resulted in further delay before either line could be operated, bad weather preventing clearance work. Subsequently, however, these teething troubles were overcome and further lines were laid over the shorter route from Dungeness to Boulogne. These provided our main supplies of fuel during the winter and spring campaigns.

For the protection of our cross-Channel shipping routes—and hence for the successful maintenance of the armies in France—we were dependent upon the ceaseless work of the Allied navies, assisted by RAF Coastal Command. These kept constant watch, to such good effect that the shipping losses which we sustained due to direct enemy action were extremely small in proportion to the vast tonnage involved.

The enemy concentrated his main efforts against the beaches and anchorages. From landward, although our penetrations soon ensured the freedom of the central beaches from artillery fire, the flank ones remained objects of attack. The reduction of the Cotentin Peninsula removed this menace on the west, but Sword beach—the easternmost of the British sector—continued to be exposed to enemy shelling as well as to attacks by E-boats, explosive motor boats, and human torpedoes based in the Seine area. The resultant losses were considerably greater than those in other sectors, and, after restrictions had been repeatedly imposed for these reasons, the decision was taken on 13 July to abandon the beach permanently for unloading purposes.

To counter the menace of enemy shelling and to afford support to our troops advancing inland, the navies carried out many heavy bombardments of the enemy batteries, defensive positions, communications, and supply dumps. On the eastern flank the configuration of the ground made observation difficult, but the armies were warm in their praise of the support given to them by the heavy naval guns. The characteristic ingenuity of the Navy was seen in the device of rocking the ships to raise the angle of the guns so that they might engage targets beyond normal range; and the effectiveness of the firing was seen when the capture of the strongly casemated battery at Houlgate (which had been primarily responsible for the shelling of Sword beach) revealed that three out of its four guns had sustained direct hits. The ships intervened vigorously in the battles ashore, both to break up enemy concentrations for counter-attacks and to supplement the barrages preparatory to our own advances, and this intervention was continued until the breakthrough came at the end of July and the enemy retired eastward.

During the early stages of the campaign the enemy made some daylight attacks upon the anchorages with bomber and fighter-bomber planes, but these proved very ineffective and were soon abandoned. Night raiding (sometimes in conjunction with surface craft attacks) continued and caused casualties.

We found in this connection that, although naval anti-aircraft fire was good, fire discipline was not easy to enforce among the large and diverse fleet of merchant shipping assembled for the build-up. Blind firing without orders resulted in the loss of some friendly planes, and eventually the Allied Naval Commander was forced to prohibit all night anti-aircraft fire by merchant ships.

Although both bombs and torpedoes were dropped by the night raiders, their chief effort was devoted to mine-laying, supplementing the activities in this respect of the surface craft based on Le Havre. The mining aircraft were awkward enemies with which to cope; they frequently operated in single sorties, up to a total of 50 a night, the planes flying in low and dropping their mines out of range of the shore defenses. Such attacks were carried out on every night but one from 6 to 30 June and took toll of our shipping by reason of their persistence.

The mines laid by the enemy off our anchorages provided the biggest problem facing the Allied navies, since they included two novel, pressure-actuated types, one of which could not be swept at all with the gear available and the other only under certain weather conditions. The task of the mine-sweeping flotillas was thus often thankless and always hazardous, for, though they detonated large numbers of mines and worked tirelessly with their accustomed bravery under often appalling weather conditions, some mines inevitably remained and our shipping necessarily suffered casualties. Serious as these losses might be, they were, nevertheless, not so heavy in proportion to the total number of ships we employed as materially to affect our build-up. The losses reached their peak in the days immediately following the great storm of 19–21 June, which had the effect of "ripening" many of the mines; but subsequently the casualty rate gradually declined. Despite the depletion of the mine-sweeper strength through the losses incurred, the development of "explosive sweeps" and the use of nets to catch drifting mines partially reduced the dangers. It was not, however, until August, when the land advances forced the enemy to abandon his air bases for others farther east that his mining activity effectively died down. The extent of the menace may be seen from the fact that by three months after D Day the number of mines swept off our invasion ports and beaches totalled one-tenth those swept in all theaters combined from the beginning of the war to 6 June.

The threat to our supply routes from enemy destroyers was virtually removed on 9 June when Force 26 met and annihilated four enemy vessels off the Ile de Batz following their interception by RAF Coastal Command aircraft. Attacks by light coastal craft, however—E- and R-boats based initially at Cherbourg and Le Havre—were carried out against the assault area with a persistence equal to that of the air-mining effort. Although the enemy never dared to interfere with our build-up by day, his craft made forays against our anchorages almost nightly from D Day onwards. A certain number of E-boats were transferred to Brest following the fall of Cherbourg, but the chief menace thereafter became concentrated in Le Havre, from which operations were directed primarily against the British anchorages. To guard against this, a protective screen was established on our eastern flank, and it was but rarely that the raiders succeeded in penetrating this barrier and destroying our shipping within. Our own coastal forces were continually engaged in repelling the enemy, and the pursuit was often followed under the guns of the hostile shore batteries. The German forces suffered severely from attrition, our close blockade effectively preventing any appreciable reinforcement. Successful air attacks were also made by Bomber Command against the docks at Le Havre, sinking a number of E-boats and other craft at their moorings. When Le Havre finally fell to our forces in September, the danger to our western Channel routes and anchorages from surface attack was practically ended.

The German fondness for war gadgets was as marked in the naval as in the military and aeronautical spheres; on one occasion the naval commander on our eastern flank reported that his protective net was "bulging with secret weapons." Among these devices, in addition to the mines already mentioned, were human torpedoes, explosive motor boats, radio-controlled glider bombs, and even an occasional V-1 flying bomb, the latter arriving probably more by accident than design. As was inevitable in our crowded anchorages, we suffered a number of casualties from these devices, used in conjunction with more orthodox weapons, but the enemy also paid heavily for his use of them. On 2/3 August, for instance, a determined attack was launched on the British anchorages by human torpedoes and explosive motor boats, under cover of diversionary air raids and E-boat assaults. We lost a destroyer, a trawler, and an LCG, while other craft were damaged; but on the German side at least 20 explosive motor boats, 30 human torpedoes, and 1 E-boat were destroyed, and 2 more human torpedoes were caught in the net.

The submarine threat proved markedly less serious than we had anticipated. When the assault was first launched, the enemy U-boats were concentrated in the Biscay area, but at once began to move toward the Channel. RAF Coastal Command, however, had established a system of air patrols covering the whole of the Western Approaches to guard against this menace, and its operations were highly successful. U-boats approaching our supply routes were spotted, sunk, or forced to abandon their missions, and during the critical first ten days of the invasion there was no evidence of penetration by a single craft. Later on, occasional U-boats got through under cover of bad weather, but the results obtained were insignificant.

In close liaison with the air watchers, Allied naval forces maintained a constant blockade along the Biscay and Channel coasts from the Gironde to Den Helder. From the outset of the campaign the Allied naval supremacy off Western Europe was not seriously challenged, and apart from the raiding of the assault area by locally based small craft the enemy was compelled to restrict his activities to attempts by blockade runners to sneak from port to port, hugging the shores, under cover of darkness or foul weather. Several such convoys were intercepted and broken up, and by the end of the year 68 enemy vessels, from destroyers to small merchantmen, had been sunk at sea, while over 200 more had been scuttled, sunk, or immobilized in ports. Considering the enormous quantities of shipping which we employed, our own losses were negligible. By mid-July the position was sufficiently satisfactory to permit release of some US destroyers for service in other theaters, and on 25 July the Admiralty resumed general control of the Channel from Admiral Ramsay (Allied Naval Commander Expeditionary Force) who, however, retained operational authority over the actual assault area.

Against the bases in England from which our convoys sailed across the Channel the enemy made no piloted air raids, but did make some use of flying bombs. A few of these missiles which fell in the Portsmouth–Southampton area early in July hit landing-craft bases but failed to cause any damage to the shipping itself. The primary object of attack, from 13 June onwards, was always London, the bombs being employed essentially as terror weapons. Two LSTs were damaged there at Deptford docks, but there was little direct interference with our build-up, and the work of loading proceeded without undue interruption. The gigantic concrete "secret weapon" installations in the Cherbourg Peninsula and the Pas-de-Calais, designed to enable "V" missiles to be assembled and launched under conditions of immunity from Allied air attack, were captured before completion.

For our freedom from effective interference by "V" weapons we were indebted to the air forces, whose persistent attacks—first upon the experimental establishment at Peenemünde and subsequently upon the operational installations in France and the Low Countries—successfully delayed the enemy's preparations until they were too late to check our operations. The attacks against London were regarded as a serious menace and one of my tasks while I had control of all the air forces was to allot air effort to reducing the enemy scale of attack against the capital. In spite of the many tasks imposed on the air forces in connection with Overlord it was still possible to make many successful attacks on the "V" weapon organization, and the apparently large diversion of effort was in fact reduced, as far as possible, by selecting opportunities for attack when the weather was unfavorable for higher priority targets. The bombardment of London following our landings was a desperate and ill-conceived measure, for more profitable results would certainly have been achieved had the main weight of the attack even then been directed against the ports along the south coast. The enemy's vindictive hatred of the British people and his underestimation of the Londoners' powers of endurance, together with his own blind overconfidence in the effects of the new weapon, enabled us to continue our build-up and successfully to establish ourselves on the soil of France.

Our communications system was satisfactory. The Admiralty, the Royal Corps of Signals, and the British Post Office jointly achieved the feat of laying a cross-Channel cable, giving three telephone and six telegraph circuits, as early as D plus 4, and a number of further cables were subsequently installed, affording adequate signal facilities with our bases in the United Kingdom. When the breakthrough came in France at the end of July the speed of the advances imposed a heavy strain on the communications personnel. Although the spearhead units necessarily relied largely on radio, a line network of great complexity was required in their rear to cope with the amount of traffic involved. Existing civilian communications were of limited value in consequence of lack of maintenance during recent years aggravated by war destruction, and within four months of D Day the Allies laid over 100,000 circuit miles of line.

Within France, the organization of our supply system did not present any major problems until our armies achieved their breakthrough. While we were consolidating our hold upon the lodgement area, the supply dumps to maintain the forces when the fighting became mobile were steadily built up, and the coastal area from the Cotentin to Caen developed into one immense depot, the biggest in history ever assembled on an invaded territory. When the breakthrough came, however, a great strain was imposed upon the maintenance system, not through any inherent fault in that system but by reason of the unexpected circumstances under which the advances occurred. The enemy's tenacious defense of the Brittany ports and my decision to concentrate all available strength fully to exploit the opportunity for a decisive victory offered in Normandy necessitated, as already indicated, the abandonment of the original plan for these harbors to be brought rapidly into use as the main arteries through which to supply the American armies on the right flank.

This meant that we had to rely for our maintenance at a most vital period of the campaign upon the original supply lines through Cherbourg, the Arromanches Mulberry, and the Normandy beaches. Some cargoes were unloaded through the minor harbors and over the beaches of northern Brittany, but they represented only a small fraction of our total needs. The bulk of the supplies for the Third Army had to be transported by the long, roundabout route down through the Cotentin and then eastward around the German pocket resisting at Falaise and Argentan. The Third Army, when it got into its stride in the dash across France, was advancing at a speed of up to 40 miles a day, and our transport services were taxed to the limit. The incentive offered by the chance of a smashing victory, however, drove the men in whose hands the maintenance of supply rested to feats of superhuman accomplishment. In the light of the difficulties they had to overcome, it seems, when one looks back upon those amazing days, well-nigh incredible that at no period up to the time when we stood upon the threshold of Germany was the momentum of the drive retarded through lack of essential needs. The spectacular nature of the advance was due in as great a measure to the men who drove the supply trucks as to those who drove the tanks.

The three essentials were food, ammunition, and gasoline; and to get these up to the armored spearheads in as expeditious a manner as possible the system known as the "Red Ball Express" was instituted. By this, a circular one-way traffic route was established across France from the beachheads to the fighting zone and back again. All civilian and local military traffic was debarred from using the "Red Ball Highway," and along it the convoys swept at high speed day and night, in an unending stream. Similarly on the railroads, many of them single-track lines never intended for such heavy usage, the trains, each loaded to capacity, pushed eastward, travelling nose to tail in a manner that defied all the normal rules of safety.

To keep all this traffic rolling would have been impossible but for the very fine work of the Engineers, who had to contend with the damage caused not only by the enemy but by our own attacks preceding the advance. The roads were strewn with mines which had to be detected, wrecked German vehicles which had to be pushed aside, and bomb craters which had to be filled. There were bridges which had to be rebuilt and the rubble of ruined towns and villages through which paths had to be driven. On the railroads there were again bridges to be constructed as well as wrecked trains to be cleared, torn-up rails to be replaced, and the frightful chaos produced by our bombing at every major junction and marshalling yard to be remedied. So greatly had the French railroads suffered that over 900 locomotives and a third of the rolling stock used had to be shipped over from Allied sources in England. Thanks to the untiring efforts of the men and the excellence of their mechanical equipment, all this work was successfully accomplished at an unprecedented rate. Bridge-building parties especially performed remarkable feats, and work which under normal conditions would have required months was completed in a matter of days.

With the resistance offered by the retreating enemy at a minimum, fuel was a more vital requisite than ammunition. Approximately a million gallons of gasoline were needed at the front every day to enable the armored columns to maintain the headlong rate of their advance. Trucked supplies could not by themselves cope with this enormous demand, but pipelines, both for aviation and ordinary purposes, were laid in the wake of the armies from the beachhead storage tanks. Our experiences in North Africa and Italy had taught us much in the matter of pipelines, and as many as 30 miles of 6-inch pipe were now laid in a single day. By early October the system was delivering 4,500 tons of gasoline daily from the main distributing point near Paris, apart from the considerable quantities being drawn from it at other points intermediate between there and Cherbourg.

Despite all these efforts and accomplishments, however, my anxiety over the successful maintenance of supplies essential to support our continued advance increased as the lines of communication lengthened. The Third Army maintenance in particular was stretched to the limit, and, as previously described, we had to employ transport aircraft to carry over 2,000 tons a day to keep the spearheads going. The enemy's failure to make a successful stand on any of the river lines freed us momentarily from the necessity for airborne operations which would have taken away the planes from the task of keeping the ground forces supplied, but it was evident that sooner or later such a situation would arise when we came up against the main frontier defenses of the Reich.

As will be indicated in due course, the difficulties of supply eventually forced a halt upon us when we reached Germany, but the very rapidity of our advance across France had made that inevitable. In consequence of the enemy's denial to us of the Brittany ports and the unexpected situation of having to support a dash of such length and speed entirely from our bases on the Normandy shore, only a miracle of hard work and brilliant improvisation by the supply services had carried our armored spearheads so far. Without the magnificent work performed by these men in coping with peculiarly arduous problems, the sweeping victory which liberated France would not have been possible.

THE ADVANCE FROM THE SEINE TO THE GERMAN BORDER

As our armies swept north through the Pas-de-Calais and into Belgium and east toward the German border, the size of our forces and the extent of our front made it necessary for me to take direct control of the land forces operating on the Continent. Until 1 September the command system had functioned effectively, exactly as planned and in accordance with the developments of the tactical and strategic situation. Full

Advance from the Seine to the German border

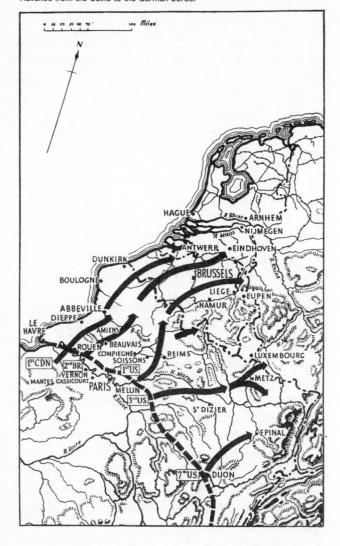

credit for this was due to the Commanders-in-Chief, to all Senior Commanders, and to the higher staffs of all services, who consistently worked together as an efficient Allied team. Change in the command set-up was necessary, however, due to the diverging lines of operation and the need for having a commander on each of the main fronts capable of handling, with a reasonable degree of independence, the day-to-day operations in each sector. These operations were to be guided by directives issued from my Headquarters.

Therefore, when on 1 September my operational Headquarters opened officially on the Continent and Field Marshal Montgomery's responsibility for arranging for coordination between 21 Army Group and General Bradley's forces terminated, Field Marshal Montgomery continued to command 21 Army Group which was also designated the Northern Group of Armies. As from this date General Bradley's command was known as the 12th or Central Group of Armies and consisted of the United States First Army under General Hodges, the United States Third Army under General Patton, and the United States Ninth Army under General Simpson.

The Franco-American forces coming from the south were not at this time under my control, but I planned with the approval of the Combined Chiefs of Staff to assume command of them on 15 September, when it was estimated that contact would have been securely established with the Central Group of Armies. Actually, first contact was reached prior to this on 11 September when troops of the French 1st

Armored Division met troops of the French 2nd Armored Division in the vicinity of Sombernon, but formal command did not pass to my Headquarters until the 15th. These forces, consisting of the French First Army under General de Lattre de Tassigny and the United States Seventh Army under Lieut. Gen. Alexander E. Patch, were designated the 6th or Southern Group of Armies, under command of General (then Lieutenant-General) Jacob L. Devers.

Each of these three Groups of Armies was supported by its own Tactical Air Force. The Northern Group of Armies was accompanied by the Second Tactical Air Force under Air Marshal Sir Arthur Coningham and the Central Group of Armies by the Ninth Air Force under Lieut. Gen. (then Maj. Gen.) Vandenberg. The Southern Group of Armies had, in the advance from the south, been supported by one Fighter Group and auxiliary units of XII Tactical Air Command. When the Southern Group of Armies came under my control, this Air Command was augmented with units of the Ninth Air Force, but later the air support of the Southern Group of Armies was to be constituted as the First Tactical Air Force.

The Tactical Air Forces in support of the Army Groups reported to my headquarters through Air Chief Marshal Leigh-Mallory, while the remaining overall air control exercised by me continued as it had originally been planned in April, the United States Strategic Air Forces and the RAF Bomber Command reporting independently. Air matters were, as already stated, coordinated through my Deputy, Air Chief Marshal Tedder.

There was no change in the Naval Command system at this time, except that Admiral Ramsay's headquarters were moved to France early in September. Later in September control of the Strategic Air Forces passed from me to the Commanding General of the USAAF and the Chief of the Air Staff jointly.

By 1 September also a new and important command unit had been formed within our Expeditionary Forces. All British and American Airborne Forces were placed under the single command of General Brereton on 8 August to form the First Allied Airborne Army. Chief components of this Army included the United States XVIII Corps (82nd, 101st, and 17th Airborne Divisions), the British Airborne Troops Command (6 and 1 Airborne Divisions), the United States IX Troop Carrier Command, and RAF 38 and 46 Groups. In view of the important roles that the airborne divisions were to play in the development of our campaign, and also in order to unify the highly specialized and integrated planning and training, I felt that an Army designation rightly belonged to General Brereton's headquarters and to the troops, even though, in the strict sense of the word, the divisions did not operate as an independent army unit once they had been committed to action. Our first use of the airborne divisions under the newly constituted command set-up was to be on 17 September, to assist in seizing the Rhine crossings at Nijmegen and Arnhem after the rapid advance by our land armies.

Although it was originally intended to employ the airborne units to close the Paris–Orléans gap against the enemy retreating from Normandy, General Patton's advance had been so rapid that the area was completely overrun by our land forces and an airborne operation was unnecessary. We had subsequently considered employing them to assist in seizing successively the crossings over the Seine and the Somme, and lastly in the Pas-de-Calais area to cut off the retreat of the German Fifteenth Army. All these areas were rapidly gained by our ground forces, a clear indication of the tremendous forward strides being made by our armor and infantry. By the time the Airborne Army was first employed in the Arnhem–Nijmegen area, enemy resistance had stiffened and we had begun the long and gruelling grind, in part unexpected, which was ultimately to take us in force across the Rhine.

It was our plan to attack northeastward in the greatest strength possible. This direction had been chosen for a variety of reasons. First, the great bulk of the German Army was located there. Secondly, there was the great desirability of capturing the flying bomb area, not only to remove this menace to England, but also to deny to the enemy the propaganda value which he enjoyed on the home front and in the army from the attacks on London and talk of new weapons which would "decide the war." A third reason for the northeastward attack was our imperative need for the large port of Antwerp, absolutely essential to us logistically before any deep penetration in strength could be made into Germany. Fourthly, we wanted the airfields in Belgium. Finally, and most important, I felt that during the late summer and early autumn months the lower Rhine offered the best avenue of advance into Germany, and it seemed probable that through rapidity of exploitation both the Siegfried Line and the Rhine River might be crossed and strong bridgeheads established before the enemy could recover sufficiently to make a definite stand in the Arnhem area. In furtherance of this plan strong United States forces marched abreast of the Northern Group of Armies to the northeast, while three United States divisions were completely immobilized in order to supply additional logistical support for the Northern Group. At the same time the entire airborne forces were made available to Field Marshal Montgomery.

Secondary to this main effort in the north was the desirability of pushing eastward with some force in order to link up with the French and American forces advancing from the south, so as to clear all southwest France as the cheapest way of protecting our flanks and rear. In addition, a drive along the Verdun–Metz axis would enhance the opportunity for surprise and maneuver, thus requiring the enemy to extend his forces, and leaving him in doubt as to the direction of the Allied main thrust.

From the time when our armies first crossed the Seine in force to the employment of the Airborne Army in Holland on 17 September, our ground forces made prodigious strides. Along the Channel coast the Canadian First Army began advancing on 30 August from the Elbeuf bridgehead above Rouen on the Seine and from bridgeheads below the city. On 1 September both Rouen and Dieppe were taken, the forces first entering Dieppe consisting of battalions of the Essex, Scottish, Royal, and Hamilton Light Infantry and the Royal Regiment of Canada which had fought there on 19 August 1942.

Le Havre was cut off, but the garrison rejected an ultimatum to surrender on 4 September and the city was invested. Attacks against it were supported by heavy aerial bombing during which more than 11,000 tons were dropped on the city, half this total being dropped on the 10th. On 10 September also the final ground attack was launched by the British 49 Infantry Division operating with the Canadian First Army. This attack was supported by naval forces including the battleship *Warspite* and the monitor *Erebus*, which bombarded enemy installations with 300 rounds of 15-inch shell. By noon on the 11th the northern and eastern outskirts of Le Havre had been reached and at 1130 hours on the 12th the city surrendered with its garrison of 7,000 troops.

Meanwhile other forces of the Canadian First Army had swept northeastward along the coast, taking, in addition to Dieppe, the small ports of Fecamp, St-Valery-en-Caux, Le Treport, and Abbeville. Etaples fell on 4 September and the Somme River, which we had anticipated as a possible barrier, was crossed in force. Calais was surrounded and the outskirts of Boulogne reached on the 6th. On the 8th the

Canadians overran Ostend and after capturing the port turned east towards Bruges which was entered by patrols on the 9th. In the meantime other troops of Canadian 2 Corps had driven toward Dunkirk, investing that city by the 11th. On the 11th also Blankenberghe, between Ostend and Zeebrugge, was taken by the Canadian 4 Armored Division.

Thus, within two weeks of the Seine crossings the Canadians had driven north, clearing large sections of the "flying bomb coast," and northeast toward the Scheldt estuary. Along the coast they had forced the enemy to hole up in a few ports which he was to defend tenaciously. Boulogne, with its garrison of 10,000, did not fall until 23 September and Calais until the 30th, both to the Canadian 2 Corps, after heavy bombardment by Bomber Command. Dunkirk was surrounded, but since the use of the small harbor as a port was not essential, I did not feel that a strong effort should be made to take it. As in the case of the Brittany ports, I decided that it would be preferable to contain the enemy, estimated at 12,000 troops, with the minimum forces necessary rather than to attempt an all-out attack. In the northeast, the Canadian advance toward the Scheldt estuary formed the lower jaw of a trap closing on the Germans, the other jaw consisting of British forces which had captured Antwerp.

The British advance on the right of the Canadians to Antwerp and the Dutch border had been spectacular during this period. From their bridgehead at Vernon their armor swept to Antwerp, a distance of some 195 miles as the crow flies, in less than four days. The advance began on 30 August and Antwerp, with its port installations virtually intact, was occupied on 4 September by the 11 Armoured Division of 30 Corps. By 29 August the British bridgehead at Vernon had extended, at its deepest penetration, 12 miles north of the Seine. On the 30th they made an advance of 25 miles from this point, taking Beauvais, while another column of the 11 Armoured Division reached a point only 25 miles south of Amiens after a 30-mile advance. On the following day they raced on to Amiens, took the town, established bridgeheads across the Somme, and pushed farther to the northeast. At the same time other British units turned northwest and attacked toward the Channel. On the morning of 1 September, British armor took Albert, about 12 miles northeast of Amiens, and Bapaume, 28 miles northeast of Amiens, while later in the day Arras was captured by the Guards Armoured Division of 30 Corps. Meanwhile Amiens was turned over to the infantry, which had come up from the south, and another armored column of the Guards Armoured Division moved north to take Doullens, about 23 miles east of Abbeville.

A part of the armored column which took Arras turned east on the next morning and captured Douai, while the main force continued to the north. On the morning of 2 September it made slow progress, but during that afternoon and the following day it gathered speed and advanced 60 miles in 36 hours, crossing the Belgian border east of Lille, taking

Tournai, where the Lille–Brussels road was cut, and then turning east along this road. At noon on the 3rd this column was 28 miles from Brussels, and late on that same day it reached the capital, which had been hastily evacuated by the enemy. On 4 September part of this column turned east and reached Louvain, the rest continuing north and entering Antwerp with the 11 Armoured Division, which had moved rapidly north from the Arras area, taking Lille on the way. By evening the dock area was being cleared, and on the 5th, with Antwerp firmly in their hands, the British spread out to the west and reached the outskirts of Ghent, which fell the following day.

Still farther west another armored division which had begun an attack northwest from the Amiens area on the morning of 2 September made rapid progress in the direction of Calais and Dunkirk and on the 3rd reached Aire, 27 miles south of the latter town. This area was subsequently taken over by the Canadians moving up from the south.

As the British forces approached closer to the German homeland, resistance stiffened and the rapid advances which had made the capture of Antwerp possible came to an end. However, by attacking northeast from Louvain on 7 September, 30 Corps was able to establish a deep bridgehead over the Albert Canal, seize Bourg Leopold after a bitter and fluctuating battle, and by the 12th cross the Dutch border to reach a point seven miles from Eindhoven. Driving east from Bourg Leopold, elements of 30 Corps advanced almost to the Meuse.

While the Canadians and British thus moved northeastward in a great sweeping drive which stretched inland from the Channel coast to Vernon, and northward to Antwerp and Eindhoven, the American First Army under General Hodges poured across the Seine bridgeheads between Mantes-Gassicourt and Melun to the east, beginning an equally spectacular drive on a three-corps front toward Namur, Liége, and the German frontier. On the right, VII Corps crossed the Aisne on 29 August, and Soissons was cleared of enemy forces by the 3rd Armored Division, which also liberated Laon the next day after stiff fighting. This division continued its rapid advance, while infantry supported it and protected its flank, and on 1 September reached a point 30 miles northeast of Laon. In the next two days the column advanced 40 miles, crossing the Belgian border in the Hirson area and reaching Charleroi and Mons.

On the First Army's left, a similar drive northward from the Mantes bridgehead area had been accomplished by a rapidly moving column of XIX Corps, spearheaded by the 2nd Armored Division. Gaining momentum, on 30 August this force advanced 13 miles, and the next day another spurt of 20 miles carried it close to Montdidier. By 2 September XIX Corps had reached the Belgian border south of Tournai, registering an advance of more than 60 miles in two days.

As a result of these operations, VII and XIX Corps cut off a large German force in the pocket that

lay between their advancing columns. This pocket
extended from Mons to the forest of Compiègne,
where German infantry resisted stubbornly the
advance of V Corps. The latter unit, forming the center of the First Army's drive northward, nevertheless
made good progress on the axis Compiègne–St-
Quentin, reaching a line east of Cambrai on the 2nd.
During the next three days some 25,000 prisoners
were captured at the top of the pocket in the Mons
area.

On 4 September the First Army began a wheel to
the east, V Corps moving to the right flank and crossing the Meuse north of Sedan on 5–6 September.
That town fell to the 5th Armored Division on 6
September, and in the next few days advance was
rapid across Belgium and Luxembourg, on a 65-mile
front. The same division liberated the city of
Luxembourg on 10 September, and by the 11th, V
Corps had reached the German frontier and the
Siegfried defenses. Farther north, VII Corps units captured Namur and the Meuse crossings near Dinant on
4–5 September, then continued to advance down
both banks of the river toward Liége. Stiff resistance
in this area was broken; Liége fell on 8 September and
by noon on the 9th our forces reached Limbourg, 13
miles southwest of Aachen. Here resistance increased,
and extensive mining and numerous road blocks with
anti-tank guns were encountered. Nevertheless, on 10
September further advances were made, and at 1723
hours VII Corps artillery for the first time shelled
German territory. On the 11th both Eupen and

Malmedy were captured. XIX Corps had paralleled this advance; by 11 September it was at the edge of Maastricht, and farther south had crossed the Meuse.

In less than two weeks, then, the First Army had crossed the Seine in force, swept across France, Belgium, and Luxembourg, and brought the war to the threshold of Germany. The bitter struggle for Aachen and the Roer bridgeheads was to follow.

In the Third Army zone of advance, on the right of our forces, General Patton's troops had crossed the upper Marne in the vicinity of Vitry-le-François on 29 August. On the 30th, 4th Armored Division of XII Corps moved on to St-Dizier, 17 miles to the east, while to the north the 80th Infantry Division captured Châlons-sur-Marne and advanced 8 miles northward. On the 31st the column which took St-Dizier pushed on to Commercy on the Meuse, while the XX Corps turned east on the axis Reims–Verdun–Metz. The following morning units of the XX Corps entered Verdun, and crossed the Meuse to reach a point six miles to the east on the road to Metz. On the 2nd this column pushed on another seven miles to Etain, while the XII Corps advanced to the vicinity of Nancy. Meanwhile, between these two columns, other crossings of the Meuse were effected, and on 2 September St-Mihiel was taken. On the 4th patrols operating up to the Moselle failed to find the enemy in any strength, except at Pont-à-Mousson, about 13 miles south of Metz. Here, after patrol clashes in the morning, the Germans withdrew to the right bank of the river and shelled the town as we moved up to it. On the 5th we reached the important communications center of Nancy, on the left bank about 28 miles above Metz.

Crossings of the Moselle were made against enemy opposition beginning on 7 September. By the 11th we had established ourselves in strength on the east bank of the river between Metz and Nancy. While some of General Patton's forces moved southward from Toul for a distance of 30 miles to compress the Belfort area through which the German Nineteenth Army was withdrawing, other forces crossed the Moselle on the 12th and began the turning movement northeast of Nancy which was to result in the fall of the city to the XII Corps on 15 September.

In the Metz area General Patton's forces had captured Aumetz on the 11th and driven to Thionville, 12 miles north of Metz, by the 13th. The city itself was stubbornly defended and the siege was to be long and arduous.

The Third Army's rapid advance involved herculean tasks in the matter of supply. At the Moselle enemy resistance had stiffened and the problem of supply became increasingly acute, to the extent that General Patton's forces were partially immobilized and physically incapable of mounting assaults on a large scale or of continuing a pursuit had the opportunity offered. This was in a measure also true of the whole front facing east against Germany and our positions here became relatively stable on a line running from the First Army's sector in the Aachen area south along the German border to Metz, Nancy, and Epinal.

On 11 September patrols from General Patch's Seventh Army had established contact with patrols of General Patton's Third Army west of Dijon, but contact in force was not finally established until a Seventh Army column, driving north against enemy opposition, joined forces with the right wing of the Third Army west of Epinal on 21 September. This action reduced the size of the pocket west of the Belfort Gap and straightened the line which as a result now extended almost due south from Epinal to the Swiss frontier. In spite of the fact that use of the Belfort Gap as an escape route was now prevented, the enemy continued to hold on stubbornly in this whole area, evidently pursuing his usual policy of not yielding an inch except under pressure. This policy reacted to our advantage since it kept the enemy fully engaged and unable to withdraw forces to aid in the north, where the airborne operation against the lower Rhine was taking place. Along the whole line the war was to resolve itself into slow, hard fighting (with the few exceptions which I shall now consider) until after the German counter-attack in December and the opening of our own offensive in February.

CONSOLIDATION ON THE FRONTIER

In part the slowdown along the front facing Germany was due to my decision to employ our greatest strength in the north to attain flanking bridgeheads across the lower Rhine beyond the main fortifications of the Siegfried Line. In view of the fact, however, that the main highway to Berlin—the plains and level fields of northern Germany—lay beyond the Rhine in the north, and that the southern country was unsuitable

Consolidation on the frontier

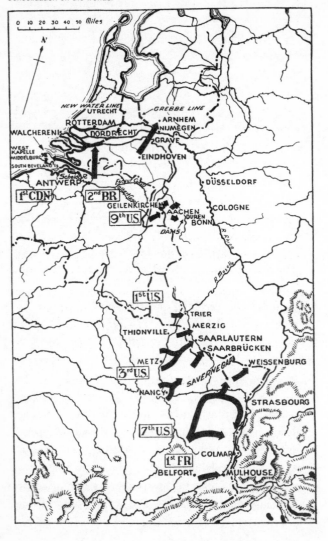

for the desired rapid advance and continued exploitation by reason of its mountainous and forested terrain,
my commanders and I were in full agreement as to the
desirability of exerting our strongest pressure in the
north. The attractive possibility of quickly turning the
German north flank led me to approve the temporary
delay in freeing the vital port of Antwerp, the seaward
approaches to which were still in German hands.

The operation to seize the bridges over the
Rhine was made up of two parts. The airborne oper-
ation, known as Market, had as its purpose the capture
of the vital bridges over the Mass, the Waal, and the
Lower Rhine at Grave, Nijmegen, and Arnhem. The
forces employed in the airborne operation included
the US 82nd Airborne Division, the 101st Airborne
Division, the British 1 Airborne Division, and the
Polish 1st Paratroop Brigade. The British 1 Airborne
Division was to be dropped farthest north in the
Arnhem area, the US 82nd Airborne Division in the
Nijmegen area, and the US 101st Division in the St
Oedenrode area north of Eindhoven. In rapid support
of the airborne troops, armor and infantry of the
British Second Army were to advance northward
from the general line of the Albert and Escaut Canals.
Passing over the bridges held by the airborne troops,
the armor was to push on to the Zuider Zee and
thus, if successful, cut off the land exit of enemy
troops in western Holland. The land operation,
known as Garden, was to take place on a very narrow
front with only one road as a line of communication
for a considerable part of the way. The axis of advance

lay through Eindhoven, St Oedenrode, Veghel, Uden, Grave, Nijmegen, Arnhem, and Apeldoorn.

The first landings of the main airborne forces were made on 17 September and follow-up troops and reinforcements continued to be flown in on succeeding days in spite of unfavorable weather on several occasions. Initial losses *en route* and at the dropping zones were very slight and bore out General Brereton's contention that heavy bomber effort on flak positions immediately preceding an airborne operation would greatly reduce casualties. These attacks had been undertaken by "heavies" of both the RAF Bomber Command and the US Eighth Air Force, which neutralized enemy airfields in the vicinity of the dropping zones and flak positions *en route*. By the 19th, British Second Army ground forces, advancing from the south, had made contact with all of the airborne troops except those to the north of the lower Rhine in the Arnhem area. Here the British 1 Airborne Division was holding out heroically against greatly superior forces, including a quantity of armor, the presence of which in the area had been estimated by my intelligence staff. This, in the outcome, proved to be effective against the tactical power we could apply.

The British Guards Armoured Division had pushed north on 17 September, but met heavy resistance slowing its advance into Eindhoven, which had been taken by the 101st Airborne Division. Firm contact was established between the two forces on the 18th, and the Guards Armoured pushed rapidly north to Grave, which had fallen to the 82nd Airborne Division. The area between Grave and Nijmegen was held by this latter division and the armored advance to the town was consequently rapid. Nijmegen itself, however, was held by the enemy, as was also the extremely important road bridge crossing the Waal. This bridge, a modern five-span structure of steel and concrete, some 6,000 feet in length, was a valuable prize, since, without it, the river would have been a formidable obstacle. An attempt by armor to get through to the bridge failed on the 19th in the face of heavy fire from anti-tank guns sited in houses near the approaches. On the following day, however, a regiment of the 82nd Airborne Division crossed the river in assault boats upstream from the bridge and surprised and overcame the German forces holding the northern approaches. The British meanwhile had seized the southern end, and that evening, after mines had been removed, the armor crossed the bridge and advanced two miles to the north where it was held up by an anti-tank screen.

During the next few days there was confused and heavy fighting in the area between Nijmegen and Arnhem, and it was not until the 24th that British infantry reached the lower Rhine in force and artillery began lending fire support to the beleaguered 1 Airborne Division on the northern bank of the river.

By 23 September the position of the 1 Airborne Division had become so precarious that the Second Army gave 30 Corps permission to withdraw the division if the situation did not improve. 30 Corps ordered every risk to be taken to relieve the division on the 24th, by which date the forces on the northern bank had been forced into a steadily contracting perimeter approximately 1,000 yards by 1,500 yards. The shelling, mortaring, and strafing of this area by the enemy was incessant, and on 25 September, Corps finally ordered the withdrawal of all forces across the lower Rhine. This was effected that night and 2,163 men of the 1 Airborne Division withdrew under cover of darkness, infiltrating in small groups through the enemy lines and across the river. Casualties had been heavy, the division losing in killed, wounded and missing some 7,000 men.

While the crossing of the lower Rhine was not completed, the operation brought very positive and important advantages to our forces. Repeated enemy attacks against the thin line of communications had temporarily necessitated withdrawal of armor from Nijmegen to keep the single road open, but the line was ultimately held and supplies went through even under constant shelling. As the line was strengthened with the arrival of stronger infantry units, the corridor was gradually widened on both sides. British forces pushed west in conjunction with northward attacks by other British and Canadian forces to establish a firm line eventually running along the Waal and Mass. To the east the corridor was also widened to bring the Northern Group of Armies into line with the Central Group and within striking distance of Kleve. Bridgeheads had been firmly secured across the Maas and Waal and the watershed between the two was to serve as a valuable corridor for a later advance to the Rhine.

Operation Market had been the largest airborne operation undertaken by the Allied forces up to this time. Between 17 and 30 September, 20,190 troops had been dropped from aircraft by parachute, 13,781 had landed in gliders, and 905 were air-landed on a strip made ready by the preceding airborne troops. In addition to this total of 34,876 troops, 5,230 tons of equipment and supplies, 1,927 vehicles, and 568 artillery pieces were transported by air. In all, the supporting air forces, who showed great gallantry in continuing to fly supplies to the isolated forces, flew over 7,800 sorties.

My decision to concentrate our efforts in this attempt to thrust into the heart of Germany before the enemy could consolidate his defenses along the Rhine had resulted in a delay in opening Antwerp and in making the port available as our main supply base. I took the full responsibility for this, and I believe that the possible and actual results warranted the calculated risk involved. Had our forces not pushed north and east to hold the line of the Maas and Waal well north of Antwerp, the port itself would have been in constant danger not only from a blow possibly synchronized with the later breakthrough in the Eifel but from independent attacks launched at close range from Holland.

With the completion of the Market-Garden operation the Northern Group of Armies was instructed to undertake the opening of Antwerp as a matter of the first priority. While the city and port installations had fallen virtually intact to 30 Corps on 4 September, the harbor had proved and was to continue to prove useless to us until the Scheldt estuary had been cleared of mines and South Beveland and Walcheren Island, commanding the sea lane to the harbor, had been reduced. The operation to achieve this involved the employment of amphibious forces, and the joint naval, air, and ground force planning was immediately undertaken and worked out during the latter part of September and early October at the headquarters of the Canadian First Army.

As an integral part of the operation, and in support of the amphibious elements, Canadian forces attacked north of Antwerp toward the South Beveland Isthmus in mid-October. On 24 October, having overcome resistance at Woensdrecht and thus ensured their flank protection, the Canadian 2 Division turned west and advanced slowly across the narrow neck connecting South Beveland with the mainland. Progress here was particularly difficult, the troops often having to fight waist-deep in water while the Germans offered strong resistance.

The Canadian forces continued their advance, however, and by midday on 27 October had reached the line of the canal at the west end of the isthmus. Crossing this at its southern extremity, they pressed forward to within 2½ miles of troops of the British 52 Division who had been landed on the south shore of South Beveland on the night of the 25th/26th, and by the 29th they effected a juncture with them. By the 30th the whole of South Beveland had been cleared and the British and Canadians continued their attack against the causeway connecting the isthmus with Walcheren.

On Walcheren the enemy consisted of the remnants of a division, forced back with severe losses from South Beveland, and elements of the German Fifteenth Army which had made their escape by sea across the Scheldt from the trap in which they had been caught with the seizure of Antwerp. Against Walcheren the Canadians attacked from the west, while amphibious forces, landed on 1 November at both Westkapelle and Vlissingen, moved east and north, converging on the strongpoints of the island. These forces, consisting of the Royal Marine 4 SS Brigade (Commandos) and two battalions of the 52 Infantry Division, had been successfully landed from naval assault craft under heavy fire. Great credit for the success of the amphibious operation is due to the support craft of the British Navy, which unhesitatingly and in the highest traditions of the service attracted to themselves the point-blank fire of the land batteries, thus permitting the commandos and assault troops to gain the shore with much lighter casualties than otherwise would have been the case. The air forces also, operating in great strength despite appallingly difficult weather conditions, lent invaluable support throughout the operation, a feature of this support being the accurate bombing by aircraft of the Bomber Command which succeeded in breaching the dykes.

The three converging ground forces, attacking over terrain made extremely difficult by flooding, and suffering heavy casualties, advanced with great gallantry against stiff enemy resistance to capture the strongpoints of Veere and Middelburg and wipe out enemy opposition. By 9 November all resistance had ceased and some 10,000 troops had been captured, including a division commander.

With the capture of South Beveland and Walcheren the land approaches to Antwerp were now freed, but the Scheldt estuary had still to be swept of mines before the port could become useful. This work was at once undertaken by the Navy and Antwerp became a port of supply for our forces with the unloading of the first ships on 26 November. The enemy, however, recognizing the importance of the harbor to us as a supply base, began at this time the launching in considerable strength of V-1 and V-2 weapons against the dock and town area. While the weapons were erratic in about the same degree as those launched against the London area, they nevertheless caused considerable damage in the district, killing both civilian and military personnel as well as disrupting communications and supply work for brief periods. Great credit is due to the citizens of Antwerp for sustaining the attacks as London had done and for unflinchingly going about their tasks which were of assistance to us in forwarding the war effort. In addition to attacks from the V-weapons against docks and shore installations, the enemy also employed large numbers of E-boats and midget submarines against our naval craft and shipping, but all these attempts at disrupting our flow of supplies were successfully countered by vigorous naval and air measures.

While the Arnhem–Nijmegen operation and the attack upon the approaches to Antwerp were the more spectacular successes during the latter part of September, the month of October and early November, the slugging matches along the rest of the front facing north and east were equally important for the general development of the campaign. Our two immediate objectives during this period were, first, to advance east to the Rhine and north to the Maas and, second, to use the space between our front and the Rhine as a "killing ground" in which to engage the enemy either in a large decisive battle or so to maul him that when the Rhine had been reached he would have little left with which to resist our crossings and prevent a breakthrough leading to mobile warfare.

Although we were not to reach the Rhine as quickly as we had hoped, or yet to engage the enemy in a decisive battle except as he himself created it in his December counter-offensive, the continued daily losses which he suffered in both personnel and equipment contributed to weakening him so that when our main blows ultimately fell victory was inevitable. By the end of September total enemy casualties, including killed, wounded, and prisoners, totalled approximately 1,000,000 men, including those swept into our net with the rapid advance of General Devers' forces from the south and their junction with General Bradley's troops west of the Belfort Gap. The isolated remnants of the German First Army in southwest France gave themselves up in piecemeal groups to the French Forces of the Interior and to our own forces, the largest single body consisting of 20,000 troops who surrendered without even attempting resistance after being trapped south of the Loire. Our continued hard-fought battles during the next three months were to increase this total by mid-January to 1,500,000, a figure indicative of the steady attrition being inflicted on the enemy. In spite of these losses, however, German troops continued to put up strong resistance, battling with a stubbornness and Teutonic fury born of the desperate knowledge that they were fighting on their own "holy soil." Our logistical situation, coupled with the fact that the terrain was suitable to the defense, aided the enemy. Additionally, during this period we experienced weather conditions which admirably suited him. The rains which fell in November were the worst known on the Continent in many years and created flood conditions along our whole front, reducing the lesser roads to quagmires and impeding tank operations and vehicular movement. All these factors made it more easily possible for the enemy, exploiting a comparatively static situation, to mine and booby-trap the areas ahead of us, contributing further to our problems.

In spite of these difficulties we achieved much. The First Army troops had entered Germany in the Trier region on 11 September and in the Aachen area east of Eupen on the 12th. At Aachen the enemy resisted bitterly but by the 20th the city was under attack from three sides and subject to heavy shelling. On the north side, which was still open, the First Army launched an attack across the German border on 2 October and in the first two days breached the Siegfried Line on a 3-mile front, the southern point of the breakthrough being about eight miles north of Aachen. Within the next few days the two remaining main roads into Aachen from the north were cut and the defenders isolated. Concurrently with these attacks the First Army attacked eastward against Stolberg, where heavy house-to-house fighting took place. On 13 October the First Army troops entered Aachen from the east and by the 19th, in spite of resistance from fortified cellars and buildings, had cleared half the city, which was now in ruins as a result of our bombing and shelling. Following the success of our assault, enemy resistance gradually weakened and the final surrender of the first large German city to Allied forces took place on 21 October when the garrison gave in to troops of the 1st Infantry Division of VII Corps. After the fall of Aachen the First Army's offensive operations were curtailed until the November offensives which were mounted along the entire front.

On the Third Army's front Nancy had fallen on 15 September, but Metz, strongly defended by its outer ring of forts, was to remain in enemy hands until our offensive ultimately reduced it on 22 November. South of Metz, along the line of the Moselle, the Third Army pushed eastward slowly until its line extended roughly parallel with the river to a depth of 20 to 25 miles. Farther south the Seventh Army and the French First Army, probing slowly into the area of the High Vosges across the Moselle from Epinal and against the Belfort Gap area, brought their line up to conform with that of the Third Army.

The relatively static warfare of October had thus brought us into position for the limited offensives which we were mounting for November.

During the month of October an administrative change had been placed in effect which was to bring the Tactical Air Forces more closely under the control of my Headquarters. Prior to 15 October the Allied Expeditionary Air Force, under Air Chief Marshal Leigh-Mallory, had maintained its separate Headquarters, reporting to me through my deputy, Air Chief Marshal Tedder. In October, however, we were informed that the Air Ministry desired to transfer Air Chief Marshal Leigh-Mallory to a post of greater responsibility in the China–Burma–India Theater, where, because of his long experience, his presence could be best employed to further the ends of the war. It was with great reluctance that I agreed to this change, but once it had been made I felt that the AEAF, without Air Chief Marshal Leigh-Mallory, might better function as an integral part of my own headquarters. SHAEF Air Staff thus came into being on 15 October and the planning and operational staffs became part of my headquarters. Shortly after this, on 14 November, Air Chief Marshal Leigh-Mallory, *en route* to his new command, was reported missing. His loss to the common war effort came as a keen personal blow to me and to the members of my staff.

With the opening of Antwerp our supply problem was considerably eased, but the Germans had profited by our earlier logistical handicap to reinforce their Siegfried defenses with hurriedly formed Volksgrenadier divisions. These divisions initially had very low combat value, but both General Bradley and I felt that unless the Siegfried positions could be speedily attacked the relative strength of the opposing forces would gradually become more favorable to the enemy.

My plan of campaign at this period included an advance on the fronts of the Northern and Central Groups of Armies to the Rhine, which it was necessary to hold from its mouth to Düsseldorf at least, if not to Bonn or Frankfurt, before a large-scale penetration beyond the river into Germany could be attempted. With the strong defensive barrier which the Rhine would afford our armies, it would become more easily possible to concentrate power at one point for the breakthrough, leaving relatively thinly held positions along the rest of the front.

The eastward drive by 21 Army Group began on 15 November, but progress was slow over ground made extremely difficult by the severe weather and it was not until 4 December that the last enemy pocket on the west bank of the Maas was cleared. A direct advance across the Maas to the Rhine was judged impracticable and extensive regrouping would have been necessary for a drive southeast from the

Nijmegen area along the relatively dry watershed separating the two rivers. To accomplish this latter penetration it would have been necessary to reduce the frontage of the Northern Group of Armies in order to gather strength at the point of attack. Due to limitations in strength, 21 Army Group itself was incapable of holding the whole of its frontage and attacking at the same time, and 12th Army Group would have had to take over a portion of the line. This could only have been done by 12th Army Group at the expense of weakening the Aachen attack, a course which was not acceptable to me. I therefore decided to postpone further major operations by 21 Army Group until the drive toward Cologne had made adequate progress in the central sector.

In the Aachen sector the offensive by the First and Ninth Armies was launched on 16 November after an hour and a half of intensive air and artillery bombardment. Over 1,200 US heavy bombers dropped bombs on fortified positions north of Eschweiler and west of Düren. Later in the day RAF bombers also attacked Düren itself and Jülich, practically obliterating these towns. The offensive was launched in two main directions, eastward from Aachen toward Eschweiler and northeastward toward Geilenkirchen. East of Aachen the enemy was driven entirely out of Stolberg, which he had partially held for some six weeks while our own forces were entrenched in the remainder of the town. By the 21st our troops had penetrated into Eschweiler, which fell after heavy fighting on the following day. Meanwhile the fighting had moved farther along the right flank into the Hürtgen Forest, southeast of Aachen, and gains in this sector placed our troops within attacking range of Düren.

To the north Geilenkirchen had fallen on the 19th and the Ninth Army continued advancing slowly until 3 December it had reached the Roer River. The First Army was conforming to the south more slowly still. Fourteen at first, and eventually seventeen, divisions were employed in the Aachen sector by the First and Ninth Armies, and at the height of the offensive no fewer than ten divisions were in the line together on a 24-mile front, this being the maximum which it was practicable to deploy. In spite of this concentration and the very large-scale strategic and tactical air attacks, the progress had been slow and the fighting bitter. The delay imposed on our advance here was a testimony to the improved defense works which the enemy had constructed following our breakthrough of the Siegfried Line in September.

While the Ninth Army had reached the Roer by 3 December, General Bradley considered it imprudent to cross the river while the Schmidt Dams, which controlled the flooding of the Roer Valley, remained intact in enemy hands. The German Sixth Panzer Army had moved west of the Rhine by this time, and had the American forces crossed the Roer the enemy, releasing the flood waters, would have been in a position to trap the attackers. Air attacks on the dams were called for at short notice and accurately executed; direct hits were secured on the structures. These attacks, however, failed to destroy the dams, partly because bad weather precluded the concentration of the necessary weight of bombs and also because of the enemy's ability to adjust the water level. General Bradley therefore ordered the First Army to maneuver to capture them. The First Army began the attack for the dams on 13 December and the attack was still in progress when the subsequent enemy counter-offensive was launched in the Eifel.

Meanwhile, south of the Ardennes, the Third Army offensive toward the Saar which started on 8 November made excellent progress. North of Metz several bridgeheads established across the Moselle in the Thionville area were linked together by the 14th, and four days later troops operating from the bridgehead crossed the German frontier in several places. To the south Metz was surrounded and cut off, but, while the city itself fell on 22 November, seven of the forts continued to resist and the difficult task of mopping them up was not accomplished until 13 December. By 5 December, also, the Third Army's right flank had pushed eastward from the Metz–Nancy area to the Saar in conformity with the advance from Thionville, closing a stretch of the river over 16 miles in length. Three bridgeheads were secured in the Saarlautern area and contact was made with the main Siegfried defenses. These defenses at the Third Army's front of attack south of Merzig on the Saar River were the strongest sections of the line, guarding the triangle between the Moselle and the Rhine. The forward line, continuous but of no very great depth, closely followed the east bank of the Saar. The rear line, of greater strength, consisted of a zone of forts about two and a half miles deep, passing in front of Lebach and continuing through the Saarbrücken Forest to rejoin the forward line ten miles east of Saarbrücken itself. Following the Third Army's rapid advance, these defenses slowed the attack so that some regrouping and additional logistical support was necessary prior to reassuming the offensive. While I had hoped that the Third Army would have been able to achieve complete victory in the Saar, I had nevertheless set a time limit for the operation. The Third Army's final attack was to begin on 19 December, after which, regardless of results, divisions were to be transferred to the north to assist in the main effort against the Rhine and into Germany. The German counter-offensive through the Ardennes on 16 December upset these plans, and made the final offensive on the 19th an impossibility in view of the need for the Third Army to contain and subsequently counter-attack on the southern flank of the breakthrough.

On the 6th Army Group front the November offensive of the French First Army was launched on the 14th. Within a week the Belfort Gap had been breached and our troops had reached the Rhine. Belfort was cleared of all resistance by the 22nd. The breakthrough, accomplished on the 18th, turned the flank of the German positions in the Vosges and forced a general withdrawal in front of the Seventh Army sector to the north, where Seventh Army troops, after launching their attack simultaneously with that of French First Army, had been struggling slowly forward along the roads leading through the Vosges passes. The towns of Blâmont, Raon-l'Etape, Gérardmer, and St-Dié, with other lesser villages which controlled the passes through the hills, had been stubbornly defended by the enemy, for as long as they remained in his hands the High Vosges stood as an impassable wall protecting the Rhine plain to the east. With the outflanking movement to the south these towns fell to advancing Seventh Army troops, and the 44th Infantry Division, rapidly exploiting the strategic possibilities, advanced to Saarebourg, which fell on the 21st. Meanwhile, the French 2nd Armored Division, operating on the right of the 44th Infantry, by-passed Saarebourg and penetrated the defenses in front of the Saverne Gap, capturing the town itself the following day. Also on the 22nd, columns pushed both north and east of the town and broke out into the Rhine plain. On the 23rd, the French 2nd Armored Division reached Strasbourg, but, while the city was rapidly and easily cleared, some of the outer ring of forts continued to offer resistance until the 27th.

On the 24th the enemy launched a counter-attack from the northeast, directed against Saarebourg, with the seeming expectation of being able to cut the corridor which Seventh Army had rapidly extended to the Rhine. Initially some ground was lost, but the 44th Infantry Division fought the enemy to a standstill and regained earlier positions. To the east the 79th Division, which had been mopping up in the rear of the French 2nd Armored Division, resumed a northward advance and, with the 44th, made rapid progress toward Haguenau, which was taken on 12 December.

On the right flank the French First Army's advance down the Rhine plain was slowed by enemy counter-attacks across its lines of communication. After reaching the Rhine on the 20th, French armor turned north and by the 22nd cleared Mulhouse in an advance so rapid that part of the staff of the German Nineteenth Army was captured as it fled from the city. The German counter-attacks against the advancing columns' lines of communication forced a temporary withdrawal from positions gained along the Rhine east of Mulhouse, but by the 27th this ground was recaptured.

Between the northern columns of the Seventh Army which had reached the Rhine in the Strasbourg area and the southern columns of the French First Army which had approached the river near Mulhouse, troops of both armies advanced steadily through the Vosges to tighten the ring around German forces stubbornly defending their positions in the area about Colmar.

On 27 November, in view of the strategic opportunity afforded our armies to attack into the Saar Basin, I directed the Seventh Army, after rapid regrouping, to attack northward to breach the Siegfried Line west of the Rhine, launching the attack west of the Pfalzerwald in conjunction with the southern flank of the Central Group of Armies.

This advance from the south and southwest directly aided the Third Army's operations against the Saar. By mid-December the Seventh Army had crossed the German frontier on a 22-mile front and penetrated well into the Siegfried defenses northeast of Wissembourg. Our progress in the Saar and Wissembourg sectors contained 14 enemy divisions, and had it been possible to continue the advance the enemy would have been compelled to divert forces from the north, thus directly aiding our main effort in that sector. Meantime, the enemy forces driven from the Vosges maintained their bridgehead west of the Rhine in the Colmar area, which the French First Army, weakened by their recent offensive operations and short of trained infantry replacements, were unable to liquidate. This bridgehead area, which was to become known as the "Colmar Pocket," later exerted a profound and adverse effect on our operations until it was finally eliminated.

THE ARDENNES
COUNTER-OFFENSIVE

As a result of the decision to deploy our maximum effort in the Aachen sector and to sustain the successful progress of the Saar–Wissembourg operations with the balance of available forces, other stretches of the front were weakly held. In particular the Eifel sector of some 75 miles between Trier and Monschau was held by no more than four divisions. In this disposition of our forces I took a

The Ardennes counter-offensive

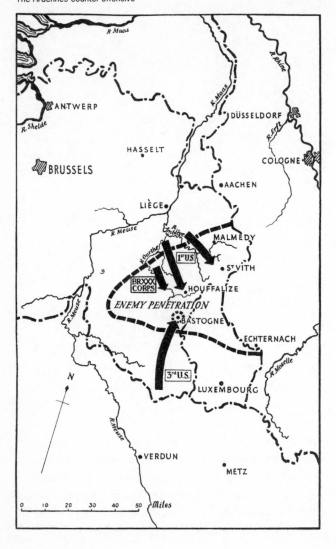

calculated risk, based on the absence of strategic objectives or large depots in the area and also on the relatively difficult terrain.

When the attacks from Aachen towards the Roer had to be suspended pending the capture of the river dams and the southern thrusts began to slow down, however, it was noticeable that the German panzer units started to withdraw from the line, their places being taken by Volksgrenadier divisions. All intelligence agencies assiduously tried to find out the locations and intentions of these panzer units, but without complete success. My headquarters and 12th Army Group had felt for some time that a counterattack through the Ardennes was a possibility, since American forces were stretched very thinly there in order to provide troops for attack elsewhere and because Field Marshal von Rundstedt had gradually placed in this quiet sector six infantry divisions, a larger number than he required for reasonable security. However, we did not consider it highly probable that von Rundstedt would, in winter, try to use that region in which to stage a counter-offensive on a large scale, feeling certain that we could deal with any such effort and that the result would ulti-mately be disastrous to Germany. Nevertheless, this is exactly what the enemy did, employing for a second time the plan of campaign and strategy which had made his first breakthrough in 1940 a complete suc-cess, and taking advantage of a period of bad weather which prevented our air power from operating. In order fully to appraise the desperate risk which the enemy undertook in making this venture it must be recognized that he aimed his blow, above all, at the will of the Allied Command. If he could weaken our determination to maintain that flaming, relentless offensive which, regardless of his reaction, had carried us from the beaches to the Siegfried Line, his sacrifices would not be altogether futile.

The attack started, after preparations of the very greatest secrecy, on Saturday, 16 December. General Bradley had just arrived at my headquarters for a conference on replacements when we received word that some penetrations of the American line had been effected, with the enemy using tanks. Sensing that this was something more than a mere local attack, I immediately advised General Bradley to move the 10th Armored Division from the south and the 7th Armored Division from the north, both toward the flanks of the attack. Army Commanders on both flanks were directed to alert what divisions they had free for instant movement toward that region if necessary. My own staff acted at once to move our reserve divisions forward. Of these movements, the most significant and important was that of the 101st Airborne Division, which was in SHAEF reserve and which was directed to Bastogne.

The following morning, the 17th, General Bradley returned to his own headquarters to keep a close grip on the situation, and during that day and the next it became clear that the enemy was making an all-out effort to split us and throw our campaign into disorder.

The enemy's general plan, as we initially analysed it and as events subsequently confirmed, was to break through our thin line of defenses in a sudden blitz drive to the Meuse in the Liége–Namur area. Having seized Liége, which was our key maintenance and communication center feeding 12th Army Group from the north, the enemy hoped to drive rapidly and with as much strength as possible to Antwerp, our great port of supply. Seizing or destroying this, he would have made our supply position practically untenable and would at the same time have split the British armies, together with the American Ninth Army and part of the First, in the north from the American and French forces in the south, isolating them and making possible their destruction in detail by attacks from Holland in the north and by his striking force in Belgium. The attack upon Antwerp itself would probably have been coordinated with an assault by paratroopers and infantry from Holland.

In all the enemy employed three armies for the battle, the Fifth Panzer Army and the Six Panzer Army supported by the Seventh Army, totalling some 14 infantry and 10 panzer and panzer grenadier divisions. Field Marshal von Rundstedt was in personal charge, and from field orders subsequently captured we obtained confirmation of our belief that this attack was in the nature of a final, desperate blow into which every available reserve was thrown. In addition to the main attacking forces, the enemy employed one panzer brigade which operated in American equipment with the mission of spearheading German combat units and spreading panic and confusion in and immediately behind our front line. Parties of paratroops were dropped throughout the battle area and particularly in the Malmedy area where about one battalion was employed, while small paratroop units and agents who had remained behind during our advance were active in attempting to sabotage key bridges and headquarters as far to the rear as Paris. For the first time also since our landing the Luftwaffe rose to give active combat support to the ground forces, not only by engaging our air forces off the ground but by attacking the airfields and installations throughout Belgium. On 1 January, for example, the German Air Force attacked our airfields in Holland and Belgium with the largest concentration of planes employed since D Day. Some 800 sorties were flown in an all-out air offensive and losses to our planes on the ground were considerable, although on this one day alone German losses amounted to 200 aircraft.

As soon as confirmation had been received of the extent of the enemy's effort to bring about a break-through, I immediately ordered the cessation of all attacks along the whole front and the gathering up of every possible reserve to strike the penetration on both flanks. My plan was to hold firmly the shoulders of the penetration, particularly the Monschau area on the north and the Bastogne area on the south, prevent enemy penetration west of the Meuse or in the Liége–Namur area, and then to counter-attack with General Patton's Army in the general direction of Bastogne–Cologne. This counter-attack was to be fol-lowed by an attack by the forces under Field Marshal Montgomery, directed as the result and progress of

General Patton's operations should indicate. I directed General Devers also to reach out as far as possible to his left to relieve Third Army, and to make available every single United States Division that he could, retaining as his own mission merely the covering of vital communications. He was told to give ground if necessary in order to keep his thus-stretched forces intact. This order was given verbally on the morning of 19 December at Verdun, where I had directed all interested ground and air commanders to assemble. Later I amplified this order by directing him to be ready to move back to the general line Belfort–Vosges in order to save the troops in the pocket lying between the Vosges, the Rhine, and the Siegfried Line. The same general instructions were given to Field Marshal Montgomery with respect to the northern flank.

On 19 December, when it became apparent that General Bradley's left flank was badly separated from his right and that the situation of his own Headquarters, located at Luxembourg, limited his command and communication capabilities to the area south of the penetration, I realized that it would be impracticable for him to handle the American forces both north and south of the large salient which was being created. I therefore fixed a boundary running east and west through the breach in our lines, generally on the axis Givet–Prüm, giving both places inclusive to the Northern Group. All forces north of the boundary, including the major part of the US First and Ninth Armies and part of the Ninth Air

Force, I placed respectively under the operational command of Field Marshal Montgomery and Air Marshal Coningham, Commander in Chief of the Second Tactical Air Force. This left General Bradley suitably located to command the forces on the southern flank of the salient, comprising mainly the US Third Army and XIX Tactical Air Command, considerably reinforced.

The full brunt of the enemy assault was met first by the four divisions deployed along the thinly held Eifel–Ardennes sector: the 4th, 28th, and 106th Infantry Divisions and the 9th Armored Division. In spite of being by-passed and divided by the penetration, these forces slowed the enemy thrust and the 7th Armored Division denied him the important area of St-Vith during the critical early days. The momentum of the breakthrough was further reduced by the arrival in the battle area on 18 December of the 101st and 82nd Airborne Divisions moved from reserve in the Reims area to the command of 12th Army Group. The 101st Airborne Division, reinforced by armor, then held the vital road center at Bastogne although completely surrounded for five days and under constant attack by forces many times superior in strength. The commitment of these divisions, however, removed the last Theater Reserve and the 11th Armored Division, newly arrived from England, was directed to assemble rapidly in the Reims area to protect the center and to meet a head-on attack on the Meuse if necessary. The 17th Airborne Division was also ordered over from England to help the 11th

Armored Division secure the Meuse line south of Givet. To re-establish and maintain a reserve, additional infantry divisions then in England were brought to the Continent in advance of planned schedule.

As the week wore on we succeeded in bolstering up the northern shoulder of the penetration, at the same time collecting a United States Corps under General Collins for use in counter-attack. From the south, General Patton began a transfer of six divisions to the north of the Moselle. 21 Army Group likewise collected reserves and placed a corps under Lieut. Gen. Horrocks in the Brussels area. The flanks of the penetration at Monschau and Echternach were held and the salient gradually stabilized by these measures. However, the penetration directly westward was still moving and, while on the north it had been possible with the 17th Airborne Division and the 11th Armored Division to cover the Meuse bridges adequately down as far as Givet, south of that the crossings remained alarmingly weak. To defend them I issued instructions that all available rear echelon troops and service units as well as six French infantry battalions be moved to the Meuse to protect the crossings at all costs and in no event to permit any bridge to fall intact into the hands of the enemy.

Because of the difficult situation in the region of Bastogne, where the 101st Airborne Division and other elements were steadfastly holding out against greatly superior forces, General Bradley felt that he should start General Patton's Third Army attacking to the northward from the Arlon–Luxembourg area no later than Friday, 22 December. General Patton was authorized to begin the attack, but prior to launching it he was instructed to make absolutely certain of the safety of his right flank in the Trier region from which a new offensive by the German Seventh Army still threatened. He was also to attack by phase lines, holding all forces carefully together in order to avoid any risk of dispersion or wastage of strength before Field Marshal Montgomery was in a position to join the attack from the north.

Prior to the 22nd the weather had been most unfavorable. From the 16th to the 22nd the enemy had the advantage of being able to attack under cover of a thick ground fog which deprived us of practically all air assistance apart from limited and extremely hazardous missions. His ground troops were able, as a result, to move against our defending forces with maximum surprise. On the 22nd, however, the weather began to improve and our air forces commenced their paralysing attacks upon enemy communications at the same time that the Third Army attack was launched northeastward from the Arlon–Luxembourg area. Since the enemy initiated the attack, prior planning of air operations (such as for the Normandy battle) was impossible. The object of our air attacks against the enemy's rail system, carried out in spite of the bad weather (both in the target area and over the bases in England), was to force back the enemy's railheads; the mounting of their offensive and the continued supply of the German forces were largely dependent on rail communications. The heavy bomber attacks achieved their object and made the closer-range attacks against road movements all the more effective in helping to strangle von Rundstedt's efforts. Throughout the period the Strategic Air Forces battered marshalling yards east of the Rhine and blocked centers of movement such as St-Vith, while the medium and light bombers of the Tactical Air Forces destroyed bridges, headquarters, dumps, and other targets in the battle area. The fighter-bombers ranged far and wide in and beyond the battle area creating havoc in enemy road and rail movement, their efficacy in starving the enemy of fuel, food, and ammunition being amply testified to by prisoners. A concerted attack on the German Air Force airfields on 24 December helped to reduce the activity of the enemy fighters and thus afforded our fighter-bombers still greater opportunity for concentration on ground targets rather than on air fighting, which had up to this time been as intense as any the enemy had proved capable of offering since D Day.

The 4th Armored Division of the Third Army, attacking northward against heavy resistance toward Bastogne, was able by 26 December to make firm contact with the defenders of the important road net there, who had meanwhile been supplied by air, and to check the enemy's advance on that flank. This attack also drew strong enemy forces away from the north of the salient. By the 26th also, additional reserves had been so disposed along the Meuse as to relieve anxiety over this sector, and it was then clear that the enemy had failed in his main intention. By the time the German drive was halted the enemy had breached a 45-mile gap in our lines from Echternach to Monschau and had penetrated over 60 miles westward to within 4 miles of the Meuse near Celles.

As soon as the enemy's advance had been checked, my intention was to cut his lines of communication into the salient and if possible to destroy him by launching ground attacks from both north and south in close coordination with continued heavy air attacks designed to extend paralysis of movement and communication over a large area. Simultaneously the strategic air effort which had been employed so effectively in the battle area was released to resume its normal tasks.

The counter-attack from the north, aimed at Houffalize in the center of the salient, was launched by the First Army on 3 January on a two-corps front, with a corps of the British Second Army conforming on the west flank. On 9 January, the Third Army, which had been maintaining strong pressure in the Bastogne area, launched a fresh attack also directed towards the Houffalize road net. Both these attacks were hampered by adverse weather over snow-covered minefields and were met by stubborn enemy resistance. Slow progress was made, however, and the gap between the attacking armies had by 10 January been narrowed to some ten miles. By this time the enemy had begun to withdraw from the western tip of his salient, but still strongly opposed our pressure against his northern and southern flanks. Nevertheless, on the 16th, attacking forces of the First and Third Armies established firm contact at Houffalize and turned their full strength eastward against the retreating enemy. St-Vith fell to the First Army forces on the 23rd and by the end of the month our line was approximately what it had been at the beginning of the breakthrough, while advance forces attacked beyond this in the direction of Bonn.

With the establishment of contact between the First and Third Armies and the reopening of direct communications between General Bradley's Headquarters and General Hodge's First Army, the operational command of the First Army reverted to the Central Group of Armies. The US Ninth Army was retained within the Northern Group of Armies under Field Marshal Montgomery.

The German counter-offensive had opened on 16 December and had been brought under control by the 26th. The initiative in the battle had passed to our forces shortly thereafter, and by 16 January, one month after the initial attack, our forces were in a firm position astride the Houffalize road network, ready to counter-attack strongly into enemy territory. Within this month, the enemy, although failing to reach even his initial objectives on the Meuse, had nevertheless succeeded in stopping our attacks against the Ruhr and the Saar. Operations to deal with the enemy offensive had occupied a full four weeks and were not, even by the 16th, completed. A certain regrouping was essential prior to the mounting of a full-scale offensive by our forces, and at that time I estimated that the enemy attack had delayed our offensive operations by at least six weeks. In addition to this disruption of our effort, the Strategic Air Forces had of necessity been drawn into the battle, thus leaving oil, aircraft, and communication targets deeper in Germany free of attack for nearly a month.

The counter-offensive, however, was not without its effects upon the enemy. Land and air forces had been carefully built up for months, and supplies, particularly of fuel, had been carefully hoarded for this all-out effort. During the month ending 16 January, my commanders estimated that the enemy suffered 120,000 serious casualties and lost 600 tanks and assault guns. He also lost about 1,620 planes—a severe blow—and his fuel stocks, after nearly a month of large-scale effort, were reduced to a bare minimum. The Tactical Aircraft claims for the month included also over 6,000 motor transport destroyed and 7,000 damaged, together with some 550 locomotives destroyed and over 600 damaged. By the end of our own counter-offensive the enemy had lost 220,000 men, including 110,000 prisoners of war. More serious in the final analysis was the widespread disillusionment within the German Army and Germany itself which must have accompanied the realization that the breakthrough had failed to seize any really important objective and had achieved nothing decisive.

During the progress of the Battle of the Ardennes, the enemy had also, as a diversionary and containing measure, mounted an attack on the 6th Army Group front with the apparent purpose of regaining the Alsace-Lorraine plains westward to the Vosges. It had initially been our plan to press the attacks against the enemy in this sector and to establish an easily held defensive line on the Rhine in order to be in a position to move forces northward for the main attack into Germany. The Battle of the Ardennes had made it immediately necessary to transfer to the north strong forces under command of General Patton prior to attaining our full objectives in the south. 6th Army Group had, as a result of the shift northward of these forces, been compelled to abandon the plans to clear the territory west of the Rhine, and was left with only the minimum forces required to maintain the defensive on its original line. Moreover, it was faced with an unhealthy situation in the area of the Colmar pocket.

After General Devers' troops had broken through the Vosges Mountains in November, it had appeared to him that the remaining German forces around the Colmar pocket could and would be quickly mopped up by the French Army. Consequently he had, according to plan, turned north with the bulk of his forces to assist General Patton who had fundamentally the same offensive role of securing the Rhine line. It was expected that as soon as the Colmar pocket had been reduced, the French Army itself would be capable of holding all Alsace-Lorraine and the entire Seventh Army could be employed north and east of the Vosges sector. As time went on, however, the enemy was able to stabilize the Colmar pocket, and to reinforce the area. Consequently, when the German thrust came through the Ardennes in great strength, we had on our extreme right flank, instead of the strong, easily defended line we expected, a situation that was inherently weak from a defensive standpoint. The entire VI Corps was lying to the east of the Vosges facing north, while the US 3rd Infantry Division had to be maintained with the French First Army in order to sustain the integrity of our lines in the Colmar pocket. The danger, clearly recognized by all of us from the start, was that the enemy would attempt to drive southward along the west of the Vosges and at the same time possibly try to erupt with a secondary attack from the Colmar pocket. In this event, VI Corps would not only have been unable to provide us with any reserves for the rest of the front, but would actually have had to turn and fight its way out of an awkward situation.

In view of this unsatisfactory position, and because General Devers' local reserves should manifestly be stationed west of the protective mountain barrier, I ordered a general withdrawal of the VI Corps line to the Vosges, retaining in the area north of Strasbourg only light reconnaissance elements that would have had to withdraw under any sizeable enemy advance. This move would, of course, have exposed Strasbourg to occupation by enemy forces and would have forced the left flank of the French Army to swing back into the mountains. It would, however, give General Devers the strongest possible defensive line along his eastern flank, since our forces had failed to gain the Rhine, and he would be enabled to collect into his own reserves at least two armored divisions in the regions south of the Siegfried Line and west of the Vosges. This would have given us opportunity to employ two US divisions as a SHAEF reserve farther to the north, leaving General Bradley free to devote his entire power to the offensive.

General Devers planned to execute this movement by stages, and until it could be completed we obviously had to leave the two divisions scheduled for SHAEF reserve under his control. Throughout the planning of the movement the French were kept informed. As the plans crystallized, however, the French became convinced that a withdrawal from the Strasbourg area would have unfortunate political repercussions in their country, bringing about perhaps even the downfall of the de Gaulle Government. They were so convinced of the necessity of at least putting up a fight for Strasbourg, rather than of voluntarily withdrawing to a better defensive line, that they were prepared to defend the city with the few French troops that could be hurriedly gathered together. These troops would have been so unready for battle and so inadequately equipped, however, that nothing could have been accomplished.

After closely studying the French views in the matter, and recognizing the political importance of Strasbourg, I felt compelled to alter the original plan for withdrawal. Originally, I had considered that the matter of Strasbourg was merely a conflict between military and political considerations and that I was completely justified in handling the question on a purely military basis. However, as I studied the French views, it became evident that the execution of the original plans for withdrawal might have such grave consequences in France that all our lines of communication and our vast rear areas might become seriously affected through interference with the tasks of the service troops and through civil unrest generally. Clearly, the prevention of such a contingency became a matter of military as well as of political necessity.

The plan was accordingly altered so that VI Corps merely withdrew from its sharp salient and its left rested in the Vosges with its right extending toward Strasbourg. In the meantime, preparation of defensive positions in the Vosges went on, conducted mainly by service troops. In view of my orders to go over to the defensive, to withdraw from the salient, and to place in reserve or send northward all available divisions, the enemy made some progress against our lines with a total force estimated at 14 divisions. Between Saarguemines and Neunhofen attacks shaping up into two prongs were made on 1 January in the direction of Rohrbach and toward the Saverne Pass, southeast of Bitche. Six days later the enemy succeeded in pushing troops across the Rhine, a few miles north of Strasbourg, and gained ground in a thrust northward from the Colmar pocket. This latter drive threatened to overrun the Alsatian Plain and to isolate Strasbourg. General Devers' forces inflicted heavy losses upon the enemy and with vigorous countermeasures, in spite of the difficulties under which they labored, succeeded in stabilizing the line so that no militarily essential ground in the Vosges was lost and Strasbourg itself no more than threatened.

PLANS FOR THE 1945 CAMPAIGN

By early 1945, the German oil supply was critically short and there was a growing transportation crisis which was already affecting every aspect of the German war effort. Our successful land advances had disrupted the German air defense system, had enabled us to install blind-bombing aids on the Continent, and had increased the depth to which fighter escorts could accompany the bombers into Germany. All these factors greatly increased our bombing power and reduced the capacity of the German Air Force to resist attacks.

By 16 January, the Battle of the Ardennes was substantially concluded. The First and Third Armies had joined hands through the salient at Houffalize, and their junction marked the achievement of tactical victory. At midnight on 17/18 January, the First Army reverted to the command of General Bradley's 12th Army Group, and the Allied line once more took up the order in which it was ranged along the threshold of Germany at the time when von Rundstedt's offensive interrupted our invasion preparations a month earlier. The task now was to regrasp the strategic initiative and resume the advance.

In planning our forthcoming spring and summer offensives, I envisaged the operations which would lead to Germany's collapse as falling into three phases: first, the destruction of the enemy forces west of the Rhine and closing to that river; second, the seizure of bridgeheads over the Rhine from which to develop operations into Germany; and third, the destruction of the remaining enemy east of the Rhine and the advance into the heart of the Reich. This was the same purpose that had guided all our actions since early 1944.

The immediate aim was to be the smashing of the enemy west of the Rhine, in order to reduce to a minimum the forces which would be available to oppose our crossing of the river and subsequent advance. A secondary purpose was to give us a maximum ability for concentration along chosen avenues across the Rhine, with maximum economy of security troops on other portions of the front. The form which these operations west of the Rhine were to take was largely dependent upon the geographical factors which would condition our progress in the later phases.

Once we had crossed the Rhine, there were two main avenues by which we could advance to the heart of Germany and defeat such enemy forces as were left to oppose us. The first of these was from the lower Rhine, north of the Ruhr and into the North German Plain; the second was from the Mainz–Karlsruhe area and thence northeast through Frankfurt toward Kassel. The former axis of advance, apart from offering the most suitable terrain for mobile operations—the type of warfare which we wished to force upon the enemy in order to exploit our superior mobility—afforded the quickest means of denying to the Germans the vital Ruhr industries. The northern and eastern exits of the Ruhr could be cut by enveloping action on the part of the ground forces, while the southern ones could be interrupted by air action. On the other hand, the importance of the Ruhr to the enemy was such that he was likely to accord it first priority in his defense plans, so that the rapid development of a superior force across the Rhine would be essential to Allied success. An advance on the southern axis from Mainz toward Kassel would also secure to us an industrial zone, in the Frankfurt area, and would therefore also be likely to afford us an opportunity of destroying considerable enemy forces. It would, moreover, offer suitable airfield sites from which to support further advances.

On the debit side, however, the advance would be over terrain less suitable for armored operations, although once Kassel had been reached the Allies could either push north to complete the encirclement of the Ruhr, or northeast toward Berlin, or eastward toward Leipzig.

From the Mainz–Karlsruhe sector, a thrust might also be eastward toward Nürnberg, but this, important as it was later to become, was not of immediate concern in the long-term planning on which we were engaged in January. We still held on to the hope for an opportunity to effect a massive double envelopment of the Ruhr, to be followed by a great thrust to join up with the Russians, but we could not then foresee to what extent the forthcoming Russian offensive, in its sweeping advances, might influence our strategy in this direction.

With respect to the local geographical factors governing our choice of Rhine crossing-sites, the Mainz–Karlsruhe sector was more favorable than that north of the Ruhr. In the latter, between Emmerich and Wesel, there were sites suitable for three divisional assaults on a 20-mile front, in addition to one possible, though difficult, further site. Flooding conditions west of Emmerich would quite likely preclude any extension of this assault area until after June. In the Mainz–Karlsruhe sector there were sites for five divisional assaults, with a possible sixth south of Karlsruhe. In addition to these two main sectors, there was one site on each side of Cologne which would accommodate a single divisional assault crossing, but this would prove tactically difficult, and, once across the river, the forces would be faced with unfavorable terrain. The nature of the country likewise militated against the use of sites between Coblenz and Bonn except under conditions of very light opposition.

Another factor which had to be taken into account in planning the Rhine assault operations was the technical opinion of the Engineers that until March there would be a danger of ice hampering the crossings and bridging. Below Mainz summer floods, following the melting of the Alpine snows, would make it imperative to complete the construction of permanent bridges by May. This estimate differed from earlier technical reports in that it indicated the advisability of a March–April attack, whereas the Engineers originally believed that conditions on the Rhine would render unwise any such attempt between 20 November and late May.

From the logistical aspect, there was available to the Allied armies sufficient bridging equipment and personnel to launch nine assault crossings, and, in addition, one unopposed crossing of the Rhine. After the crossings had been effected, it was estimated that our lines of communication would enable us to build up to a maximum of some 35 divisions north of the Ruhr, leaving some 55 divisions (counting scheduled arrivals) for holding and secondary operations.

None of the considerations mentioned above indicated any change in the decision arrived at during our pre-D-Day planning, that is that the main thrust of the Allied armies for the crossing of the

Rhine and the isolation of the Ruhr should be on the axis north of the Ruhr. Without that vast industrial region, Germany would be incapable of continuing to wage war, especially when the expected Russian offensive had engulfed the Silesian industrial area which alone was comparable to the Ruhr in productive capacity. Since we could not attack the Ruhr frontally, we must by-pass it; and the most favorable terrain lay to its north. I was equally certain that this main effort on the north should be accompanied by a secondary effort as strong as our means permitted after the main, northern thrust had been provided for, from the Mainz–Karlsruhe area in the general direction of Kassel. Thus the maneuver would constitute a great double envelopment, which would encircle the Ruhr and the mass of the enemy forces which were certain to concentrate in its defense.

With this in mind, the first task must be to initiate operations west of the Rhine and north of the Moselle which should destroy the enemy in that zone and bring our armies on to the Rhine north of Düsseldorf to permit preparation for the ensuing main attack. That done, we must direct our main effort to eliminating other enemy forces west of the Rhine which might still constitute an obstacle or a potential threat to our subsequent crossing operations. When the enemy had thus been cleared from the west bank, we must seize bridgeheads over the river both in the north and the south. North of the Ruhr, we must deploy east of the Rhine the maximum number of divisions which we were capable of maintaining there, while to the south, on the axis Mainz–Frankfurt–Kassel, we must deploy such forces as might be available after providing the estimated 35 divisions required for the principal thrust north of the Ruhr.

The primary task of the southern force was to draw away enemy units which might otherwise oppose the main advance in the north. It was essential to force the enemy to disperse his strength, so that we might use all possible crossings and lines of communication to establish in western Germany a concentrated force of sufficient size to complete the conquest. Flexibility had to be an essential of our plans, as the possibility of failure to secure the necessary bridgeheads in one or another sector could not be overlooked. Logistical preparations must therefore be made rapidly to switch the main effort from north to south if this should prove necessary. Whatever the opposition might be, the fact remained that in any case the crossing of the Rhine, on the narrow frontages available, would be a tactical and engineering feat of the greatest magnitude. Use of airborne forces, air support, and amphibious equipment on the maximum scale would be required if the successful passage of the main Allied armies was to be assured.

The strength of our land forces, at the time of planning in January, was 71 divisions, but this figure did not accurately represent their effective value. Many of the American divisions were seriously under strength in infantry, and, although strenuous efforts were being made to find the necessary replacements both by accelerating the flow of reinforcements from the United States and by taking fit men from rear echelon employment, it was obvious that some time must elapse before these men could become available for front-line duty. For the moment the French divisions on our southern flank were depleted to relatively low combat effectiveness. By the time at which we estimated we should be ready to cross the Rhine, in March, the Allied strength would, under the existing build-up program, have risen to 85 divisions, including 6 airborne, with 5 to 8 new French divisions organizing, training and equipping for possible later employment. It was also hoped that the existing French divisions would have their combat value largely restored.

As against the Allied power, it was difficult, as the situation then stood, to calculate the likely strength of the enemy in the spring. This depended partly upon the extent to which he might be able to draw reinforcements from Italy and Norway for the Western Front. It would depend also upon the destructive effects of our continuing winter operations, which, as always, I was determined to pursue vigorously. Finally, it depended upon the degree to which events on the Eastern Front would engross the enemy's attention. If the worst happened and the anticipated Russian spring offensive proved weak and ineffectual, the enemy was estimated to be capable of maintaining as many as 100 divisions in the west. But if the Russian offensive proved as successful as we hoped, it seemed unlikely that more than 80 divisions could be spared to meet our attack, while the German logistical potentialities would be correspondingly impaired.

Now that the time was approaching for what, we trusted, would be the final blow to Nazi Germany a closer coordination with the Russian High Command and mutual understanding of our respective plans became essential. Our first liaison with Moscow had been effected late in 1944 when air operations necessitated the establishment of a coordinated bomb-line, but little further had been accomplished. The only link between my headquarters and that of Marshal Stalin was through the medium of the Allied Military Mission in Moscow, and it appeared most difficult to learn of Soviet intentions. Up to the end of 1944 I had received no information on matters affecting the Russian grand strategy, although I had expressed my willingness to afford any such information concerning my own overall plans as the Red Army might desire. At Christmas time, however, following upon a message which I sent to the Combined Chiefs of Staff explaining the difficulty with which I was faced in attempting to evolve plans while still ignorant of the Russian intentions, President Roosevelt secured from Marshal Stalin his agreement to receive our representative in order to discuss the correlation of our respective efforts in the forthcoming spring.

Accordingly, in January, my deputy, Air Chief Marshal Tedder, accompanied by Major-General Bull (G-3) and Brig. Gen. Betts (G-2), journeyed to Moscow for this purpose. The conference proved conspicuously successful. In the course of a discussion ranging over many aspects of the forthcoming campaigns, Marshal Stalin was acquainted with the nature of our own plans, including the timing. He, in turn, responded with a full explanation of the great four-pronged offensive, involving from 150 to 160 divisions, which the Red Army was preparing to launch. He further gave us an assurance that, in the event of the main offensive being halted by bad weather, the Red Army would still conduct local operations which he believed would so pin down German armies as to permit no major movement of divisions from east to west during the difficult period of the spring thaw. As events showed, the success of this gigantic offensive proved even greater than had been anticipated. In the meantime, fortified by Marshal Stalin's assurances, we were able to proceed with our own operational planning.

In addition to his preoccupation with the Russian forces, the enemy was certain to be seriously hampered in the forthcoming operations on our front by the logistical difficulties which had been imposed upon him by the attacks of the Allied Strategic Air Forces from the west, while in the east the vital Silesian industrial region was soon to be overrun by the Soviet armies. Despite superhuman efforts to keep the lines open, the German railroad system was gradually breaking down under the weight of ever-increasing air blows. The attacks upon the facilities behind the Ardennes front had forced the railheads back nearly to the Rhine. Heavy destruction had also been inflicted upon the enemy's airplane industries, although dispersion of plants and the construction of underground factories had enabled him to make some progress with his jet aircraft production—the most serious threat with which we were faced. But planes would be of little avail without fuel, and it was against the German refineries and synthetic plants that our greatest effort was directed. Although some recovery had been effected during the autumn and early winter, the heavy blows struck at the end of the year once more brought production down to an extremely critical figure. The gasoline produced during January was likely to be no more than 100,000 tons (20% of the pre-raid amount), and there was a prospect of a further drop to about half this figure with the intensification of our attacks in the near future. In fact, with the immobilization of probably the whole Ruhr synthetic fuel industry, the simultaneous stoppage of the great installations at Bruz, Leuna, and Politz, and the threat of the Russian advances to the synthetic plants in Silesia, the German oil industry was facing a graver crisis than ever before, and this at a time when operational requirements were likely to rise to a point higher than in any previous period of the past six months.

It was to this oil offensive that we pinned our faith to counterbalance the numerical superiority which the enemy enjoyed over us in respect to his jet aircraft. Had the program of production which the Luftwaffe envisaged been put into effect, our air mastery in the spring of 1945 would have been precarious, for our own production had not enabled us to meet the jets on equal terms. Fortunately our bombing campaign, both upon the production centers and upon the airfields from which the jet planes operated, so limited their numbers and potentialities that the German effort was too little and too late. So far as orthodox aircraft were concerned, despite a numerical strength that was still considerable, the fuel situation and the growing dearth of trained pilots were so acute that the German Air Force was never in a position seriously to interfere with our operations after the great but costly effort made on New Year's Day, when some 800 aircraft raided Allied airfields in Belgium and Holland.

On the Allied side, I was satisfied that our Tactical Air Forces were strong enough to fulfil the tasks which would face them when our offensives began, and that the Strategic Air Forces were fully capable of carrying out their planned programs. Attacks on oil installations, jet aircraft and armament factories, and naval and communications targets were to be the chief objectives of the heavy bombers, with an overriding priority of coordination with the ground force offensive operations. The air staff fully explored the possibility of destroying the 31 Rhine bridges behind the enemy armies west of the river, in the same way that in the previous summer we had cut the lines of communication over the Seine and Loire behind the German Seventh Army in Normandy, but did not consider such a program practicable. It was believed that to undertake the destruction of so many bridges as an additional target system would involve too great a diversion from the existing strategic effort, and that the weather was unlikely to afford the requisite number of visual bombing days. Certain key bridges were to be attacked, however, in conjunction with a transverse blocking of communications within each battle area which would limit the enemy's tactical mobility.

In the latter respect, the enemy was favored by the advantages accruing from his strong defensive lines, first the Siegfried fortifications, and behind them the great barrier of the Rhine itself. These defenses were extremely formidable, and apart from the cost of piercing them on a selected front, their chief value to the enemy lay in the fact that they would enable him to concentrate safely for counter-attack at our lines of communication. That capability was well demonstrated when the Ardennes thrust had been launched, and, although that attempt had been defeated, the possibility of further, though necessarily weaker, offensives remained. To meet this we would have to station all along our extended line more troops than we could afford, and any concentration on our part for an attack on a given point would entail a dangerous weakening of other sectors, *unless* before striking our decisive blow at the heart of Germany we ourselves possessed such a defensive line as the enemy himself enjoyed. I was convinced that only the Rhine could fulfil this requirement. Once we held the Rhine substantially throughout its length we should possess such a line as could be held with minimum forces along the inactive sectors. Thus we could safely concentrate the great strength required for our intended main thrust across the river north of the Ruhr and, by the exercise of economy elsewhere, provide reasonable strength for a secondary effort. Moreover, the enemy would find himself at the same disadvantage as that at which the possession of the Siegfried Line had formerly placed us. We would have the opportunity of threatening him at a number of points along the line, forcing him to disperse his defending forces and thus making easier the task of our troops invading the Reich at the points selected for our attack.

For these reasons, we considered that before attempting any major operations east of the Rhine it was essential to destroy the main enemy armies west of the river, although it might not be worth the time and cost to indulge in protracted operations to reduce any strong but constricted bridgeheads that might remain in German hands. When the Combined Chiefs of Staff expressed doubts as to our ability to maintain two thrusts—north of the Ruhr and in the Mainz–Frankfurt area—with the forces at my disposal, it was pointed out that such would indeed be the case if we did not clear to the Rhine before embarking on a major offensive to the east of that river. Given a situation, however, where we could operate without fear for the security of our flanks and without expending for defensive purposes more strength than we could afford, I felt confident of our ability to carry out the plans already indicated, putting the chief weight into the northern thrust but at the same time striking in the south and retaining flexibility enough to switch the main effort if the situation so required. Moreover, the simple fact remained that destruction of enemy forces should be easier on the west of the Rhine than on the east.

Of the 85 divisions which were to be at my disposal, 35 were tentatively allocated for the northern thrust. Of the remainder, I estimated that only 25 were necessary for defense and reserve purposes if we held the line of the Rhine, whereas as many as 45 would be required were the northern assault to be attempted while the rest of the front was substantially west of the river, with the enemy capable of striking at us from behind his Siegfried fortifications.

Together with their suggestion that I should concentrate upon the single heavy drive in the north rather than run what might, except in the circumstances described, have proved a dangerous risk of weakening the Allied efforts of overdispersal, the Combined Chiefs of Staff submitted for my consideration a proposal by the British Chiefs of Staff that a single ground commander for the whole front north of Luxembourg be appointed to exercise, under me, operational control and coordination of all ground forces involved in the offensive which was to take us across the Rhine. This suggestion was based upon the assumption that all the remainder of the front would remain on the defensive, contrary to my plans. I pointed out that, under these plans, the Ruhr marked the logical division of command zones, and that Field Marshal Montgomery would be in charge of all the forces—the Canadian Army, British Army, and US Ninth Army—that were to participate in the northern offensive to capture the Ruhr. In the center, during the operations preceding the Rhine crossing, General Bradley's 12th Army Group, comprising the US First and Third Armies, would concentrate primarily on an offensive through the Siegfried Line along the axis Prüm–Bonn with its left swinging north to support the Ninth Army and its right swinging south to flank the Saar. South of the Moselle General Devers' 6th Army Group, with the US Seventh and French First Armies, would remain on the defensive at first, subsequently operating to clear the Saar Basin and close the Rhine when the Germans had been driven out of the zone north of the Moselle.

The existing Army Group system of command thus fitted naturally into the operational plans which we had evolved, and I could not see how the appointment of a C-in-C of Ground Forces over the Army Group Commanders to direct the forthcoming battles would in any way secure better coordination of effort. On the contrary, the appointment would, in fact, have necessitated a duplication of personnel and communications which could have resulted only in decreased efficiency, while such functions as the allocation of forces and supplies between the Army groups were already performed by my own headquarters.

In this connection, my views as to the place of a so-called "ground" C-in-C in a theater commanded by a single Supreme Commander are roughly as follows: ground forces should ordinarily be commanded according to the possibilities, frequently determined by geography, of close battlefield supervision. Battlefield command extends upward through the Division, Corps, Army, and Army Group Commander. This last commander is the highest ground commander who has a logical function separate from that of the Theater Commander and who, at the same time, can be sufficiently freed from broad strategic, logistic, and civil problems to give his entire attention to the battle. The next higher commander above the Army Group Commander, by whatever name he is called, such as Supreme or Theater Commander, necessarily controls broad strategy and commands air and sea forces, and therefore is the only one in position to bring additional strength to bear to influence the action. When the ground front is such that configuration and extent permit close battle supervision by a single Army Group Commander, then this officer is also known as the Ground Commander of the entire force. But when there is more than one Army Group in a single theater, there cannot logically be an overall "ground commander" separate from the Theater or Supreme Commander. Each Army Group should normally occupy a well defined channel of strategic advance. A special case would be one where a series of armies would be operating, each in a distinctly separate geographical area and without close tactical relationship, one to the other. In this case each Army Commander would be directly subordinate to the Theater Commander, since an Army Group Commander could serve no useful function.

These convictions, together with the outline operational plans which had been worked out, were explained to the Combined Chiefs of Staff when they met at the Malta Conference in the last week of January, on their way to the Tripartite Conference in the Crimea. My Chief of Staff, who attended the Malta Conference as my representative, assured the Combined Chiefs that we would seize the west bank of the Rhine at the crossing sites in the north as soon as this was feasible and without waiting to come up to the river throughout its length. We undertook further to advance across the Rhine in the north with maximum strength and complete determination as soon as the situation in the south allowed us to collect the necessary forces and carry out the assault without incurring unreasonable risks.

OPERATIONS TO REACH
THE RHINE

In conformity with our strategic plans for operations into the heart of Germany, the main effort in the Allied operations west of the Rhine was to be in the northern sector, with a view to seizing the crossings north of the Ruhr. All our other operations were designed primarily to assist this northern operation, to gain secure flanks so as to permit of the heaviest concentration with which to force a crossing in the north,

Operations to reach the Rhine

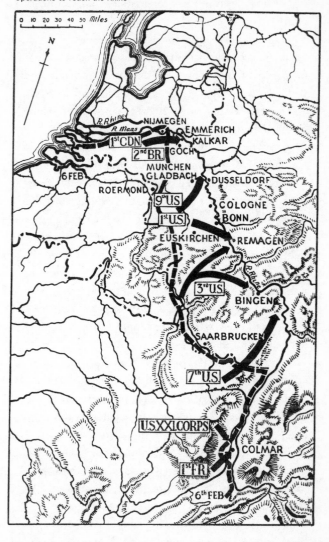

and eventually to provide the bases for our secondary effort.

Operations west of the Rhine were to be developed in three distinct phases. Phase I was to consist primarily of the operations known as Veritable and Grenade, by which respectively the Canadian Army and the US Ninth Army were to advance to the Rhine below Düsseldorf. In addition, the US First Army was to seize the line of the Erft west and northwest of Cologne, thus ensuring the security of our communications between Aachen and München-Gladbach. As soon as these operations began, the existing offensive in the Ardennes was to give place to a policy of aggressive defense designed to contain the German divisions fighting there and to widen the breaches made in the Siegfried Line. South of the Moselle our forces were to remain on the defensive, such local operations as were necessary to contain the German forces on their front being conducted with the maximum economy both of personnel and of ammunition.

During Phase II, while the Rhine-crossing operations were prepared and instituted in the north, the enemy was to be driven back to the river north of its confluence with the Moselle in order that the main bridgehead's lines of communication should be absolutely secure. On completion of these operations our southern forces were to initiate an offensive to capture the Saar Basin and begin their advance to the Rhine in that sector.

Finally, in Phase III, while the northern bridgehead was consolidated and expanded and the Central

Group of Armies remained on the defensive north of the Moselle, the remaining forces in the south were to complete their operations to reach the Rhine so that the Allies would hold the entire left bank.

During the latter half of January and the beginning of February the Central Group of Armies continued to fight hard in the Ardennes sector to take advantage of the check we had imposed upon the enemy there. General Bradley was instructed to inflict the maximum losses upon the Germans, to seize any opportunity of breaching the Siegfried Line and, if successful, to advance northeast on the axis Prüm–Euskirchen. The attack was to be pressed with all vigor as long as there was any reasonable chance of securing a decisive success, but, as an alternative, we had to be ready to pass quickly to the defensive in the Ardennes and to launch the new attacks in the northern sector.

The latter offensive, comprising operations Veritable and Grenade, was to be under the control of 21 Army Group. The US Ninth Army was to remain under the command of Field Marshal Montgomery for this purpose and was to be built up to a strength of four corps, totalling twelve divisions, the rate of build-up being determined by the progress of operations in the Ardennes. In operation Veritable, the target date for which was to be not later than 8 February, the Canadian First Army was to conduct a strong offensive from the Nijmegen area southeast between the Rhine and the Maas, carrying the thrust as far as the general line Xanten–Geldern, clearing the whole area and establishing a firm flank along the

Rhine. The attack was to be made on a two-corps front, British 30 Corps on the right and Canadian 2 Corps on the left, while British 1 Corps was also to be under command of the Canadian Army. In all, seven infantry and four armored divisions, with four infantry and five armored brigades, were to be employed. If, as was hoped, dry ground conditions prevailed, the basis of the operation was to be speed and violence, the armored columns passing through the enemy lines and disrupting his rear areas. As events turned out the state of the country was the very reverse of what had been desired.

In order that operation Grenade might be launched, 12th Army Group was to extend its left wing northward as far as Jülich, and the Ninth Army would then hold a front on the Roer River from Jülich to Roermond. From the right portion of this front it was to launch a strong attack toward the Rhine, with its right flank on the line Jülich–Neuss. The offensive was to be carried up to the Rhine between Düsseldorf and Mors. 12th Army Group was initially to protect the Ninth Army's right flank. It was hoped to commence Grenade not later than 10 February.

Operation Veritable was duly launched on the target date of 8 February, but the weather conditions could hardly have been more unfavorable. January had been exceptionally severe, with snow lying on the ground through the month, and when the thaw set in at the beginning of February, the ground became extremely soft and water-logged, while floods spread far and wide in the area over which our advance had been planned to take place. The difficulties thus imposed were immense, and the men had sometimes to fight waist-deep in water. The privations which they underwent were appalling, but their spirit was indomitable, and they overcame their personal hardships with great gallantry to inflict a major defeat upon the enemy in some of the fiercest fighting of the whole war.

Under such conditions it was inevitable that our hopes for a rapid breakthrough should be disappointed, and the fighting soon developed into a bitter slugging match in which the enemy had to be forced back yard by yard. When the attack was first launched the enemy's reaction was slow, but our own difficulties gave him a chance to consolidate his defenses. The Germans' trouble lay, as usual, in their lack of mobility, for the stocks of gasoline which they had laboriously accumulated for the Ardennes offensive were now exhausted and the incessant Allied air attacks upon the fuel-producing plants, the roads, and the railways caused the situation daily to deteriorate still further.

Apart from the German army's logistical difficulties, moreover, it was considerably weakened in numerical strength on the Western Front by the date when Veritable was launched, as compared with that army's state at the beginning of January. During the closing stages of the Ardennes battle, when the failure of the offensive was seen to be inevitable, the Sixth Panzer Army had been withdrawn from the line to commence a weary and unhappy trek across Germany to the Eastern Front. With it went the remnants of some seven panzer and panzer grenadier divisions, two panzer brigades, and three infantry divisions, a force which included considerably over half the armor which had confronted us when von Rundstedt launched his attack in mid-December. As against these departures and some 150,000 serious battle casualties, the reinforcements sent to the Western Front were insignificant in both quality and quantity. Now that the Allies were once more on the general offensive, all hope of any renewed major offensive by the enemy disappeared, and it soon became merely a question of how long von Rundstedt's skill and the stubborn spirit of his depleted forces could maintain a purely defensive battle west of the Rhine. Again the desperate commitment of formations piecemeal to the fighting, which we had first witnessed in Normandy, was repeated. The enemy's chief assets for the moment lay in the weather and the terrain, but these could never compensate for the seasoned fighting forces which he had lost.

During the first days of Veritable good progress was made through the forest called Reichswald and to the outskirts of Kleve, but fierce resistance was then encountered. The opposition on the southern edge of the forest was particularly violent. Nevertheless, Kleve fell by 12 February and on the 13th the forest was cleared. On the following day the Rhine was reached opposite Emmerich, and on the 16th the

Kalkar–Goch road was crossed, although German forces of the First Parachute Army continued to resist strongly in the Goch sector. The town itself fell on 21 February, two days before operation Grenade was launched.

Despite the comparative slowness of our progress, Veritable achieved its strategic objectives. We gained a footing on the west bank of the Rhine in the area where our major crossing operations were subsequently to be launched, and, equally important, heavy losses were inflicted on the Germans west of the river. Moreover, the offensive steadily drew in the enemy's slender reserves and thus cleared the way for very rapid progress by the Ninth Army when operation Grenade was initiated on 23 February.

Grenade had of necessity been repeatedly postponed on account of the ground conditions. The Ninth Army was ready to strike on the target date appointed, 10 February, but the state of the terrain enforced delay until the floods should subside. Apart from the effects of the thaw, aggravated by the heavy rains which followed the melting of the snow, the enemy was in a position to flood the area further by reason of his control of the Roer dams. The First Army was instructed to concentrate on the capture of these prior to the launching of Grenade, and in heavy fighting its forces pushed hard toward their objectives through extremely difficult country of broken hills covered with forests. The first of the seven dams was reached on 4 February and the last and most important one—the Schwammenauel Dam—on 10

February. The controls on some of the dams had been hit by our air bombing in December, but the damage had been partially repaired, and before the enemy was compelled to abandon the Schwammenauel Dam, he opened the sluices. The water poured down the valley, causing the level of the Roer to rise about four feet, and it was not until 23 February that the flood subsided sufficiently to permit the launching of Grenade across the river.

The attack was begun, in clear moonlight, by VII Corps of the First Army, over the Roer south of Düren at 0330 hours. An hour later, XIX and XIII Corps of the Ninth Army commenced their crossing of the river in the Jülich sector. The attacks were preceded by 45 minutes' intensive artillery bombardment which effectively reduced enemy interference with our initial assault, but considerable difficulties were experienced from the mines sown in the river and from the swiftness of the current which rendered the passage of the assault boats extremely hazardous. However, bridgeheads were speedily gained and consolidated. Once across the river, our forces met their chief opposition from the German artillery, which also bombarded the bridging sites, while the enemy infantry generally fell back after rallying for only one real counter-attack. The enemy also made a considerable air bombing and strafing effort against the bridges, but they were unable to hold the advance.

Our offensive rapidly gathered momentum. VII Corps cleared Düren by 25 February, Jülich had fallen the day before, and the enemy recoiled north and northeast of Linnich as the Ninth Army armor passed through the infantry to thrust forward its spearheads. While the First Army forces pushed towards Cologne, those of the Ninth Army were directed towards München-Gladbach and Grevenbroich. The speed of the advance increased daily, and whole units of the German Fifteenth Army surrendered as their losses in both men and ground began to tell. By 1 March the industrial center of München-Gladbach had been cleared, Grevenbroich had fallen, Neuss was entered, Venlo reached, and Roermond found abandoned by the enemy. With General Simpson, the Ninth Army Commander, I visited München-Gladbach to catch a glimpse of the fighting north and east of that city. The troops definitely sensed ultimate victory and were irresistible.

Meanwhile, the First Parachute Army had been fighting stubbornly to hold the continued pressure by the Canadian Army between the Rhine and the Maas farther north, but the advance of the Ninth Army now threatened its rear and its withdrawal became inevitable. Although an armored division fought hard to retain the wooded area south of Marienbaum and keep us back from the Rhine, on 4 March the two Allied armies made contact in the Geldern area and the success of the combined Veritable–Grenade operations was assured. By 5 March there were no enemy left west of the Rhine between Neuss and Homberg, but the Parachute Army struggled bitterly to retain its last bridgehead across the river in the Wesel–Xanten area. It was not until 10 March that this bridgehead finally collapsed, the enemy blowing the bridges behind him as his last forces withdrew to the east bank. On the following day the task of mopping up the whole area on the west bank was completed. The prisoners brought our total captured since D Day to over 1,000,000.

While the Ninth Army was pushing to the Rhine in its sector, the First Army was exploiting its successful crossing of the Roer and thrusting towards Cologne. This operation, however, may more correctly be considered as part of those which comprised Phase II of the whole campaign west of the Rhine. It was intended that the First Army should close in upon the river from the northwest and the Third Army from the southwest, eliminating the enemy north of the Moselle. While these operations, known under the general name of Lumberjack, were being executed, 6th Army Group, south of the Moselle, would remain basically on the defensive, while in the north 21 Army Group would complete its preparations for the forthcoming major assault across the Rhine north of the Ruhr.

The plan of operation Lumberjack was for the First Army to seize the high ground east of the Erft River northwest of Cologne and to close to the Rhine south of Düsseldorf. Farther south, the road center of Euskirchen was to be captured, bridgeheads established over the Erft in that sector, and forces concentrated for an advance to the southeast. Cologne was then to be invested from the northwest, and, at the appropriate moment, a strong attack on a narrow front was to be driven southeast from Euskirchen to converge with the Third Army advance, and the Rhine was to be reached in the army zone. The Third Army was to seize bridgeheads over the Kyll River, on which its forces at present stood, and then, when so ordered, to drive hard eastward to seize the Mayen–Coblenz area and complete the clearance of the enemy from the west bank of the Rhine between the Moselle and the Ahr. If the enemy defenses proved weak, the Third Army was also, in a subsequent stage, to obtain a bridgehead over the Moselle to the southeast, to facilitate the operations which were to be initiated in that sector.

We had good reason to hope for sweeping success in these operations, for the enemy's forces, reduced as they were both by their contributions to the Eastern Front and by the heavy casualties inflicted on them by our armies, had, in the Veritable–Grenade campaign, shown themselves inadequate to contain simultaneous Allied attacks on a broad front. The same policy of converging major thrusts which had proved successful in 21 Army Group sector was now about to be repeated by 12th Army Group. Apart from the damaging losses which the enemy had incurred, the fighting spirit of his armies, taken as a whole, had undergone a decline, and at certain points his defensive system was manifestly disorganized. Few—if any—trained reserves outside the west were believed to be available, and in the hard fighting which had taken place since the New Year virtually all the reserves in the west had been committed to the defensive battle. Under the circumstances, it seemed to me that the enemy's only course would be to do as he had done in the north and make as orderly a retreat as possible to the east of the Rhine, though it appeared likely that he would try to hold small bridgeheads on the west bank. Our plans were designed to prevent a safe withdrawal over the river.

Meanwhile, the increased hammering of the fuel installations in Germany, which followed the improvement in weather conditions after January, had made the enemy's situation more grave than ever in this respect. The February output fell to a total only 14% of normal, representing barely half the minimum requirements to maintain full-scale military effort. The effects of this and of the transportation crisis in Germany were seen not only on our own front but also on that facing the Russians, where, despite the transfer of the Sixth Panzer Army, the enemy had shown himself incapable of mounting an effective counter-attack to stem the growing tide of Soviet successes.

Operation Lumberjack fulfilled expectations. In the First Army drive, with VII Corps, toward Cologne, heavy opposition was for a time encountered east of the Erft Canal, but the three armored formations brought up to block our advance were dispersed by our air attacks, carried out in strength. The Erft bridgeheads were expanded, and on 5 March the advance elements of VII Corps were entering Cologne. By the afternoon of the 7th the city was entirely in our hands, the enemy resistance having collapsed once the Allied forces had reached the outskirts. The untrained Volkssturm left as a forlorn hope when the regular forces withdrew over the Rhine, blowing the bridges behind them, were capable of little fight. On the same day that Cologne fell, the remainder of the enemy evacuated the west bank north to Düsseldorf. This success had a profound effect on our subsequent operations, as the divisions which would have been used to invest Cologne became available to assist in exploiting the great opportunity we were shortly to be offered.

Farther south, the progress of the First Army was even more spectacular. III Corps attacked southeast in accordance with the operational plan, rolled up the disorganized enemy confronting it and closed to the Rhine at Remagen on 7 March. It was here on that day that occurred one of those rare and fleeting opportunities which occasionally present themselves in war, and which, if grasped, have incalculable effects in determining future success. In his confusion before the rapidity of the Allied thrust, the enemy failed to complete the destruction of the Ludendorff railroad bridge across the Rhine. Before he could rectify his mistake, a small spearhead of 9th Armored Division with the greatest determination and gallantry had seized the bridge—the only one to be left intact by the Germans throughout the entire length of the river.

The Remagen bridge was not in a sector from which it had been intended to launch a major thrust eastward, but I at once determined, at the expense of modifying details of the plan of campaign, to seize the golden opportunity offered to us. It was obvious that possession of a foothold over the Rhine here would constitute the greatest possible threat as a supporting effort for the main attack north of the Ruhr. In order, therefore, to exploit the situation and establish an adequate bridgehead, consolidated in readiness for an offensive therefrom as soon as the progress of our operations south of the Moselle permitted, I ordered General Bradley, when he telephoned me to report the occurrence, to put not less than five divisions on to the far bank.

Partially anticipating this decision, General Bradley had begun the exploitation of the bridgehead immediately the bridge fell into his hands. A combat command was rapidly passed across, and by 9 March we held a lodgement area some three miles deep. It was several days before the enemy recovered sufficiently from his surprise and overcame his transport difficulties to send reinforcements to the threatened sector, and by the time they arrived the bridgehead had been enlarged and strengthened to a degree which rendered its elimination impossible. Enemy armored forces were again, as in Normandy, committed to battle piecemeal as they arrived on the scene, and no concerted major attack was mounted on a scale sufficient to effect a serious penetration. Such efforts as the enemy did make were unable to check the further expansion of the bridgehead; and as its area grew, the north–south autobahn east of the river, so vital to the enemy, was severed. By 24 March, when our main attacks eastward from the Rhine began in the north, the area held by the First Army at Remagen was 25 miles long and 10 miles deep, and within it three corps were poised ready to strike.

In the meantime the enemy had made desperate efforts to destroy the bridge while the security lodgement area was still dependent upon it. Long-range artillery was brought to bear on it, and the German Air Force put up the strongest effort of which it was capable in attempts to cut the structure by bombs, rocket projectiles, and cannon fire. All these efforts proved equally unsuccessful. The air battles over Remagen provided the Luftwaffe with its greatest test, and it failed. The umbrella established over the vital area by the US Ninth Air Force effectively disrupted the attacks, and the enemy's losses, both to our fighter planes and to the heavy concentration of anti-aircraft guns established on the river banks, were severe.

The enemy onslaught nevertheless made the area extremely uncomfortable, especially for the Engineers who carried out, with conspicuous gallantry and determination, the dangerous work of repairing damage and of strengthening the bridge to bear the enormous strains to which it was subjected and which it had never been intended to undergo. These strains eventually proved too much for the damaged structure, and on 17 March the center span (which had been damaged in the Germans' unsuccessful last-minute attempts at demolition on the 7th) collapsed into the river. Although a disappointment, this had no serious effect upon our operations, for by this time a number of supplementary floating bridges had been constructed, and the build-up of the forces on the east bank continued without interruption.

While III Corps of the First Army was establishing the bridgehead at Remagen, V Corps, on its right flank, struck to the south to make contact with the advancing spearheads of the Third Army. The German Fifth Panzer Army, disorganized, offered little resistance, and the Allied thrust made rapid progress. Bad Godesberg and Bonn fell on 9 March, and on the following day the link-up along the Rhine with the Third Army forces which had closed to the river in the Andernach area was accomplished. Considerable elements of the Fifth Panzer Army were cut off to the west by these converging drives; they fought courageously to the last, but it was the courage of despair, and they made no organized attempt to force a way out of the trap.

During February, the Third Army had been engaged in making the necessary preparations for its subsequent push to the Rhine. XX Corps had eliminated enemy resistance in the Saar–Moselle triangle by 23 February, and bridgeheads had been established over the Saar at Ockfen and Serrig in the teeth of violent opposition. The Siegfried defenses were penetrated, and Trier fell on 2 March. Farther north, the German Seventh Army had been forced back successively over the Our and Prüm Rivers, despite extensive minefields and obstacles, and on 4 March the first bridgeheads were gained across the Kyll.

The Third Army advance to the Rhine now began. VIII Corps, spearheaded by 11th Armored Division, broke through north of Kyllburg on 7 March. Advancing northeast with increasing rapidity, it reached the Rhine at Andernach on the 9th and linked up with the First Army, as already described, on the following day. To the south of VIII Corps, on 5 March, 4th Armoured Division of XII Corps, with great boldness, charged along the north bank of the Moselle, parallel to VIII Corps, toward its confluence with the Rhine. This objective was attained on 10 March, large quantities of enemy equipment being captured in the process. By the next day, the left bank of the Rhine from Coblenz to Andernach had been cleared, and the enemy had virtually been eliminated along its length north of the Moselle, thus accomplishing Phase II of the operations to close the river in its entirety through German territory.

The stage was now set for the initiation of the joint offensive operations by the Third and Seventh Armies south of the Moselle which had been anticipated as Phase III of the campaign west of the Rhine. In the 6th Army Group sector, operations during January and February had, in accordance with our overall plan, been mainly of a defensive nature. Such local operations as had been conducted were designed to eliminate the dangerous situation created in the south, as I have earlier described, following the enemy attacks in support of his Ardennes offensive and our weakening of 6th Army Group when divisions had to be moved northward to meet the major threat.

Chief among the tasks which had to be accomplished was the destruction of the Colmar pocket. An attack was launched by the French I Corps against the southern edge of the pocket on 20 January, but this at first made little progress, partly because of bad weather. North of the pocket the French II Corps fared similarly. However, we had assembled and turned over to the French First Army the US XXI Corps, composed of the 3rd, 28th, and 75th Infantry Divisions, and the 12th Armored Division, under Maj. Gen. Frank W. Milburn, to carry the brunt of the battle by an attack between the two French corps. Its efforts quickly became effective. Lack of reinforcements caused the enemy resistance to crumble at the end of the month and at the same time the weather improved. Before our three-corps attack the German disintegration developed rapidly: Colmar itself fell on 3 February, and by the 6th the enemy was mainly east of the Rhine–Rhône canal. The evacuation of the disorganized remnants across the Rhine was then in progress, and with the collapse of opposition at Neuf Brisach on 9 February all organized resistance west of the Rhine in that zone ceased. In the course of the operation the enemy suffered over 22,000 casualties and considerable losses of equipment: the German Nineteenth Army was virtually destroyed.

After the elimination of the Colmar pocket, interest in the 6th Army Group area centered in the Seventh Army zone, in front of the Siegfried defenses. The French Army maintained the defensive along the Rhine, and its left wing assumed responsibility for the front as far north as Bischweiler. During the latter half of February and early March the chief activity on the Seventh Army front was in the Saarbrücken-Forbach area, where bitter fighting took place and restricted Allied advances were made.

Following the Third Army successes north of the Moselle, the time had arrived for launching operation Undertone, the major offensive south of the Moselle, with the objectives of destroying the enemy west of the Rhine and closing on that river from Coblenz southward. By this means crossing-sites for the establishment of bridgeheads would be obtained in the Mainz–Mannheim sector and more enemy forces would be drawn away from the area where our main effort was shortly to be made in the north. To this end, the Seventh Army was to assume control of elements of the French forces known as the Groupement Montsabert and then to attack in the general direction Homberg–Kaiserslautern–Worms. It was to breach the Siegfried Line, destroy the enemy in its zone, close on the Rhine and seize a bridgehead. Meanwhile the French Army was to protect the right flank of the Seventh Army and to conduct an aggressive defense along the Rhine. In cooperation with the Seventh Army effort, General Bradley was instructed to launch a thrust by the Third Army forces southeast across the lower reaches of the Moselle, with the object of turning the German line and thrusting deep into the rear areas of the forces facing the Seventh Army. He was also to attack the nose of the Saar salient.

On 15 March the offensive began. While XX Corps of the Third Army struck from the Allied bridgeheads over the Saar and Moselle into the forested hills of the Hunsruck from the west, VI and XV Corps of the Seventh Army, with the French elements under command, attacked north between Haguenau and Saarbrucken. The former attack met with stiff opposition from the enemy's prepared positions, but the southern thrust took the German First Army by surprise and, following the capture of Haguenau on the first day, a number of deep penetrations were made. Zweibrucken and Saarbrucken were occupied by 20 March and resistance in the western portion of the front became disorganized; but the defenders in the Siegfried Line farther to the east stood firm against the Allied attacks.

It was at this point that the intervention of the Third Army across the lower Moselle became devastatingly effective. XII Corps had attacked across the river on 14 March, and the bridgehead gain was rapidly expanded. The Germans were, in fact, completely misled by the Allied tactics. Following the Third Army's swift arrival on the Rhine north of the Moselle they had expected its forces to erupt through the Remagen bridgehead. Instead, when the Third Army turned southeast, the enemy was taken off balance, being utterly unprepared for such a development. No real opposition to the XII Corps drive was offered, and the unready enemy forces were brushed aside as the Allies swept up the Rhine. At the same time, Coblenz was occupied, and by 19 March the river bank was cleared from there as far as the Bingen bend. On the 22nd all resistance ceased in Mainz and on the following day Speyer was reached.

The enemy was still holding out in the Siegfried positions in the Rhine valley west of Karlsruhe, but, with the escape routes across the river cut by the Third Army advances in their rear, his situation was now hopeless. General Patton's aggressive tactics culminated in a surprise night crossing of the Rhine on 22 March. He sent over the US 5th Division without formal preparations of any kind and with negligible losses. Thus, before our main "power" crossing of the Rhine was attempted by 21 Army Group, we were already in possession of two sizeable bridgeheads in the south. Farther west the German units were in a state of chaos and their positions were rapidly overrun and enveloped. By 25 March an end came to all organized resistance west of the Rhine, and Phase III of the operations to close the river was over, with the added accomplishment of two Rhine crossings completed as Phase III closed; while we were rounding up the broken remnants of the enemy the First Army surrounded to the west, we had launched our carefully prepared main effort in the north in our invasion of the German hinterland over the last great barrier remaining to its defenders.

All these operations west of the Rhine had, like those in France, been greatly assisted by the vast weight of Allied air power which we had been able to bring to bear in their support. While the long-range strategic effort was maintained against the fuel and industrial targets in the heart of Germany, a steady offensive was kept up against the enemy lines of communication westward across the Rhine. In addition, the heavy bombers were also employed in direct support of the ground tactical operations whenever the weather conditions permitted. They were further, during this period, engaged in the extensive and remarkable Ruhr interdiction program, which will be mentioned later.

The weather, although persistently bad, could not halt the operations of the tactical air forces, whose performance was never more magnificent than during this time. The ground advances were supported resolutely by these tactical forces; their operations at once warded off the German Air Force attempts at interference and at the same time greatly contributed to the disorganization of the German armies opposing us, strafing and bombing the enemy positions and causing havoc in his supply system. Particularly noteworthy was the work of the First Tactical Air Force in support of the Saar offensive, when 8,320 sorties were flown in a single week, with claims of 2,400 motor vehicles, 85 armored vehicles, 146 locomotives and 1,741 railroad cars. In addition, over 2,000 motor vehicles and 100 armored vehicles were damaged and over 300 rail cuts made. These great efforts played an important part in assuring the success of the ground campaign in the southern sector.

By this time the broad pattern of air-ground operations had become almost a fixed one—subject to adjustment of details to terrain, weather, hostile communications, and so on. Faith in the ability of the Air Force to intervene effectively in the ground battle was the vital feature of the original invasion plan; the general scheme thus used for the isolation of the battlefield, for direct action against selected targets, for air cover and for other important missions, including supply, had by now been so perfected that teamwork was easy and the results obtained were regularly decisive in the area of attack.

In connection with the Allied air activities during the early months of 1945, the operation known as Clarion, carried out on 22 February, is worthy of special mention. Nearly 9,000 aircraft, from bases in England, France, Holland, Belgium, and Italy, took part in this gigantic onslaught, which involved targets covering an area of a quarter of a million square miles, extending from Emden to Berlin, Dresden, Vienna, and Mulhouse. The aim was to attack incidental communications facilities, such as railroad signal points and grade crossings, canal locks, and junctions, in order to aggravate the growing difficulties experienced in keeping open the German life-lines. It had been found by experience that such local attacks, complementary to large ones, had far-reaching effects in slowing down enemy movement, and it was hoped that Clarion would spread the paralysis throughout Germany. It was a bold scheme, demanding great skill and daring on the part of all involved. Confounded by the widespread nature of the blow, the enemy's attempts at defense were completely ineffective.

The whole of the Allied campaign west of the Rhine had gone according to plan to an extraordinary degree, and my fullest hopes were realized. Two features of the operations upon which I had not originally calculated were the rapid capture of the Cologne area and the seizure of the Remagen bridge. Both these events turned wholly to our profit, for, thanks to the flexibility of our plans, we were able to take full advantage of the opportunity which the prizes offered without sacrifice of our planned objectives. In each of the three phases of the campaign, two converging armies had thrust to the Rhine and cut off and destroyed the German forces which had been disposed to bar their way. We had attained along the whole length of the Rhine in German territory the economically defensible front upon which I had insisted as an essential prerequisite to the launching of the concentrated thrusts over the river which were to strike at the heart of Germany, and in the process we had eliminated her own future defensive abilities. The armies which she now so sorely needed to man the last great natural barrier left to her had been broken to pieces in fruitless attempts to halt our slashing blows among the floods of the lower Rhineland, in the Eifel, and amid the hills and forests of the Saar Palatinate.

Field Marshal Montgomery's attack, in the extreme north, got off on 8 February, exactly as planned. The Ninth Army was to join this attack on 10 February, and was ready to do so. Field Marshal Montgomery and I had already agreed that while the

ideal situation would be for the Second Army and the
US Ninth Army to attack almost simultaneously, yet
realizing that flood conditions on the Roer River
might hold up the Ninth Army indefinitely, we were
fully prepared to accept a two-weeks' delay in the
Ninth Army attack in the confidence that the shifting
of German reserves to the north would facilitate victory in that sector. Events fully justified this estimate.
The Ninth Army's attack across the Roer River on
the 23rd rapidly converged with the Canadian Army
and we held the Rhine in the Wesel region.

In the 12th Army Group General Bradley's plan
for supporting the Ninth Army and then for the
destruction of the German forces north of the
Moselle by swift converging blows materialized in
almost exact accordance with his diagrammatic plans.
Moreover, his constant concern was to see that at the
culmination of each offensive his forces were so situated as to undertake the next succeeding step without
delay for regrouping, and from such direction as to
surprise and confuse the enemy. He went into the
attack with instructions for each unit to look for and
to seize any opportunity to cross the Rhine.

Finally, the 6th Army Group, which had been
confined heretofore largely to a holding, protecting,
and supporting role, was suddenly unleashed with the
Seventh Army brought up to a strength of 15 US
divisions. We knew that the enemy was at that time
discounting the strength of the Seventh Army and
that he felt relatively safe lying in the Siegfried Line
facing General Patch's forces. No defeat the Germans

suffered in the war, except possibly Tunisia, was more devastating in the completeness of the destruction inflicted upon his forces than that which he suffered in the Saar Basin. Yet this attack was conducted by portions of two Army Groups and, though a boundary between such large forces is ordinarily considered one of the weakest tactical spots in a major front, no real difficulty was encountered in coordination and unification of the battle. Although I personally kept in touch with details and was in position to make tactical decisions when such proved necessary, the real reason for this lack of confusion and for the incisiveness of the whole operation is to be found in the identity of tactical training, organization, and mutual confidence among all the divisions and commanders participating in the battle. The whole operation was characterized by boldness, speed, and determination, and the victory was so complete that when General Patton thrust a division across the Rhine on the night of 22/23 March, he was able to do so with almost no reaction from the enemy.

I unhesitatingly class General Bradley's tactical operations during February and March, which witnessed the completion of the destruction of the German forces west of the Rhine, as the equal in brilliance of any that American forces have ever conducted. The cooperation during the latter part of this period between General Bradley's 12th Army Group and General Devers' 6th Army Group was a superb example of grand tactical cooperation on the battlefield.

CROSSING THE RHINE

When the time came for launching the main assault across the Rhine, the Allied armies under my command had been built up to a total strength on the Continent of nearly four million men. The difficult manpower situation with which we had been confronted during the Ardennes battle had been remedied and we were once more at full strength, with every unit demonstrating an unbelievably high morale and battle effectiveness.

Crossing the Rhine

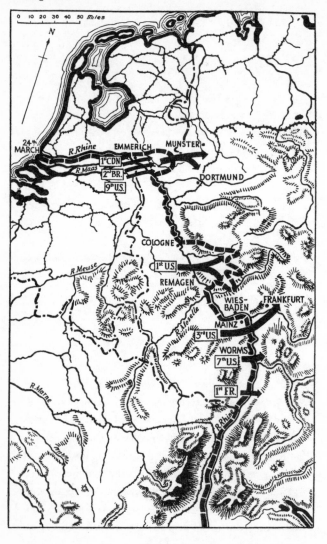

In the 6th Army Group sector the French divisions had been reformed and strengthened, while the passing of winter facilitated the re-employment of the colonial troops for whom active operations had been impracticable during the very severe weather. To the American armies had been added fresh divisions from the United States; and to 21st Army Group had come British and Canadian reinforcements from the Mediterranean Theater. The Combined Chiefs of Staff decided, at their Malta conference at the end of January, that the situation on the Italian Front was such as to permit the transfer of up to five divisions from the Eighth Army to the Western Front. The move of three divisions was to commence forthwith, and two more were to follow as soon as the situation in Greece allowed. In addition, a corresponding proportion of the Twelfth Air Force was to be transferred with the ground forces. The complicated process of moving the units to France and northward across the lines of communication of the Southern and Central Groups of Armies (called Operation Goldflake) was carried out efficiently and smoothly, and the security precautions taken were completely successful in concealing from the Germans what was afoot. By the time the 21st Army Group offensive across the Rhine came to be launched, these latest units to arrive were ready to play their part in it.

The enemy now found himself in an unenviable position. He had, as we had hoped, and attempted to compel, elected to stand and fight west of the Rhine, and the results had been disastrous to him. Beaten in the open field and behind his frontier fortifications, he was now in no condition to hold fast in the defensive line to which he had been compelled to retreat. His powers of resistance had been reduced by increasing shortages of weapons, ammunition and oil which resulted from our attacks against his war economy. His losses in battle had been crippling, and these inevitably caused a deterioration in the morale of all but his élite units. The SS and the armored divisions were for the most part made up of fanatical Nazis whose faith in the cause they served could be shaken by little less than annihilation; yet the time was soon to come when even their commanders, realizing the fruitlessness of further struggle, would surrender their units rather than see their men slaughtered to no purpose. In the ordinary infantry divisions, spirits were again as low as when they had fled eastward from France to gain the shelter of the Siegfried Line in the preceding autumn. Moreover, as his losses grew, the enemy was forced more and more to entrust his defense to the ragged army of the local Volkssturm who might, in some cases, fight courageously enough in the protection of their homes, but as field units were at times as much a liability as an asset.

Such were the troops now ranged along the Rhine to bar our crossing. The front was too long for them, shrunken as their numbers were since January. While the Allies had gained the economically defensible line behind which to concentrate in safety for the overwhelming thrusts about to be launched in the selected sectors, the enemy, lacking the reconnaissance to obtain definite information as to our intentions, could only spread his forces as far as they would go and wait for the blow to fall.

Under these conditions the success of our operations appeared certain, a conviction which I felt was undoubtedly shared by the German General Staff. Continuance of the struggle was now merely evidence of Hitler's fanaticism. The enemy's northern sector, where our chief weight was to be brought to bear, had been weakened by his movement of forces southward to meet the threat which had already developed from the Remagen bridgehead. Even had the situation there been such as to allow the enemy to disengage and return his forces to the north (which was far from being the case), his lack of mobility was too greatly reduced to enable them to arrive in time to meet us while our foothold on the east bank north of the Ruhr was still precarious.

The plan of campaign for crossing the Rhine and establishing a strong force on the far bank was, thanks to the success of the operations west of the river, basically the same as that envisaged in our long-term planning in January, and even before D Day. Its fundamental features were the launching of a main attack to the north of the Ruhr, supported by a strong secondary thrust from bridgeheads in the Frankfurt area, directed initially on Kassel to complete the envelopment of the Ruhr. Subsequently, offensives would strike out from the bridgeheads to any remaining organized forces and complete their destruction.

In the execution of this plan, the seizure of the Remagen bridgehead was a factor of great significance. Apart from the effect its existence had already produced upon the German defenses, it afforded us a base from which we might the more rapidly accomplish the aim of encircling the Ruhr. Moreover, its existence forced the Germans to man an east–west line along the Sieg River, because of the immediate threat imposed upon the industries of the Ruhr. The forces now gathered within the bridgehead could maintain a pressure to the north, squeezing the Ruhr frontally while enveloping it on the eastern flank, and at the same time strike southeast to Frankfurt. In the latter area the crossing of our forces over the Mainz sector of the river would thus be assisted, and our general build-up for the southern attack would be accomplished rapidly. Consequently we were able to launch a southern supporting offensive in strength on a much earlier date than we had originally expected to be feasible; and this, in turn, had an important effect in determining the future Allied strategy within the interior of Germany.

The plan of Operation Plunder, the great assault across the Rhine north of the Ruhr which was to constitute our main effort, involved the use of three Allied armies. Under the command of Field Marshal Montgomery, the US Ninth Army on the right and the British Second Army on the left were to attack over the river between Rheinberg and Rees. They were to capture the communications center of Wesel and then to expand their initial lodgement area on the east bank southward to a distance sufficient to secure the roads through Wesel from enemy ground action, northward to enable the river to be bridged at Emmerich, and eastward and northeastward to secure a firm bridgehead of adequate size from which further offensive operations could be developed. The Ninth Army's assault was to be launched south of Wesel, with its main bridging area at Rheinberg, and its principal initial task was to be the protection of the Army Group right flank. The Second Army was to assault north of Wesel and to concentrate first on the capture of that town in order that the Ninth Army might commence bridging there. The Second Army was also to bridge the river at Xanten and Rees.

To assist the advance of the Second Army, the First Allied Airborne Army was to drop XVIII Airborne Corps (comprising the US 17th and British 6th Airborne Divisions) north and northwest of Wesel to seize the key terrain in that area. This airborne operation (known as Varsity) was, unlike those previously conducted by the Allies, timed to follow the commencement of the ground assault, it being hoped thereby to achieve an additional element of surprise.

The Canadian Army, on the left flank, was to take no active part in the assault, but was to hold firmly the line of the Rhine and Maas from Emmerich westward to the sea, to ensure the absolute security of the existing bridgehead over the Rhine at Nijmegen, and to guard the Scheldt estuary, the port of Antwerp being now practically the only place where effective enemy interference behind our lines could be achieved. Following the successful establishment of the Second Army bridgehead, the Canadian 2nd Corps was to be passed over the Rhine at Rees by Second Army and to operate to secure Emmerich, where the Canadian Army would then be responsible for the construction of another bridge.

It will be seen from the nature of these operations that the cutting of communications from the Ruhr was a matter of the first importance in facilitating the establishment of a bridgehead on the east bank of the Rhine north of the industrial area. I shall deal in due course with the progress of the land forces in accomplishing its encirclement and reduction, but it must here be noted that already, when the attack was launched over the river in the north, the Allied air forces had achieved the practical denial to the enemy of the Ruhr resources and at the same time had isolated the battle area from the rest of Germany.

The plan of the air forces' Ruhr isolation program was that, prior to the establishment of the 21st Army Group bridgehead, the northwestern area of Germany should be cut off from the central and southern regions by the drawing of a line of interdiction running in a rough curve southward from Bremen to the Rhine at Coblenz. In principle, it was a repetition of the air plan for the original invasion. Along this line were 18 vital railroad bridges and viaducts, the destruction of which would, it was estimated, cut every main rail route from the Ruhr to the remainder of the country. Three of the lines, running through the targets at Bielefeld, Altenbeken, and Armsberg, carried about half of the total traffic between them and were thus of particular importance.

Some of the bridges had earlier received incidental damage, but the main interdiction program began on 21 February. During the next month, 40 major blows were struck by heavy and medium bombers, apart from many fighter-bomber attacks designed to cut the bridge approaches and hamper the Germans' frantic efforts to carry out repairs. In the course of the attacks the RAF used, for the first time, its 22,000-pound monster bombs, with devastating results. The operations proved singularly successful: by 24 March, ten of the bridges had been destroyed, two seriously damaged, and two more were damaged, though possibly passable. The aim in view, that of interrupting the enemy's all-important traffic out of the Ruhr and at the same time preventing the large-scale movement of supplies from central and southern Germany to the armies in the threatened area on the lower Rhine, was fully realized, and the results were immediately evident when our ground forces set foot on the east bank.

The German communications network running west of the interdiction line toward the Rhine was also heavily attacked from the air during the weeks preceding the assault across the river. A very important operation comprised blows delivered by Bomber Command on 11 and 12 March. On the 11th a record was established for the load of bombs dropped on a single target in one raid when 1,079 heavy bombers rained some 5,000 tons on the Essen rail center. The record was surpassed on the 12th when 1,108 heavies dropped 5,487 tons on Dortmund. These communications attacks were also energetically supported by fighters and fighter-bombers of the RAF Second Tactical Air Force and the US XXIX Tactical Air Command. The resulting chaos was such as to prove far beyond the powers of the Reichsbahn repair organization to remedy, despite its immense efforts to keep the lines open.

Mention should be made of the excellent work performed, in preparation for the ground assault, by the Allied photographic reconnaissance aircraft. Now, as throughout the campaign in Europe, their work provided the armies with extremely full and accurate intelligence information. Conversely, the enemy's failure, from D Day onward, was partly due to his own lack, by reason of his air weakness, of the facilities which the Allies enjoyed in this respect.

As 23/24 March approached, the target date for Operation Plunder, the strategic and tactical air force attacks upon the communications in the battle area were intensified. In addition, during the 72 hours preceding the assault, a number of attacks were made upon enemy barracks and camps in the vicinity of the planned bridgehead. Defenses which the Germans were observed to be constructing around the towns and villages, with a view to turning them into strongpoints, were also bombed and strafed. Individual targets of particular importance were allotted to the pilots of rocket-firing Typhoons especially experienced in the technique of pinpoint attacks. Among the buildings destroyed in the course of these operations was one believed to house the headquarters of the German Twenty-fifth Army. Apart from the casualties inflicted in such attacks, it cannot be doubted that they produced a serious morale effect upon the enemy, who, after enduring three days of unremitting hell from the air, was in no condition to meet the frontal assault when it was launched.

Important in the aerial preparation for Operation Plunder were the Allied attacks upon the enemy air force bases in northwest Germany. As earlier stated, the chief threat which the enemy could exercise against our air power lay in his jet aircraft. The Allied production of these machines lagged behind that of our opponents, and in the air it was difficult to counter their attacks. We therefore decided that the best insurance against their possible interference with our Rhine-crossing operations was to employ our heavy bombers to render the enemy's jet airfields unusable. A number of fields possessing the extra-long runways necessary to enable jet planes to take off were located within range of the battle area, and reconnaissance revealed that the Germans were concentrating their machines on them. These fields were accordingly subjected to severe blows from 21 March onward, while the fuel dumps and auxiliary installations were attacked at the same time. The consequence was that the enemy lost a large number of planes on the ground, and the runways were cratered and rendered temporarily unusable. Before repairs could be effected our ground forces were across the Rhine. On 24 March the Allied air forces flew some 8,000 aircraft and 1,300 glider sorties while sighting fewer than 100 enemy planes in the air.

In all these preparatory operations, as on 24 March itself, our air forces were favored with excellent weather conditions, clear skies, and perfect visibility permitting visual bombing and greatly assisting the tactical forces in picking out their targets for pinpoint attacks.

Apart from the airborne landing operations, which I shall consider below, the air force blows reached their peak on 24 March. Prior to the arrival of the transport planes and gliders, the Ninth Air Force and the Second Tactical Air Force planes attacked the enemy flak positions, with the result that interference with the airborne elements from this source was considerably reduced. Also, in immediate cooperation with the armies, medium bombers attacked 18 towns which were either strongpoints or communication centers. Gun and mortar sites and the enemy forward positions generally were relentlessly strafed and bombed, while armed reconnaissance was maintained against the German supply lines. The whole weight of the Eighth Air Force bombers, apart from one division of Liberators used for airborne resupply, was employed in the attacks on the jet airfields.

Two major diversionary air operations were also conducted during the day. One hundred and fifty bombers of the Fifteenth Air Force, with five groups of fighters, flew 1,500 miles from their Italian bases to Berlin and back, while other forces from Italy were raiding airfields in the south. Over Berlin itself fighters of the Eighth Air Force provided cover. This raid successfully fulfilled its object of drawing enemy fighters away from the Rhine battle area. The second diversion was carried out by RAF Bomber Command, which attacked the rail center of Sterkrade as well as oil targets in the Ruhr. In all, during the four days, 21–24 March, American and British air forces, based in Britain, Western Europe and Italy, flew over 42,000 sorties against Germany.

The task of the armies assaulting across the Rhine represented the largest and most difficult amphibious operation undertaken since the landings on the coast of Normandy. The width of the Rhine and the nature of its currents indeed were such that, without the operations already mentioned which were to reduce enemy resistance on the far bank to a minimum, the success of the crossing might well have been a matter of doubt. The variations in the river level also presented unusually difficult problems for, apart from the seasonal fluctuations, there was a danger of artificial floods being created by the enemy's ability to demolish the dams located on the eastern tributaries. A special flood-warning system was instituted to guard against this threat.

It was therefore necessary to treat the assault as an amphibious operation in the fullest sense, involving naval as well as military forces, since the equipment available to the engineer elements of the armies was alone insufficient to cope with the task. Months previously, exhaustive experiments had been carried out on rivers in Britain giving bank and current conditions similar to those of the Rhine in order to determine what ferry craft were most suitable and what loads they could carry. The LCM and LCV(P) craft were chosen for the purpose and these were transported to the Rhine, partly by waterway and partly overland on special trailers built to stand the great strains involved in transit across roads ravaged by war. The immense difficulty of this feat may be judged from the fact that the craft measured as much as 45 feet in length and were 14 feet wide. British and American naval forces were built up to operate the ferry service, and valuable experience was gained when some of the craft were used in the Remagen area early in March. The fact that an LCM could take such loads as a Sherman tank or 60 men, and an LCV(P) a bulldozer or 35 men, may serve to indicate their value in the initial stages of our main assault in the north.

The offensive was heralded, at 2000 hours on 23 March, with a great artillery barrage of an hour's duration, directed against the east bank of the Rhine and extending through the zone where the airborne forces were to be dropped and landed on the next day. At 2100 hours, as soon as the barrage lifted, the British I Commando Brigade commenced the assault on Wesel. This town had been so heavily and accurately bombed by Bomber Command that it was captured with only 36 casualties. During the night the main attacks went in. In the Second Army zone, 15 Division led the 12 Corps assault north of Xanten, and 51 Division crossed in the 30 Corps sector astride Rees. South of the Lippe Canal, 30th and 79th Divisions launched the Ninth Army assault under the command of XVI Corps.

After spending the night on the west bank of the river in the Ninth Army area I met, next day, the Prime Minister of Great Britain, who was accompanied by the Chief of the Imperial General Staff, Field Marshal Brooke. We toured the west bank of the river to witness the ferrying of troops and supplies and to visit troops, all of whom reflected the highest state of enthusiasm and morale. Both the Prime Minister and Field Marshal Brooke, who expressed themselves as extraordinarily delighted with the complete success of our operations of the past 45 days, made a brief visit that afternoon to the east bank of the river.

The initial crossings, thanks to the weight of the preparatory artillery fire and bombing, were generally effected against only slight opposition, and firm footholds were obtained on the far bank of the river. On 24 March, while the ferrying of further troops proceeded steadily, the Allied bridgeheads were expanded and contact was made with the airborne forces flown in during the morning. Wesel was successfully cleared, and in most sectors the enemy's confusion and disorganization were reflected in the uncoordinated resistance offered. Only at Rees did the defenders hold out stubbornly and bring heavy and accurate fire to bear upon the bridging sites.

The airborne landings in the Wesel area, coordinated by the First Allied Airborne Army, commenced just before 1000 hours and continued until 1300 hours. The 6 Airborne Division was flown from bases in East Anglia in 669 planes and 429 gliders of the RAF 38 and 46 Groups and the US IX Troop Carrier Command, while the 17th Airborne Division was brought from the Paris area in 903 planes and 897 gliders of the IX Troop Carrier Command. Fighter escorts on the approach flights were provided by the 213 RAF Fighter Command and by 676 Ninth Air Force planes. Nine hundred aircraft of the British Second Tactical Air Force provided cover over the target area, while 1,253 fighters of the Eighth Air Force established a screen east of the Rhine. As a result of this protection, coupled with the measures taken against enemy airfields, not one transport was molested by hostile aircraft. Some losses were sustained from anti-aircraft fire over the target, but the total of 46 planes destroyed (3.98% of those employed) was remarkably low considering the fact that, to ensure accuracy of dropping and landing, no evasive action was taken. I witnessed as much of this operation as could be seen from observation posts west of the river and was struck by the courage of transport pilots flying relatively slow aircraft steadily along their allotted routes in spite of heavy flak barrages.

The two divisions established contact with each other during the afternoon and with the 15 Division by nightfall. Their positions were rapidly consolidated, and on the 25th, the 6 Airborne Division commenced a swift advance eastward with 15 Division, while the 17th Airborne Division, after linking with the main forces of Ninth Army, followed suit.

Operation Varsity was the most successful airborne operation carried out to date, and its brilliant results reflected the great strides made in this aspect of warfare since the landings on D Day, nine months earlier. Much of this was due to the coordination secured by the units of the First Allied Airborne Army. The glider landings and parachute drops had been carried out with accuracy, while the supplies dropped shortly after the main landings were virtually 100% recovered. The timing of the attack had achieved the element of surprise which had been planned, and the rapidity with which the forces reformed and established their positions after landing also resulted in the casualties being extremely low. As may be seen from the composition of the forces involved, Varsity was an Allied operation in the fullest sense, and the victory won represented yet another triumph in the annals of Anglo-American cooperation in the common fight.

From 25 March onward the success of our assault north of the Ruhr was assured. Rees was reduced on that day and the Allied bridgeheads were quickly expanded. Enemy resistance was stiffest on the flanks, but during the following week XVI Corps of the Ninth Army, on the right, began to press south into the Ruhr, while on the left Emmerich was cleared by Canadian 2 Corps by 30 March. The Allied troops continued to pour across the Rhine, and, with the airborne units coming under command of the Second and Ninth Armies, the main thrusts eastward to encircle the Ruhr and strike into the heart of Germany began. The great operation of forcing the lower Rhine had proved successful to the fullest extent of my desire.

Meanwhile, in the sector of the Central Group of Armies, operations were proceeding equally well. There, as has been stated earlier, the main object was to establish a firm lodgement area in the Frankfurt region from which an advance in strength could be made toward Kassel. This lodgement area was to extend from the Neckar River in the south to the Sieg River in the north, and eastward as far as Eberbach, Hanau, Giessen, and Siegen. To create this base for our future operations, the First Army was to undertake an offensive south from the Remagen bridgehead, while the Third Army and the Seventh Army crossed the Rhine mainly between Mainz and Mannheim. This direction of movement from the Remagen bridgehead had been decided upon promptly after the securing of that foothold. It completely surprised the German High Command.

In the execution of these plans we were again greatly aided by the results of the dash and daring with which the operations west of the Rhine had been carried out. The sweep which General Patton had conducted across the lower Moselle and up the west bank of the Rhine, together with the heavy blows of the Seventh Army and the continued aggressiveness in the First Army bridgehead, had so utterly disorganized the enemy and so largely destroyed his forces in the region that, although he had managed to blow the last bridges as the escaping remnants struggled across, he was in no condition to defend the east bank. General Patton, as before mentioned, seized the opportunity thus offered, and on the night of 22/23 March, as our main, carefully prepared crossing in the north was poised for its massive blow, 5th Division of XII Corps crossed the Rhine in the neighbourhood of Oppenheim, south of Mainz. The bridgehead gained grew swiftly, and by the evening of 24 March it was 9 miles long and 6 miles deep, while 19,000 prisoners were taken in 24 hours. The remainder of XII Corps crossed the river, seized Darmstadt on the 25th, and swept on to capture intact the main bridges at Aschaffenburg.

While this success was being exploited, the First Army steadily expanded the Remagen bridgehead with advances by V, III, and VII Corps. The enemy's efforts against the northern flank continued to prove fruitless, and by 26 March he was compelled to withdraw over the Sieg River. On the same day the resistance on the southern flank of this bridgehead, which had previously been light, collapsed completely. In a rapid thrust by V Corps to the southeast, Limbourg was overrun and the advance continued toward the Main River. At the same time, the Third Army was clearing this river from Frankfurt to the Rhine.

These sweeping advances completed the demoralization of the enemy forces in the sector. Taking advantage of this, VIII Corps of the Third Army established new bridgeheads over the Rhine at Boppard and north of Brauback on 25 March. The Rhine here flows between hills which fall sharply to the banks of the river, presenting country more difficult for a crossing operation than any which can be well imagined. Despite the advantages thus offered to the defense, the enemy's resistance, though initially heavy, was short-lived. On the following day two more crossings at St Goarshausen and Oberwesel were effected with equal success by VIII Corps. The forces thus put across the Rhine struck hard to the east and, after Bad Schwalbach had been taken on 28 March and Wiesbaden on the 29th, all enemy activity in the area soon ceased. Farther east, Aschaffenburg and Frankfurt were also cleared by 29 March, and the whole Allied lodgement area in the Frankfurt region was securely established. Marburg had been taken by VII Corps, and the armored advance on Kassel was already under way.

The success of the Undertone operations west of the Rhine had equally favored the Seventh Army in its river crossings. Plans had been prepared for an airborne operation in this zone, by the US 13th Airborne Division, to assist the frontal assault, but the weakness of the enemy following his defeat in the Saar rendered it unnecessary. I intended that this situation should be so exploited as to enable the Seventh Army to take over the sector south of the Main, and its first bridgeheads were accordingly established near Worms on 26 March. Once again, initially heavy opposition on the east bank dwindled in the face of Allied superiority, and the four small footholds gained by XV Corps were swiftly consolidated into a firm lodgement area extending southward to the Neckar, a link-up with the Third Army being effected south of Darmstadt on the 27th. On 28 March the Neckar was crossed, and on the following day Mannheim surrendered. The advances from this bridgehead also into Germany had begun.

Finally, on 1 April, the French II Corps established a bridgehead for the French Army at Philippsburg, and there built up a base on the east bank from which subsequently to strike southeast toward Stuttgart and to clear the right bank of the Rhine as far as the Swiss border.

Thus the Rhine barrier, the greatest natural obstacle with which the Allied armies had been faced since the landings in France, had been breached all along the line, and the cost to our forces had been fantastically small. The enemy had committed the same error as in Normandy, and with the same fatal results. His characteristic refusal to admit tactical defeat had proved his undoing. Instead of carrying out a planned withdrawal to the strong defensive positions afforded by the great river, which his inferiority in men and equipment indicated as the logical course, he had chosen to stand and fight a hopeless battle in front of the Rhine. The result was that he was then too weak, when the withdrawal was eventually forced upon him, to hold the line which Nature had offered to him. Spread out along the vast front, his broken and depleted forces could not hope to withstand the overwhelming weight hurled against them in the concentrated Allied assaults. Moreover, once we had gained a bridgehead his lack of mobility rendered him incapable of rushing reinforcements to the threatened area, and the breach once made could never be closed. The élan of the Allied armies had sealed Germany's fate in the operations which had preceded the crossing of the Rhine, and now they were pouring over the river to surge with the same victorious impetus to the innermost parts of the country.

Von Rundstedt had failed in Normandy and had been removed from his command as the penalty. Later he had been reinstated to conduct the ill-fated offensive in the Ardennes where, in 1940, he had achieved his most spectacular success in the invasion of France. Now, with the Allies over the Rhine, he was again dismissed; and with him went the last hopes of Germany's survival. Kesselring was brought from Italy to assume the forlorn task of holding together the beaten armies of the west in the last month of their existence.

THE ENVELOPMENT OF THE
RUHR AND THE JUNCTION WITH
THE RUSSIANS

If the Nazi leaders, in appointing Kesselring to the
command of the German forces in the west, expected
him to repeat his defensive successes of Italy, they
were to be sadly disappointed. With the Rhine
crossed, he had here no Gustav Line, no Monte
Cassino, upon which to make a stand. So completely
had the Germans relied upon their ability to hold out

Envelopment of the Ruhr

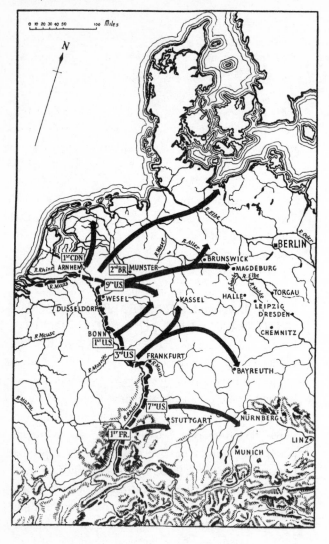

in the Siegfried Line that east of the Rhine there were no artificial barriers ready to halt our progress other than hastily constructed local defense works. Any other defenses on a larger scale existed only as plans, now never to be realized.

Nor had Kesselring the unified resolute forces which had withstood the Allied attacks in his former command. During March, an average of 10,000 prisoners had fallen into our hands every day, apart from the heavy losses in killed and wounded, and the divisions which had been weak when the Rhineland battles began were now reduced to mere skeletons. The total of enemy casualties from the opening of the Allied spring offensive on 8 February represented the destruction of a score of full divisions.

Within a week of the crossing of the Rhine, the Allied spearheads were thrusting eastward, isolating corps and divisions, and cutting off one army from another. Despair gripped the German forces as never before, and the disintegration of the entire Western Front developed rapidly. Already the task of exercising unified command over the German detachments was becoming almost an impossibility. Communications were breaking down, and reports filtered through so slowly that Kesselring could never be sure what the position at a given moment might be. By the time information had been received and instructions sent back to the armies, the Allied advance guards had probably pressed forward 50 miles and the entire situation had been transformed. Under such circumstances, the local commanders were increasingly compelled to make their own decisions, irrespective of what might be happening elsewhere, and to act independently of the higher command. In consequence, Kesselring found himself increasingly unable to exercise any real control over the situation, and the organization of the Western Front collapsed completely. Only one thing was certain: by Hitler's order, the fight was to go on.

It thus seemed evident that the enemy had no hope of ever re-establishing a line in Germany capable of withstanding the Allied avalanche. His only chance of prolonging resistance for any length of time lay in retreating to the so-called "National Redoubt" in the Alps, where he might be able to hold the immensely strong natural defenses against our attacks for a considerable period. At the same time, he would probably continue to resist in the "fortresses" of western France and Dunkirk, where his troops were still under siege, in the Channel Islands, in the Frisian Islands, in Norway, and behind the floods of Holland. Knowing the Nazi mentality, I had little expectation of an immediate all-embracing collapse and an abrupt termination of the struggle through complete surrender while these outposts remained unsubdued.

The task which the Allies had now to undertake lay in so exploiting the success of the Rhine crossings as to effect, in the shortest possible time, the complete defeat of the broken armies immediately before us. We had to thrust forward our armored spearheads with the maximum speed that logistics would permit, and to divide and destroy the enemy before he could withdraw into such defensible positions as those afforded by the mountains of the Redoubt.

In order fully to carry out this policy of speed and violence, however, our attacking armies had, as far as possible, to be freed from the responsibility of holding down the ever-growing rear areas in Germany. There was a danger that the detachment of forces for security purposes in the overrun territory would so weaken the combat formations as seriously to limit their powers of rapid advance. For this reason, on 30 March the US Fifteenth Army was activated, its function being to occupy, organize, and govern the parts of Germany already conquered and thus permit the other armies to concentrate on their task of bringing the war to the speediest possible conclusion. At first the Fifteenth Army was responsible, under the 12th Army Group, for the administration of territory west of the Rhine between Bonn and Homberg, together with command of the reinforced 66th Division containing the enemy garrisons in Lorient and St-Nazaire. Later it was to extend the area under its control as the other armies advanced eastward. The Allied military government organization was working smoothly and, apart from isolated outbreaks by individual Nazi fanatics, was experiencing little trouble with the population.

The Ruhr had been isolated by air action early in 1945. In addition to the direct damage to factories, the transportation system had been wrecked, and the coal and steel produced there, on which the German war economy largely depended, had been, for the time being, denied the enemy. Before operations deep into the German interior could safely be undertaken, however, the Allies had, following the Rhine crossings, to complete the encirclement of the Ruhr and the elimination of any danger from the pocket which would be thus created. With this vast armory in Allied hands, and the Russians in control of its Silesian counterpart, Germany's power of continuing to wage war would be destroyed even were her armies to be preserved intact. The essential weapons, ammunition, and fuel produced by the Ruhr would be denied to them, and even the local factories dispersed about Germany to escape the Allied bombs would be brought to a standstill through lack of raw materials, for the bulk of which they were yet dependent upon the Ruhr and Silesian resources.

I determined, therefore, before launching any further offensive eastward into Germany, to carry out the policy originally envisaged of enveloping the Ruhr by converging thrusts from the two bridgeheads at Wesel and Frankfurt. The southern drive, thanks to the rapidity of the 12th Army Group build-up east of the Rhine which our position upon the river line had permitted, was now capable of being made in far greater strength than would otherwise have been possible. Accordingly 21st Army Group and 12th Army Group were instructed to concentrate on achieving a junction in the Kassel–Paderborn area, while 6th Army Group was to protect the right flank as far north as the Hohe–Rhön hill mass. The First Allied Airborne Army was to be prepared to assist the advances by carrying out a one-division air drop in the Kassel area to seize the airfields there and the Eder River dam. The rapidity with which the ground forces progressed rendered this relatively small airborne operation unnecessary. Previously we had seriously considered the greatest airborne operation yet attempted. The outline plan was to employ about seven airborne and infantry divisions in seizing a large area in the Kassel region, where by blocking all roads and operating on remaining German units from the rear, all these could be destroyed in place. The rapidity and decisiveness of our air–ground operations made this operation completely unnecessary. Under the Ninth Army in the north, while XVI Corps probed southward into the industrial area, XIX Corps swung around its left flank and drove eastward. Meanwhile VII Corps of the First Army, spearheaded by the 3rd Armored Division, struck north from Marburg, which had been taken on 28 March. On 1 April the two armies made contact near Lippstadt, and the encirclement of the Ruhr, which might be said to have begun with the air forces' interdiction program in February, was completed.

The operation constituted the largest double envelopment in history. Inside the pocket we had trapped the whole of the German Army Group B and two corps of Army Group H, including the picked troops who had been massed in March to defend the southern approaches of the Ruhr against the immediate offensive which the enemy had erroneously expected us to launch northward from the Remagen bridgehead.

The decision of the High Command to hold on in the Ruhr can be explained only by the German's innate insistence upon fighting where he stood in preference to carrying out a withdrawal, no matter what the odds against him; and coupled with this, perhaps, went some realization of the difficulties which any move would entail in the armies' present condition. The tactics of the battle of the Falaise pocket were therefore repeated on a far greater scale. Yet in the Ruhr there was no objective like the cutting of the Avranches corridor to justify the German obstinacy; here our armies were in strength all around the enemy, and there could be no question of a threat to our supply lines. As for the Ruhr resources, even though still in German hands these were obviously of no value to the bulk of the armies which were now cut off from them to the east.

The enemy may have entertained ideas of holding out in the Ruhr for some time and thus constituting a threat in our rear which would prevent our further progress while his remaining armies regrouped. If so, he had seriously miscalculated. Events were to show that the Ruhr could not support its defenders, despite its armament works and fuel production plants, while the armies to the east were in no condition to regroup and reform any sort of effective line. Each of them was hard put to maintain its own position, and there was no hope of filling the gap in the center of the front created by the trapping of the 21 divisions of Army Groups B and H. Through that gap the Allied armies were shortly to pour eastward, since the German troops which should have been barring their path were, instead, on the march to Allied prison camps.

Immediately the encircling move had been completed, operations were instituted to render innocuous the forces in the pocket. The densely built-up Ruhr area offered many advantages to the defense, and it was my intention, should the enemy continue to resist firmly, to content myself with compressing him into a small area where only a few divisions would be needed to contain him, and there to starve him into surrender. Even if the Ruhr itself could supply its garrison with adequate means of defense, it was clear that so populated an area, containing many hungry civilian mouths, could not also feed indefinitely the huge armies which it suddenly found in its midst. Meanwhile the remainder of our forces would devote themselves to the more important tasks facing them farther east.

At first the trapped enemy showed spirit, and Field Marshal Model, who was in command, attempted to strike out from Hamm in the north and Siegen in the south. These attempts, however, like the cooperating counter-attacks by the enemy armies outside the pocket, were abortive, and were forced back everywhere except along the bank of the Rhine. Meanwhile the ammunition factories ceased production, and what little was available could not be transported to the front. Fuel and food likewise could not be supplied where they were needed; the rail system was ineffective for this purpose since, apart from the damage it had suffered, the network was thinnest where the fighting was hottest, in the southern Sauerland. The shortage of weapons was as grave as elsewhere in the German armies; rear echelons were stripped to arm the forward ones, but even then the latter often lacked ammunition of the correct calibers.

By 13 April, signs of disintegration were evident, resistance becoming scattered and the enemy giving themselves up in such numbers that the disposal of the prisoners constituted a difficulty. It was clear now that there would be no question of starving a stubborn remnant into submission. The main industrial towns in the north were cleared, and on 14 April the pocket was split in two at Hagen. The eastern half collapsed on 16 April, when 80,000 prisoners were taken in the 24 hours, and on 18 April the pocket was finally liquidated. The total bag of prisoners reached the immense figure of 325,000 including 30 general officers. Originally we had estimated that only 150,000 could be taken. Twenty-one divisions were destroyed, including three panzer, one panzer grenadier and three parachute divisions, and enormous quantities of booty fell into our hands. What Hitler may have expected to prove a fortress to hold us back from central Germany had given way after 18 days, and by now the main front was over 100 miles distant to the east.

Once the process of eliminating the enemy forces in the Ruhr had reached a stage when they presented no potential threat to our security, three main avenues by which we could thrust deeper into Germany lay before us.

In the north, a route lay across the North German Plain toward the Baltic and Berlin. Berlin was the symbol of victory before the eyes of every Allied soldier from the day we set foot in Normandy; but other gains would spring from an advance to the northern sector, gains which were at least as important as those to be derived from capture of the German capital. By a thrust to the Baltic, we should cut off from the main enemy armies those elements which were located in Denmark, Norway, northwest Germany, and Holland, at once depriving them of supplies and preventing their coming to the assistance of the forces in the center of Germany. Furthermore, we should gain the north German ports and thus deny the enemy use of his naval bases and ship-building yards, bringing to an end the activities of the submarines and other craft which had for so long preyed upon our supply routes. Finally, we should link hands with the Russian forces sweeping across Pomerania to the north of Berlin.

In central Germany, a route was open to us through the gap in the enemy's line created by the trapping of Army Group B in the Ruhr. An easy advance was thus offered from Kassel, through Erfurt and Leipzig, to Dresden. This would again bring our forces to an important industrial area, the richest still left to the Germans after their loss of the Ruhr and Silesia. There also we should be able to meet the advancing Red Army, and in so doing we should cut in half what remained of Hitler's Reich.

In the south, an axis of advance was available through Nürnberg and Regensburg, by the Danube Valley into Austria, where the Russians were already threatening Vienna. A thrust on this axis would also enable us to isolate, and then penetrate, the Redoubt in western Austria into which we now knew the enemy intended eventually to withdraw as many of his forces as possible. The prevention of such a withdrawal was a major objective in any operations which we might execute in the south.

Weighing the relative advantages which would accrue from an advance in strength in either north, center, or south, I decided that an offensive first in the center would prove the most effective. With Germany once cut in two, the enemy remaining in each portion could then more economically be eliminated. Such a central thrust, moreover, would afford us the maximum degree of flexibility for future operations, as we could subsequently switch forces rapidly to the north or to the south as the situation should indicate.

General Bradley was accordingly instructed to launch an offensive with the Central Group of Armies from the Kassel area, where he now stood, toward Leipzig, establishing the right flank of his advance on the line Bayreuth–Erzgebirge. He was to seize any opportunity of capturing a bridgehead over the Elbe River and to be prepared for operations farther east, but it was anticipated that these would be unnecessary as the speed of the Russian advance would probably lead to a junction with them on the Elbe, if not west of the river. To assist the First and Third

Armies in executing this thrust, Ninth Army reverted from 21st Army Group to the operational command of 12th Army Group on 4 April.

While General Bradley's forces were thus engaged in the center, the operations of the Allied army groups in the north and south were to be of a limited nature, designed primarily to support the principal offensive. Field Marshal Montgomery's 21st Army Group, after completing its present operations to the Leine River and Bremen was to strike toward the Elbe on the northern flank of 12th Army Group. It was also to be prepared to establish bridgeheads over the river. General Devers' 6th Army Group was to protect the southern flank of the central advance west of Bayreuth, and meanwhile to prepare for a later thrust of its own along the axis Nürnberg–Regensburg–Linz to prevent any concentration of German resistance in the south.

When the central thrust had achieved its object, the principal task was to be an advance to the Baltic and the cleaning out of the whole northern area from Kiel and Lübeck westward by 21st Army Group. The Ninth Army would, if necessary, again be used to assist Field Marshal Montgomery in this work. After the requirements for these northern operations had been met, we should be able to direct 6th Army Group, with perhaps the Third Army, southeastward down the Danube Valley and into the Redoubt.

It will have been observed that in all the possible lines of advance into Germany following the Ruhr encirclement the question arose of effecting a junction with the Russians. In fact, with the approach of our respective forces from east and west, it was now essential that operations on the two fronts should be coordinated, and necessary to learn something of the Russians' intentions in order to know best how to exploit such success as our own plan of campaign might achieve. I therefore informed Marshal Stalin of my general plan to strike first in the center and subsequently to effect a link-up with his forces in the Regensburg–Linz area with a view to neutralizing the Redoubt. Marshal Stalin replied that this scheme coincided entirely with the Russian plans in respect to both the central and southern sectors.

The decision to concentrate first upon a major thrust in the center nevertheless gave rise to some misgivings. The desirability of bringing the U-boat war to an end, of opening up supply lines through the north German ports, of acquiring the use of Swedish shipping, of relieving the Dutch, and of occupying Denmark and Norway, and the political and psychological effects of an early entry into Berlin were all advanced as reasons in favor of early operations in the 21st Army Group sector.

Our reply pointed out that we had not forgotten the important advantages to be gained by the conquest of north Germany. It was merely a question of timing that was at issue. Our plan for an advance in the center was itself intended to facilitate such a conquest which, I was convinced, could more easily be achieved once Germany was cut in two. It was vital that we should concentrate for each effort in turn rather than allow our power to be dispersed by attempting to undertake too many projects at once.

Despite appearances on the map, the North German Plain does not in reality afford such favorable terrain for a rapid advance as does the central sector at this time of year. Between Kassel and Leipzig we should be moving over a plateau with no major river obstacles, whereas the northern area is intersected with water-ways and the ground was in a condition to make heavy going. Previous experience of the Germans' thoroughness in bridge destruction also served to indicate the advisability of advancing across headwaters rather than the lower reaches of rivers when speed was an essential factor.

Berlin, I was now certain, no longer represented a military objective of major importance. The Russian advance and the Allied bombing had largely destroyed its usefulness, and even the governmental departments were understood to be in process of evacuation. Military factors, when the enemy was on the brink of final defeat, were more important in my eyes than the political considerations involved in an Allied capture of the capital. The function of our forces must be to crush the German armies rather than to dissipate our own strength in the occupation of empty and ruined cities. Moreover, the Russians were practically on its outskirts (30 miles away) and it was a matter of serious concern to avoid entangling of forces in areas where, due to difficulties of communication and difficulties in language, unfortunate incidents might occur.

Kassel was cleared on 4 April, and within the following week the main Allied advances to the east were begun. On the southern flank, the Third Army, headed by XX Corps, encountered only scattered opposition, with little more than road blocks to bar its progress in the country north of the Thuringian Forest. Weimar was reached on 11 April and Erfurt cleared the next day. By the 13th, Jena had been cleared and the 4th Armored Division was at the outskirts of Chemnitz. The enemy retired southeast into the Erzgebirge along the frontier of Czechoslovakia, although he still clung to the town of Chemnitz as a pivot to the north, where the south Saxon cities were putting up a stiff resistance to the First Army. At the same time that XX Corps was advancing to the north of Czechoslovakia, XII and VIII Corps of Third Army, farther south, pushed through Bayreuth and Neustadt toward the mountains of the Bohemian Forest forming the southwestern border of the country. On 18 April the Allied armies set foot in Czechoslovakia.

On the left flank of the First Army, Ninth Army continued the advance to the northeast which it had commenced under 21 Army Group following its successful envelopment of the north of the Ruhr. XIX Corps established a bridgehead over the Weser at Hameln on 6 April and pushed rapidly ahead, south of Brunswick, to reach the Elbe south of Magdeburg on 11 April. On the next day, Brunswick fell and the first bridgehead was gained on the east bank of the Elbe by the 2nd Armored Division. A second bridgehead, south of Wittenberge, was achieved by the 5th Armored Division of XIII Corps on 13 April.

From Magdeburg to Wittenberge, the enemy showed himself ready to evacuate the west bank of the river, but he fought hard to deny us possession of Magdeburg itself, which only fell to XIX Corps on 18 April. Very strong counter-attacks were also launched against the bridgeheads, and these were so severe as to compel the Ninth Army, on 14 April, to abandon the two footholds originally obtained. But a third, at Barby, held firm, as enemy attempts to destroy the bridges by floating mines down the river proved abortive. So rapid had been the thrust to reach the Elbe that a number of German pockets had been by-passed on the way. The forces in these, before being mopped up, attempted to harass the Allied lines of communication, but with little success.

The First Army offensive, south of the Harz Mountains, got under way by 11 April, and rapid progress was made against generally disorganized resistance. On 14 April, the 3rd Armored Division of VII Corps reached Dessau, just south of the confluence of the Elbe and Mulde Rivers. In the course of this thrust, the Harz Mountains, containing some 10,000 enemy troops, were almost encircled, but attempts to reduce this pocket met with strong resistance. The garrison succeeded for some time, with the aid of the difficult terrain, in holding the Allied inroads to a minimum, while striving to keep open a corridor to the east near Bernburg. The encirclement was nevertheless completed when this corridor was severed on 18 April. A desperate attempt by the von Clausewitz Panzer Division to relieve the garrison by a dash across some 50 miles of Allied-held territory was foiled, and opposition within the pocket soon weakened. The last organized resistance in the Harz ceased on 21 April.

Meanwhile, although the Allies had penetrated to the southeast of Leipzig, the enemy fought back strongly to its west and southwest. After two days of bitter struggle, the 69th Division of V Corps cleared the city on 19 April. The enemy salient which had extended westward from the line of the Mulde to the Leipzig–Halle area had now disappeared and Allied elements cleared to the river.

On 25 April patrols of the 273rd Regiment, 69th Division, under V Corps, which had probed eastward from the Mulde, met elements of the Russian 58th Guards Division in the Torgau area, on the Elbe. The junction of the Eastern and Western Fronts had been effected, and Germany was cut in two. The object of the central thrust had been achieved.

The problem of liaison with the Russians had grown more pressing during the advance across central Germany, strategical questions being replaced by tactical ones as the time of junction approached; but solutions were not forthcoming until the last minute. One of our principal anxieties concerned the mutual identification of our respective force, both in the air and on the ground. Already, at the beginning of April, our tactical air forces had come into contact and shots had been mistakenly exchanged, and we considered it of the utmost importance that all possible arrangements should be made to ensure proper recognition in order to prevent errors and possibly tragic incidents which might result in later recriminations. Following recommendations by the Army Group Commanders, a system of recognition signs and signals was eventually arranged by 20 April.

In regard to the territorial questions affecting the junction of the fronts it did not seem to me practicable to restrict our operations to a demarcation line prepared in advance, either on the basis of the subsequent occupational zones or otherwise. Both fronts should be free to advance until contact was imminent, after which an agreement should be reached between the local commanders concerned as to any readjustment of lines which operational considerations might render desirable. This policy met with the approval of the Combined Chiefs of Staff and of the Soviet High Command, and instructions accordingly were issued to the armies under my command. The arrangement worked smoothly and, in accordance with an agreement reached with the Soviet High Command when contact was imminent, the boundary was temporarily fixed in the central sector along the easily identified line of the Elbe and Mulde Rivers. The subsequent readjustment to the zonal boundaries for occupational purposes was carried through without incident after the cessation of hostilities.

While the Central Group of Armies had been pushing eastward to divide Germany, the Northern and Southern Groups had each in their respective sectors been carrying out the operations assigned to them during this period.

Under 21st Army Group, Second Army was, by my instructions, to advance towards Bremen and Hamburg, thereafter thrusting to the Elbe (gaining a bridgehead if the opportunity offered) and thereby protecting the northern flank of the Ninth Army in the 12th Army Group. Meanwhile the Canadian Army was to open up a supply route to the north through Arnhem and then to operate to clear north-east Holland, the coastal belt eastward to the Elbe, and west Holland, in that order of priority. The operations were, in many respects, similar to those carried out in France by the same Army Group in the preceding summer, when the Second Army drove across the rear to the Pas-de-Calais while the Canadian Army mopped up the enemy along the coast.

The Second Army advance was made with 30 Corps on the left flank, 12 Corps in the center, and 8 Corps on the right. Resistance at first was slight and good progress was made. North of Münster, the German First Parachute Army troops were scattered, Rheine was taken on 3 April, and enemy hopes of a stand on the Weser–Ems Canal were frustrated. On 6 April, 8 Corps established a bridgehead over the Weser on the southern flank, and continued the advance to the Elbe, which 11th Armored Division reached at Lauenburg on 19 April. Farther north, 12

Corps, against stiffer resistance, reached Harburg, on the south bank of the Elbe opposite Hamburg, on 20 April. South of Bremen, the advance of 30 Corps was stoutly contested. The Allies were at the outskirts of the city by 22 April, but very bitter fighting took place before 3 and 52 Divisions finally crushed all opposition on the 26th.

Meanwhile the Canadian Army was probing into Holland. In a thrust northward, Canadian 2 Corps, conforming with the Second Army on its right, initially met heavy opposition from the First Parachute Army, but broke out on 6 April and, while some elements turned northwest, others advanced northeast toward Oldenburg. Resistance in north Holland collapsed and the sea was reached on 15 April. By the 21st, the whole area, apart from a small tip in the northeast, was cleared as far south as Harderwijk on the eastern shore of the Ijssel Meer. To the west, the Ijssel River line was stubbornly defended at Deventer and Zutphen, but the former town fell on 10 April and a bridgehead was established over the river. In the southern sector of the army zone, Canadian 1 Corps attacked from Nijmegen, clearing to the lower Rhine by 5 April, and Arnhem was captured on the 15th. The enemy now withdrew into "Fortress Holland" behind the Grebbe and New Water Lines, protected by the floods, beyond which no further Allied advance was made in this sector. It was rightly felt by Field Marshal Montgomery that an advance into Holland would occasion great additional suffering for that unhappy country and that the quickest and most economical way to free the country was to complete the destruction of the enemy forces elsewhere.

The principal task of 6th Army Group during the first half of April was, as previously indicated, the protection of the right flank of the 12th Army Group thrust as far east as Bayreuth. To accomplish this, Seventh Army was ordered to advance with all speed to a line Ludwigsburg–Crailsheim–Nürnberg–Bayreuth, linking with Third Army in the Bayreuth area. The Bayreuth–Nürnberg autobahn was to be cut and Nürnberg itself captured, after which the army was to be prepared to attack towards Regensburg and Linz. The French First Army was to advance its Rhine bridgehead force to the line Lichtenau–Pforzheim–Ludwigsburg, capturing Karlsruhe and Pforzheim. When the principal bridgehead had been adequately built up, the area east of the Rhine was to be cleared far enough south to enable a new bridgehead to be established at Strasbourg. The troops there would then cross the Rhine, after which the main effort would be an advance on Stuttgart from the Pforzheim–Ludwigsburg areas.

In the execution of these plans the opposition encountered was generally steady, despite the losses incurred by the enemy. While XXI Corps, in the Seventh Army sector, penetrated to Schweinfurt by 11 April, stiff resistance met the Allied thrusts at Würzburg and Heilbronn. At the latter place the enemy defended the Neckar River line against VI Corps for some days and then fought in the town for a week before it was cleared on 12 April. A salient thrust as far as Crailsheim by the 10th Armored Division on 7 April had to be temporarily abandoned in the face of enemy pressure. By 16 April XV Corps reached Nürnberg, but again several days' hard fighting was required before the city was cleared.

In the French Army sector, resistance in the Rhine Valley was initially stiff, but soon weakened. Karlsruhe fell on 4 April and Baden-Baden on the 12th. The enemy defenses to the south now collapsed before French 1 Corps. By 15 April, Kehl was taken and the way cleared for bridging to be started at Strasbourg. As the withdrawal to the south up the right bank of the Rhine continued, the enemy was forced to conform by retiring in the Black Forest to the east, and the situation was prepared for the capture of Stuttgart by Allied pincers converging from northeast and southwest.

THE FINAL PHASE

The division of Germany accomplished by the junction with the Russians at Torgau produced immediate and far-reaching consequences. The enemy's difficulties of command which followed the loss of Army Group B in the Ruhr now reached their climax, and all chance of restoring effective unity to the armies facing the Western Allies irrevocably disappeared. The enemy found himself split into virtually independent commands in the north and south, with no means of coordinating the operations in the two zones. Each had to fight its own battle as best it could.

The morale effect of this situation was immense, and a weakening of the resistance previously offered in both north and south was at once evident. During the first three weeks of April over a million prisoners were taken by our armies, and losses sustained at such a rate inevitably brought on collapse in every sector. The Russians, moreover, were now fighting their way into Berlin, and the government, already partly evacuated, was rendered powerless.

At the same time, the paralysis of the German administrative system as a whole, which had set in as a result of Allied air action, and since spread rapidly as 12th Army Group advanced eastward, gripped the entire country. The autocratic nature of the system was such that, with its mainspring disabled in Berlin, the parts throughout the rest of Germany automatically ceased to function. Communications finally broke down, the postal services came to a standstill, and the complete isolation from his home in which the German soldier now found himself sapped his last powers of resistance. With his world collapsing about him, he lost all heart in the fight. The horror pictures which the Nazis had painted with such lurid colors in their anti-Bolshevik propaganda began to have an effect very different from that envisaged by their originators. Instead of being steeled to a last superhuman effort, the soldier, confused and disillusioned by the helplessness of the units to which he had once been proud to belong, became concerned solely with his individual desire to be with his family in whatever fate might be overtaking them.

Prior to the Allied advance across central Germany, evidence had been received that the government was preparing to evacuate Berlin and move southward, ultimately perhaps to Berchtesgaden in the National Redoubt. Some of the departments had already left the city, but the main body now found that, with the Allied link-up on the Elbe, it was too late. An impassable barrier had been drawn across the country, and the way to the Redoubt was cut off. In consequence, Hitler and his intimate henchmen stayed on in Berlin.

Although the Redoubt was not, therefore, to be the last seat of the Nazi government, the possibility remained that it would still be the scene of a desperate stand by the fanatical elements of the armies south of the dividing line, together with those which might retreat northward out of Italy. These armies, totalling about 100 nominal divisions, included the bulk of the remaining German armored and SS formations, and up to 30 panzer divisions might conceivably be concentrated behind the mountain barriers. In addition, most of the surviving German jet fighter plane strength was located in the south. The conquest of the Redoubt area thus remained as an important objective of the Allies, despite the collapse of the rest of Germany. In the event of determined resistance, its reduction would constitute a formidable problem, and speed of movement was therefore essential to forestall the enemy's retiring into the area in time to fortify it against our attacks.

Extending some 240 miles in length and 80 miles in depth, the Redoubt comprised the western half of Austria, with small portions of Germany to the north and Italy to the south. It was bounded on the north by the Bavarian plains, on the south by the Dolomites and Carnic Alps, on the west by the Swiss frontier and the Rhine Valley, and on the east by the Lageneurt Basin and the eastern extremity of the Niedere Tauern. Within it lay Berchtesgaden and Hitler's "Eagle's Nest".

The whole area was extremely mountainous and thus unsuitable for large-scale airborne operations, while the roads into it followed narrow valleys which could easily be held by determined defenders. The snows and danger of avalanches limited the possibility of any military operations to the summer months between May and October. Although there was no evidence of any completed system of defenses along the natural ramparts, some progress appeared to have been made in this respect along the northern flank. Air reconnaissance also revealed underground constructional activity. It was believed that some subterranean factories had been established in the area, but if any considerable numbers of troops were to be maintained there they would have to rely for their supplies, both of food and ammunition, upon previously accumulated stocks.

North of the dividing line in central Germany some 50 enemy divisions were likely to remain to be mopped up, and of these the only formidable elements were those of the First Parachute Army.

Although it was not conceivable that resistance could long be maintained in the North German Plain, it was possible that some withdrawal might be attempted into Denmark and Norway with a view to make a last stand in those countries, while "Fortress Holland" would also continue to hold out behind the water barriers. The prevention of such a withdrawal, by means of a rapid Allied advance to the Baltic, thus became the primary objective of our operations in the northern sector.

For the subsequent reduction of Norway, in the event that the German garrison there continued to hold after its isolation had been effected, a task force was assembled in Scotland under the command of Lieut. Gen. Sir Andrew Thorne.

On the Central German Front, although elements pushed forward, as described, to meet the Russians at Torgau, it was necessary to halt the main Allied forces on the lines of the Elbe and Mulde Rivers and the Erzgebirge. For this decision logistical factors were mainly responsible, as well as the aim of concentrating forces now on the north and south flanks. The rapidity of our advance and the large scale upon which the operation was conducted had strained our supply organization to an unprecedented degree, and it could not, at the moment, be further stretched.

As in the dash across France in 1944, it was possible now to maintain the momentum of the armored columns in their swift advances only by the expedient of airborne supply. In executing this task, the carrier planes accomplished remarkable feats, and, invaluable as they had proved throughout the campaign in Northwest Europe, the "flying boxcars" were never more essential than in these concluding stages of the war. Landing on improvised airfields close to the front line and sometimes within pockets temporarily surrounded by the enemy, 1,500 IX Troop Carrier Command C-47s, supplemented by heavy bombers stripped for the purpose, flew over 20,000 sorties during April to carry nearly 60,000 tons of freight (including 10,255,509 gallons of gasoline) to the forward elements of the ground forces. Making their outward flights from French bases in the mornings, the planes returned in the afternoons bearing thousands of evacuated casualties and Allied prisoners of war who had been liberated during the advances. Without such assistance it would have been impossible for the armored divisions to achieve the sweeping successes which attended their operations.

While our forces in the center were halted on the Mulde and Elbe Rivers, we turned to the completion of operations in the north and south, concentrating upon the two principal objectives of further subdividing the enemy's remaining armies and of neutralizing the areas already described where he might the most effectively make his last stands.

Accordingly, in the northern sector 21 Army Group with US XVIII Airborne Corps under command, was directed to fulfil the tasks upon which it was at present engaged west of the Elbe, to seize crossings over that river in the British Second Army zone, secure Hamburg, and advance with the utmost speed on the general area of Kiel–Lübeck. This done, Field Marshal Montgomery was to be prepared to conduct operations northward to liberate Denmark, using, if necessary, an airborne assault to force the Kiel Canal. Meanwhile operations were to continue to achieve the clearing of the coastal belt, and to reduce the enemy naval bases and fortifications which threatened the approaches to Hamburg. The Allied naval and air forces were to assist in these operations, but the nature of the defenses made it possible that their reduction might prove lengthy and difficult, in which case the availability to the Allies of the German ports might be delayed. The question of the subsequent opening of either Hamburg or Bremen, or both, was also dependent upon the condition in which we should find their port installations, but first priority was to be accorded to Hamburg. On the eastern flank of 21 Army Group, operations toward Berlin would have to await the developments of the situation following the accomplishment of the more important tasks outlined above.

In view of the great importance of the opening up of the port of Bremen, Bomber Command carried out a heavy attack on Heligoland on 18 April in order to neutralize its defenses and thus facilitate a Commando landing if such an operation became necessary.

At the same time that 21 Army Group concentrated on its principal thrust to Lübeck, a similar advance was to be made in the southern zone down the Danube Valley toward Linz with the object of effecting a further junction with the Russians. The static situation in the center now permitted the use of the Third Army for this purpose, while 6th Army Group devoted the whole of its attention to the problem of the Redoubt farther south and west.

Even when the Danube offensive had subdivided the enemy's forces in the south, it might still be possible for the Redoubt to hold out, and Third Army was therefore instructed, in addition to its principal thrust, to seize Salzburg, while the Seventh Army, under 6th Army Group, was to advance along the axis Würzburg–Munich, penetrate the mountains, and subsequently to occupy the fortress area. We made available to General Devers the use of the US 13th Airborne Division to assist in these operations if it should prove necessary. Farther west, the French Army was to mop up the Black Forest region and clear along the Swiss frontier, and subsequently to enter Austria if the situation required.

In the execution of the 21 Army Group operations in the north, the resistance encountered by the British Second Army in its attacks toward Bremen and Hamburg was persistent. Following the fall of Bremen on 26 April, however, the situation changed. The main Allied effort was now transferred to the sector of 8 Corps, which launched an attack across the Elbe at Lauenburg on 29 April. Weak opposition only was offered—chiefly by local defense battalions and labor services—and across the river the bridgehead was quickly enlarged. Simultaneously the US XVIII Airborne Corps, now fighting in a ground role, effected a crossing to the south and was attached to the Second Army to provide flank protection for further advances. On 1 May, 11th Armored Division broke out of the British 8 Corps bridgehead to dash across Schleswig-Holstein to the Baltic and entered Lübeck on the afternoon of 2 May, thereby sealing off the enemy in Denmark. On the same day, the British 6 Airborne Division, under XVIII Corps, reached Wismar, farther east along the coast, while inland Schwerin was attained.

While the hold thus gained on the neck of the Danish peninsula was being consolidated, other forces crossed the Elbe and turned down its right bank toward Hamburg, which surrendered and was occupied by 7th Armored Division on 3 May. At the same time, 30 Corps completed clearance of the area between the Elbe and the Weser.

On 3 May, US XVIII Airborne Corps was in contact with the Russians along the general line Wismar–Schweriner–Lake Grabow. While Berlin was in flames, a new offensive by the Red Army during the last week of April had taken Stettin and swept rapidly westward across Mecklenburg, driving the disorganized remnants of German armies before it. Now, with the junction of the Allied fronts, all resistance in northern Germany ceased.

By the end of April the enemy had finally abandoned all attempts to stem the Allied advances from east and west simultaneously. He turned his back upon the western Allies to concentrate all his remaining forces in a last desperate effort to hold back the

Russians, but it was too late. As his armies were forced farther and farther back, the troops gave themselves up in thousands to the Anglo-American armies in their rear. While the Second Army was thrusting unopposed to the Baltic, the American units standing on the Elbe were receiving wholesale surrenders from the enemy retreating westward across the river and into their arms. One corps alone took 300,000 prisoners in the course of a single day.

In northeast Holland and along the coastal belt eastward, the Canadian Army continued its operations to clear the area, taking Oldenburg on 2 May, after overcoming stiff resistance, and driving on beyond. In western Holland, however, no further ground advances were made across the flood barriers behind which the German Twenty-fifth Army lay entrenched.

The situation confronting us in western Holland was one of peculiar difficulty. Civilian conditions there had deteriorated steadily for some months, and after the advances of our armies to the east had isolated the area from Germany, the position of the population became desperate. It was imperative, therefore, that steps should be taken by the Allies to relieve the growing distress before wholesale starvation took place. The strength of the German defenses was such, however, that to mount an operation on a sufficiently large scale to ensure success would have necessitated a serious weakening of the main armies in Germany just at the time when it was all-important that we should press home the attacks which were bringing about the final collapse of the enemy there. Moreover, even had we been able to launch an offensive against western Holland at this moment, the enemy would have opened the dykes to flood the whole country, ruining its fertility for many years to come, and bringing further miseries to its people.

We warned General Blaskowitz, the German commander, that the opening of the dykes would constitute an indelible blot upon his military honor and that of the German Army, and pointed out to him that the retention of Holland could not impede the coming collapse of Germany before our advances. Meanwhile, Seyss-Inquart, the Nazi commissioner for Holland, offered a solution by proposing a truce. If the Allied forces were to continue to stand on the Grebbe Line as at present, no further flooding would take place and the Germans would cease all repressive measures against the Dutch, at the same time cooperating in the introduction of relief supplies. The Combined Chiefs of Staff having accorded me a free hand in the matter, my Chief of Staff met Seyss-Inquart on 30 April, a Russian representative being present and concurring in the action taken on behalf of his government. Methods of introducing food by land, sea, and air routes were agreed upon, and the movement of the supplies which the Allies had held ready commenced forthwith; the free dropping of food had indeed already begun.

Seyss-Inquart was impressed by the arguments put forward by the Allies that, recognizing the hopelessness of the position, the German garrison should surrender at once instead of waiting for the inevitable; but that, he said, was a decision for the military commander, over whom he had no control. Blaskowitz would not consider capitulation so long as any form of resistance continued in Germany.

With the relief of the Dutch thus assured, no useful purpose could be served by attempting inroads into "Fortress Holland" at this time when the final collapse of all German resistance was imminent. The Canadians accordingly held fast on the Grebbe Line until the enemy garrison surrendered with the remainder of the forces in northern Germany.

In the south, the thrust of the Third Army down the Danube Valley began on 22 April and made rapid progress against a tottering enemy. Although the defenders held out at Regensburg until 26 April, XX Corps established bridgeheads across the Danube east and west of the city on the 25th, and then advanced southeast down the right bank while XII Corps did likewise north of the river. By 2 May the north bank had been cleared of the enemy as far as Passau, and the 11th Armored Division shot ahead to receive the surrender of Linz on 5 May. With this lengthening of the XII Corps line, the Third Army took command of V Corps, from the First Army, for operations into Czechoslovakia on its northern flank. By an attack eastward across the frontier, Pilsen was captured on 6 May.

These operations were carried out in full coordination with the Russians approaching from the east. The American troops advanced to the line Budejovice–Pilsen–Karlsbad, but were there halted while the Red Army cleared the east and west banks of the Moldau River and occupied Prague. South of Czechoslovakia, the agreed provisional line of junction ran down the Budejovice–Linz railroad and thence along the valley of the Enns, where contact was effected in due course.

South of the Danube, XX Corps crossed the Isar River on 29 April, at the same time clearing the north bank to the Danube confluence. On 1 May the corps reached the Inn River at Braunau and proceeded to close that river in its sector. On its right flank, III Corps crossed the Danube in the Ingolstadt area on 26 April, and, advancing southeast, established bridgeheads over the Isar on the 28th, in conformity with the Seventh Army offensive farther west. On 2 May III Corps reached the Inn at Wasserburg, securing the Mühldorf bridges intact, after which the sector was taken over by the Seventh Army.

The final thrust by the Seventh Army also began on 22 April, following the fall of Nürnberg two days earlier. On the right flank, XV Corps moved down the Danube and then struck south to Munich, which was captured, in the face of some opposition, on 30 April. The enemy attempted to move an SS Panzer Division to block the Allied advance along the Alpine foothills, but was powerless to check our progress. On 4 May, the 3rd Division of XV Corps cleared Berchtesgaden, while other troops occupied Salzburg, and the entire enemy sector between there and Linz fell apart.

Meanwhile XXI and VI Corps had crossed the Danube in the Dillingen area on 22 April, and at

Donauwörth two days later. Pockets of the enemy created south of the river by the converging advances were eliminated, and Augsburg was cleared by XXI Corps on the 28th. Farther west, the Ulm area was reached by VI Corps, which, after a pause occasioned by the moves of the flanking French units, drove on toward the Alpine foothills. The infantry passed through the armor to penetrate the mountains, where the terrain served to slow progress more than did the opposition of the enemy. On 3 May, Innsbruck was taken, and the 103rd Division of VI Corps pushed on to the Brenner Pass.

Here, at Vipiteno on the Italian side of the border, a junction was effected during the morning of 4 May with the 88th Division of the US Fifth Army which, after the defeat of the enemy forces in Italy, had struck into the Alps from the south. The danger of a last stand by the enemy in the Redoubt was finally eliminated, and on the following day the enemy Nineteenth Army capitulated, followed by the whole of Army Group G on 6 May. Among the prisoners taken in the course of the Alpine campaign was the most formidable of my former antagonists, the now retired Field Marshal von Rundstedt.

While the Seventh Army was smashing its way into the Redoubt, the French First Army was completing the destruction of the enemy farther west. Following the collapse of the German resistance in the Black Forest sector, the French broke through with great speed. On 22 April, French I Corps thrust to the east of the Black Forest to reach Lake

Constance, and the corridor was widened on the next day. Then, turning northeast, an advance was made to Ulm, where contact was made with Seventh Army forces on 24 April. This action created three pockets of the enemy: one in the southern Black Forest, one in the Stuttgart area, and one north of Sigmaringen. Meanwhile another French force drove up the right bank of the Rhine to the Swiss frontier at Basel and then east to complete the process of encirclement. By 26 April, the Allies were along the Swiss border from Basel to Lake Constance. Stuttgart itself had been cleared on 21 April, and by the 27th organized resistance had ceased in all the pockets despite the strong opposition offered in some places, aided by difficult terrain.

After being relieved by the Seventh Army in the Ulm sector, the French armor now drove along the northern shore of Lake Constance and turned south across the Austrian border on 30 April. Feldkirch was captured on 4 May, and the advance was continued up the Ill and Kloster Valleys to penetrate the western end of the Redoubt and to make contact with the Seventh Army there as the enemy capitulated.

Apart from the main activities of the French First Army, operations were also carried out at this time by French forces under the control of 6th Army Group on the Franco-Italian border and against the German pocket which had continued to hold out at the mouth of the Gironde. Extensive air operations supported the latter offensive. The penetrations over the Alps into northwest Italy were executed as a diversionary measure to assist 15th Army Group in its breakthrough across the plain of Lombardy. As such, they fulfilled all that was expected of them. The operations against the Gironde enclave were launched on 14 April, after repeated postponements since October 1944 necessitated by the demands of the more important battles elsewhere. Long isolated, and now demoralized by the Allied successes on the main fronts, the defenders were incapable of any extended resistance. Fighting ceased in the Royan sector north of the river on 18 April and three days later the Pointe de Grave on the south bank fell. The final elimination of the enemy in the area was achieved with the reduction of the Island of Oléron on 1 May. Farther north, however, the St-Nazaire–Lorient "fortress" held out until the final surrender of all the German armies.

In these concluding stages of the war, the Allied air forces continued to afford the invaluable support which had been such a vital factor in ensuring our successes throughout the entire campaign. As the Eastern and Western Fronts closed together, however, the opportunities for employment of the strategic bomber forces grew more and more limited, former strategic targets having now become tactical ones. The chief occupation of Bomber Command and the Eighth Air Force by the beginning of May consequently consisted of flying food supplies to the Dutch civilian population and of evacuating casualties and liberated Allied prisoners.

The Tactical Air Forces' work in close support of the advancing armies in the north and south went on, but their operations also were restricted by the danger of hitting advanced Russian elements and the large bodies of prisoners who, having broken loose from their camps, were streaming westward along the roads. The last major offensive by the tactical planes was in the south, where attacks were concentrated ahead of the Third Army advance down the Danube Valley, destroying the enemy's remaining dumps of fuel and other supplies in that area, and cutting the few communications still available for their distribution.

Of enemy offensive activity in the air there was no sign. As the area left to the Germans decreased, the congestion of planes on the remaining airfields grew worse, and the number of aircraft destroyed on the ground amounted in proportion. The demoralization of the German Air Force personnel was too far developed for any suicidal effort to be made with the jet aircraft squadrons left in Austria and Czechoslovakia, and by the beginning of May practically the only flights undertaken were for the purpose of desertion.

The end of the German Navy was even more unspectacular. Having put to sea only on rare occasions throughout the war, then invariably to be hounded to their destruction or driven crippled back to their bases where the Allied air forces repeatedly undid any repair work attempted, the heavy units lay helpless in the northern ports as these fell into the hands of the advancing armies. Only three of the larger ships were in anything approaching a condition for effective action when the last naval bases surrendered. The coastal craft had ceased to operate during

April, and it was left to the submarine forces—the only truly successful naval weapon of which the enemy had enjoyed the use—to carry on the fight to the end.

By 5 May the principal objectives of the Allies had been achieved in every sector, and the war in Europe was virtually at an end. Nowhere on the Continent was there still in existence a German army capable of continuing the fight.

To the east, the armies under my command were joining hands with their Russian allies from the Baltic to the Alps. To the south, they had linked with their comrades in Italy, where already the enemy had made formal surrender. Of the Nazi "fortresses," the National Redoubt had been penetrated while its intended garrison lay dispersed and broken outside its walls; Norway was isolated and doomed; Dunkirk, the Brittany ports, and the Channel Islands were helpless; and Holland and Denmark had just capitulated.

The German war machine which had sought to dominate the world lay overwhelmed and crushed to a degree never before experienced in the history of modern armies. The moment had come for Germany to make her final acknowledgment of defeat.

THE SURRENDER

During the spring of 1945, as the sky grew darker over Germany, the Nazi leaders had struggled desperately, by every means in their power, to whip their people into a last supreme effort to stave off defeat, hoping against hope that it would be possible, if only they could hold on long enough, to save the day by dividing the Allies. Blinded as they were by their own terror and hatred of "Bolshevism", they were incapable of understanding the strength of the bond of common interest existing between Britain, the United States, and the Soviet Union.

As soon as it became clear that a war on two fronts had become impossible to maintain, the Nazi government set itself to obtain, if possible, a truce in the west in order that all its remaining forces might be concentrated in an attempt to check the rolling tide of the Russian advances in the east. In March an approach was made to this end through the British Embassy in Stockholm, but the offer was, of course, rejected out of hand.

Even after this rebuff, however, the Germans clung to their fond hopes of an Allied rift, and a last desperate attempt to create a schism between the Anglo-Americans and the Russians came as late as the last week in April. Himmler, claiming that he spoke for the German government because Hitler was now "incapacitated", approached the Swedish government, through Count Bernadotte, with an offer to surrender all the forces now fighting on the Western Front. Once more the Allies replied that the only acceptable terms were of immediate and unconditional surrender on all fronts simultaneously. Whereupon Himmler disappeared from the scene until, after the final capitulation, he was apprehended as a fugitive from justice and met his death by suicide.

Hitler and his close followers determined to carry on the fight. They personally had everything to lose, nothing to gain, by peace now. Amid the disillusionment of their armies and the ruins which daily multiplied in Germany, they deliberately chose to sacrifice the remnants of their country.

Not all of their henchmen, however, followed their lead. Waffen SS General Karl Wolff, the chief SS officer in northern Italy, in mid-February approached Allied representatives with a view to a capitulation in the Mediterranean Theater. Negotiations with AFHQ made clear to the Germans that the Allies would discuss no terms and would accept unconditional surrender only. By 26 April the deterioration of the enemy's position which followed the Allies' splitting of his armies in Lombardy and Venetia led to renewed approaches; and, on the 29th German representatives signed the terms of surrender, by which all hostilities in Italy were to cease on 2 May.

This capitulation by the German armies facing south in the Alps led inevitably to an abandonment of the struggle by those who, behind them, had been driven back into the mountains before the Allied 6th Army Group offensive. On 2 May Wolff asked with whom the surrender of the North Alpine area should be negotiated. He was told to apply to General Devers, but warned that only unconditional submission would be acceptable. On 5 May the representative of General Schulz, commanding Army Group G, accepted the Allied terms at Haar, in Bavaria, and the German First and Nineteenth Armies accordingly laid down their arms. The surrender was officially to take effect at noon on 6 May, but both sides at once announced the termination of hostilities in order to obviate further loss of life.

Rumors of an impending local capitulation in the north also reached the Allies in mid-April. Field Marshal Busch, commanding the Hamburg area, was stated to be anti-Nazi and willing to surrender, but unable to do so until the Western Allies reached the Baltic and cut him off from the possibility of the arrival of die-hard SS formations from central Germany. General Lindemann, the commander in Denmark, was also understood to be ready to yield at the same time as Busch, and on 30 April an emissary appeared in Stockholm to confirm this. It was urged that the British Army should make all speed to reach the Baltic before the Russians did so, for the Germans would under no circumstances surrender to the Red Army.

By 3 May, however, when the capture of Lübeck had severed Denmark and northwest Germany from the remainder of the country, more important figures came within our reach. As the Red Army had drawn nearer to the Western Allies, Admiral Doenitz, upon whom the mantle of the Führer had now fallen, had instructed his armies which had been facing east to turn about and surrender to the Anglo-American forces.

While thousands of Germans fleeing westward gave themselves up daily, Admiral Friedeburg, the new head of the German Navy, accompanied by Field Marshal Busch's chief of staff and two other officers, appeared at Field Marshal Montgomery's headquarters on 3 May. They asked to be allowed to surrender the Third Panzer, Twelfth, and Twenty-first Armies, which had been fighting the Russians, and to be permitted to pass refugees through the Allied lines into Schleswig-Holstein. Their sole desire was to avoid the necessity of surrendering to the Russians. Field Marshal Montgomery, however, refused to discuss capitulation with them on these terms, though he informed them that individual soldiers who gave themselves up would be treated as prisoners of war. The German representatives then sent back to Field Marshal Keitel, the Chief of the German High Command, for further instructions, meanwhile urging the Allies to follow the retreating German armies closely to avoid chaos.

On 4 May Friedeburg announced that he had received permission from his superiors to make unconditional surrender of all German armed forces, land, sea, and air, in northwest Germany (including the Frisian Islands, Heligoland, and all other islands), Holland, Schleswig-Holstein, and Denmark. I had instructed Field Marshal Montgomery that a capitulation covering these areas might be regarded as a tactical matter and, as such, be dealt with by him. It was arranged that a Russian officer should be present to accept the German submission on behalf of his government. The instrument of surrender was accordingly signed on 4 May, and it became effective at 0800 hours on 5 May.

As laid down in my directive from the Combined Chiefs of Staff, no commitments of any nature were made on the Allied side in accepting these local capitulations, and their terms were made subject to the provisions of the subsequent general unconditional surrender of all the German armed forces. The time for this final yielding had now arrived: unlike Hitler, Admiral Doenitz was ready to bow to the inevitable.

On 4 May it was learned that Doenitz was sending a representative to my headquarters on the following day, and that he had already ordered the German U-boats to return to port in earnest of his intention to bring the war to a close as speedily as possible. I at once notified the Russian High Command of this fact, and they agreed with my suggestion that a Red Army officer should be appointed to join with me in handling the surrender in order that a simultaneous capitulation on all fronts might be arranged. General Suslaparov was accordingly delegated to act on behalf of the Soviet High Command for this purpose.

At the same time that Doenitz's emissary was coming to Reims, Field Marshal Kesselring, as Commander-in-Chief West, transmitted a message stating that he desired to send a plenipotentiary to discuss terms of capitulation. He was informed that unless his surrender covered all German forces facing east as well as west, in addition to those isolated elsewhere, negotiation was out of the question.

Meanwhile Admiral Friedeburg arrived at my headquarters on the evening of 5 May. He began by stating that he wished to clarify a number of points, but was bluntly told that only unconditional surrender was acceptable. To this he replied that he had no power to sign any document of capitulation. The hopelessness of the German military position was pointed out to him, and he was shown the act of military surrender which had been drafted.

Friedeburg cabled a report of his interview to the government, and was informed by Doenitz that General Jodl was on his way to assist in the negotiations. Jodl arrived on the evening of 6 May. It was at once obvious that the Germans were merely playing for time so that meanwhile they could evacuate the largest possible number of soldiers and civilians from the Russian front to behind our lines. They persisted even now in attempting to surrender the Western Front separately, going so far as to say that, whatever my answer might be, they intended to order their armies to cease firing upon the Anglo-Americans. They asked for an adjournment for 48 hours before signing the final surrender, allegedly to enable them to get the necessary orders to their outlying units, but actually, it was clear, only to gain further respite for the purpose above mentioned.

They were informed that unless they agreed to my terms forthwith I would break off all negotiations and seal my front, preventing, by force if necessary, any further westward movement of German soldiers and civilians. They then drafted a cable to Doenitz, asking for authority to make full surrender, but specifying that actual fighting would cease 48 hours after signing. Since this solution obviously placed the decision as to when fighting should cease in the hands of the Germans, I refused to accept it; and finally told them that unless all hostilities should terminate on both fronts within 48 hours of midnight that night, my threat to seal the Western Front would be carried out.

This declaration at last had the desired effect. Doenitz gave his approval for acceptance of my terms, and at 0241 hours on the morning of 7 May the act of surrender was signed by Jodl on behalf of the German High Command. My Chief of Staff signed for me, and Maj. Gen. Ivan Suslaparov signed for the Soviet High Command. General Savez of the French Army, Deputy Chief of Staff for National Defense, signed as witness. The terms were to become effective at midnight, 8/9 May.

In addition to the act of military surrender, Jodl signed an undertaking that the Chief of the German High Command, with the Commanders-in-Chief of the Army, Navy, and Air Force, would appear at a time and place to be designated by the Soviet High Command and myself for the purpose of executing formal ratification of the unconditional surrender on behalf of the German High Command. This meeting was held in Berlin on the night of 9 May, when Air Chief Marshal Tedder signed on my behalf, and Marshal Zhukov for the Soviet High Command. General Spaatz of the US Air Forces and General de Lattre de Tassigny (representing the French Government) were present as witnesses.

With this final capitulation by the German leaders, the mission of the Allied Expeditionary Force placed under my supreme command on 14 February 1944 was accomplished.

CONCLUSION

In attempting very briefly to assess the factors underlying the Allied success in this campaign, I would
stress the importance of three episodes as being the
most decisive in ensuring victory.

The first of these was the battle of the Normandy
beaches. We sailed for France, possessed of all the tactical information which an efficient intelligence
service could provide, but we had yet to take the
measure of the foe we were to meet. We were

embarking upon the largest amphibious operation in history against a coastline bristling with all the defenses modern ingenuity could devise, and behind the beaches lay the German armies of the west which had not been tried in full-scale battle since the dark days of 1940.

As we struggled first to gain and then to hold our footing in Normandy, we learned the strength and also the weakness of these armies. We learned that the German soldier was still the same stubborn fighter whom we had met in Africa and in Italy, but we saw, too, how slender was the thread upon which his existence in France depended. During the months of June and July all the difficulties of communications and supply which were ultimately to prove his undoing became manifest. It was thus that we were enabled to establish ourselves on the Continent and to build up the great armies necessary to achieve the liberation of Europe. We learned also, at this time, how inadequate was the enemy's intelligence concerning the Allied intentions. Thanks to his air weakness and consequent lack of reconnaissance, he was completely misled by our diversionary operations, holding back until too late the forces in the Pas-de-Calais which, had they been rushed across the Seine when first we landed, might well have turned the scales against us.

The second vital battle was that of the Falaise pocket. Here the enemy showed that fatal tendency to stand and fight when all the logic of war demanded a strategic withdrawal. By so doing, he allowed his Seventh Army to be encircled and ground to pieces, and the battle for France was decided among the bloody orchards and hedgerows of Normandy. As the broken forces fled eastward we strained every effort to complete their overthrow before they could reach the shelter of the Siegfried Line, but the logistical burden was too great, and we had to wait until the weary winter drew to a close before we could strike the final blow.

The third decisive phase in the campaign consisted of the battles west of the Rhine during February and March. Once again the enemy played into our hands by his insistence upon fighting the battle where he stood. In the lowland country between the Rhine and the Meuse, in the Eifel, and in the Saar, the armies which had been intended to defend Germany were shattered beyond recovery. The potential barrier of the Rhine lay practically undefended before us, and from that time onwards there was no German force in existence capable of halting our forward march. The war was won before the Rhine was crossed.

Throughout the struggle, it was in his logistical inability to maintain his armies in the field that the enemy's fatal weakness lay. Courage his forces had in full measure, but courage was not enough. Reinforcements failed to arrive, weapons, ammunition, and food alike ran short, and the dearth of fuel caused their powers of tactical mobility to dwindle to the vanishing point. In the last stages of the campaign they could do little more than wait for the Allied avalanche to sweep over them.

For this state of affairs we had, above all, to be grateful to the work of the Allied air forces. Long before we landed in France, the heavy bombers had begun their task of destroying the centers of production upon which the enemy relied, and the fruits of this effort were evident immediately the land campaign began. Following the invasion, these strategic blows at the heart of German industry were continued, and the task was also undertaken of cutting the supply lines which linked the factories to the fronts. Meanwhile the tactical aircraft, by their incessant bombing and strafing of the enemy before us in the field, broke his powers of resistance and prepared the way for the ground advances which struck toward the center of Germany. Those thrusts, moreover, were made with a rapidity which only the expedient of airborne supply could support. The overwhelming Allied superiority in the air was indeed essential to our victory. It at once undermined the basis of the enemy's strength and enabled us to prepare and execute our own ground operations in complete security.

It is difficult even for a professional soldier to appreciate the tremendous power which was achieved on the battlefields and in the skies of Western Europe by the concerted efforts of the Allied Nations. As stated earlier in this report, most of the 90 divisions which fought in the later phases of our operations were habitually reinforced to a strength of 17,000 men by tank, tank destroyer, and anti-aircraft attachments. An idea of their shattering impact upon the

Nazi war machine comes from consideration of the terrific firepower which they represent, of the mass of heavier Corps and Army artillery which supported them, of the inexhaustible supply system that sustained them, and of the flexibility with which their efforts could be applied by means of the efficient communications system. For behind the combat units the efforts of three millions of other men and women in uniform were devoted to maintaining them in action. We could, in effect, apply against the enemy on the Continent a force 30 times as large as the Allied armies which defeated Napoleon on the battlefield at Waterloo. In addition, we had available nearly 11,000 fighter and bomber airplanes whose mobile firepower could be applied at virtually any point we desired, as I have just described, and whose annihilating effects are evidenced by the wreckage of a powerful nation's cities, industries and communications, and by the destruction of the air forces which defended them. To this power was added the striking and strangling force of two formidable naval fleets working as one.

Mention has already been made of the skill and devotion of our service forces whose efforts, both in the field and at home, made an essential contribution to our victory. To them, and to the civilian workers of factory and farm who provided us with unstinted means, we are forever indebted. Our enormous material superiority gave us an unchallengeable advantage over our foes. While Germany's own war potential crumbled, that of the Allies rose to heights unprecedented. No army or navy was ever supported so generously or so well. Never, during the entire campaign, were we forced to fight a major battle without the weapons that were needed.

More important even than the weapons, however, was the indomitable fighting spirit of the men of the Allied nations who wielded them. The courage and devotion to duty which they exhibited throughout the campaign, in the grim days of the Ardennes counter-offensive as well as in the excitement of the dash across France and later the advances into the midst of Germany, were unsurpassable. It was the spirit that had enabled them to withstand the shocks of Dunkirk and Pearl Harbor which brought us at the last to Lübeck, to Torgau, and to Berchtesgaden.

Underlying this invincibility of spirit was the confidence in Allied unity and the justice of the common cause which permeated all who were engaged, directly or indirectly, in the struggle. The comradeship which had been first exemplified in North Africa carried us to new triumphs in Northwest Europe. Within my own headquarters the American and British personnel worked harmoniously together, obliterating all distinction of national outlook in their zealous service to a single organization, while in the field of battle the men of the Allied armies fought shoulder to shoulder under my supreme command.

Those civilian volunteers who shared the rigors and dangers of campaign that they might brighten the existence of our men have the assurance of our warmest gratitude.

The United States of America and Great Britain have worked, not merely as Allies, but as one nation, pooling their resources of men and material alike, in this struggle against the forces of evil engendered by Hitler's Germany. In the Expeditionary Forces which it has been my privilege to lead, both in the Mediterranean Theater and in Northwest Europe, an Allied experiment unprecedented in the history of the world has been carried out with decisive results.

In concluding this report it is with regret that I am unable to record here the details of my personal and official obligations and gratitude to those who served so devotedly at Supreme Headquarters and at the other headquarters which cooperated so loyally and effectively with us. Nor can I make adequate recognition of the collaboration of those many individuals in civil and military positions in Great Britain and the United States with whom my duties brought me into contact, and whose efforts aided in a major degree the accomplishment of our common task. Yet I know that all these would have me pay a final tribute to the memory of two very senior and gallant officers who started the campaign with us and who lost their lives before its conclusion. These were Admiral Sir Bertram H. Ramsay of the Royal Navy, and Air Chief Marshal Sir Trafford Leigh-Mallory of the Royal Air Force. At the beginning of the operation these officers were respectively my Naval Commander-in-Chief and my Air Commander-in-Chief. The former lost his life in an airplane accident near Versailles, France, while still serving in the same capacity. The latter, relieved from my Command to take over the Allied Air Forces in Southeast Asia, was lost in an airplane accident near Grenoble, France. The war service, the devotion to duty, and the sacrifice of these two outstanding men typify the irreplaceable cost of the campaign represented in the lives of thousands of officers and enlisted men and members of the women's services, of the American, British, and French forces.

All of them died in the spirit of that unity which joined the Allies in our common ideals. To them, and to those who still bear the wounds of battle, we, their comrades in arms, render most grateful and humble tribute.

Under the arrangements made by the Combined Chiefs of Staff for the control of the field forces, General of the Army George C. Marshall acted as their executive in transmitting to me their orders and instructions. Moreover, under that most distinguished Secretary of War, Henry L. Stimson, General Marshall was always my direct administrative superior in my capacity as a Commander of United States Army forces. To this great soldier-statesman, I owe a particular debt for his friendly counsel and constant support. There was nothing throughout the war so morally sustaining as the knowledge that General Marshall concurred in the plans I was adopting and the means I was taking to put them into effect.

Dwight D. Eisenhower

DWIGHT D. EISENHOWER,
SUPREME COMMANDER,
ALLIED EXPEDITIONARY FORCE

13 *July*, 1945

Other titles in the series

The Amritsar Massacre: General Dyer in the Punjab, 1919

"We feel that General Dyer, by adopting an inhuman and un-British method of dealing with subjects of His Majesty the King-Emperor, has done great disservice to the interest of British rule in India. This aspect it was not possible for the people of the mentality of General Dyer to realise."

Backdrop

At the time of the events described, India was under British rule. Indians had fought alongside the British in World War I, and had made tremendous financial contributions to the British war effort. Mahatma Gandhi was the leader of the Indian National Congress party, which was seeking independence from the British Empire.

The Book

This is the story of the action taken by Brigadier-General Dyer at Amritsar in the Punjab in 1919. Faced with insurrection in support of Mahatma Gandhi, the British Army attempted to restore order. General Dyer, on arriving in the troubled city of Amritsar, issued an order banning any assembly of more than four people. Consequently, when he discovered a large crowd gathered together during a cattle fair, he took the astonishing action of shooting more than three hundred unarmed people. Regarding the subsequent native obedience as a satisfactory result, he was surprised to find himself removed from command a year later, and made lengthy representations to Parliament.

ISBN 0 11 702412 0   Price £6.99

British Battles of World War I, 1914–15

"The effect of these poisonous gases was so virulent as to render the whole of the line held by the French Division incapable of any action at all. It was at first impossible for anyone to realise what had actually happened. The smoke and fumes hid everything from sight, and hundreds of men were thrown into a comatose or dying condition, and within an hour the whole position had to be abandoned, together with about 50 guns."

Backdrop

On 4 August 1914, Britain declared war on Germany. Germany had already invaded Belgium and France and was progressing towards Paris.

The Book

These are the despatches from some of the battles of the first two years of World War I. They include action in northern France, Germany, Gallipoli, and even as far afield as the Cocos Islands in the Indian Ocean. They describe the events of battle, the tremendous courage, the huge losses, and the confusions and difficulties of war. These startling accounts, which were written by the generals at the front, were first published in the "London Gazette", the official newspaper of Parliament.

ISBN 0 11 702447 3   Price £6.99

Florence Nightingale and the Crimea, 1854–55

"By an oversight, no candles were included among the stores brought to the Crimea. Lamps and wicks were brought but not oil. These omissions were not supplied until after possession had been taken of Balaklava, and the purveyor had an opportunity of purchasing candles and oil from the shipping and the dealers in the town."

Backdrop

The British Army arrived in the Crimea in 1854, ill-equipped to fight a war in the depths of a Russian winter.

The Book

The hospital service for wounded soldiers during the Crimean War was very poor and became the subject of concern, not just in the army, but also in the press. "The Times" was publishing letters from the families of soldiers describing the appalling conditions. This embarrassed the government, but even more it irritated the army, which did not know how to cope with such open scrutiny of its activities.

The book is a collection of extracts from government papers published in 1855 and 1856. Their selection provides a snapshot of events at that time. In particular they focus on the terrible disaster that was the Charge of the Light Brigade, and the inadequate provisions that were made for the care of the sick and wounded. The documents relating to the hospitals at Scutari include evidence from Florence Nightingale herself.

ISBN 0 11 702425 2   Price £6.99

Lord Kitchener and Winston Churchill: The Dardanelles Commission Part I, 1914–15

"The naval attack on the Narrows was never resumed. It is difficult to understand why the War Council did not meet between 19th March and 14th May. The failure of the naval attack showed the necessity of abandoning the plan of forcing the passage of the Dardanelles by purely naval operation. The War Council should then have met and considered the future policy to be pursued."

Backdrop

The Dardanelles formed part of the main southern shipping route to Russia, and was of great military and strategic importance. However, it had long been recognised by the British naval and military authorities that any attack on the Dardanelles would be an operation fraught with great difficulties.

The Book

During the early stages of World War I, Russia made a plea to her allies to make a demonstration against the Turks. So attractive was the prize of the Dardanelles to the British generals, notably Lord Kitchener, that this ill-fated campaign was launched. Just how powerful an influence Kitchener was to exert over the War Council, and just how ill-prepared the Allies were to conduct such an attack, are revealed in dramatic detail in the report of this Commission.

The book covers the first part of the Commission's report. It deals with the origin, inception and conduct of operations in the Dardanelles from the beginning of the war in August 1914 until March 1915, when the idea of a purely naval attack was abandoned.

ISBN 0 11 702423 6   Price £6.99

The Russian Revolution, 1917

"It is the general opinion in Ekaterinburg that the Empress, her son, and four daughters were not murdered, but were despatched on the 17th July to the north or the west. The story that they were burnt in a house seems to be an exaggeration of the fact that in a wood outside the town was found a heap of ashes, apparently the result of burning a considerable amount of clothing. At the bottom of the ashes was a diamond, and, as one of the Grand Duchesses is said to have sewn a diamond into the lining of her cloak, it is supposed that the clothes of the Imperial family were burnt there."

Backdrop

By November 1917 Russia had lost more than twenty million people in the war. Lenin's Bolshevik party had overthrown the Tsar and had called for an end to all capitalist governments.

The Book

Government files contain a number of detailed documents describing the nature of the Bolshevik Revolution and the government of Lenin, which was observed to be not only abhorrent but also menacing because of the international implications. The book is compiled from two of these files, one of which describes the events leading up to the revolution and how the Bolsheviks came to power in October 1917. The other contains a series of eye-witness accounts of the frightening days of the Bolshevik regime from the summer of 1918 to April 1919.

ISBN 0 11 702424 4   Price £6.99

UFOs in the House of Lords, 1979

"Is it not time that Her Majesty's Government informed our people of what they know about UFOs? The UFOs have been coming in increasing numbers for 30 years since the war, and I think it is time our people were told the truth. We have not been invaded from outer space. Most incidents have not been hostile. Indeed it is us, the earthlings, who have fired on them. . . . Whatever the truth is, I am sure that an informed public is a prepared one. Another thing: it is on record that both sighting and landing reports are increasing all the time. Just suppose the 'ufonauts' decided to make mass landings tomorrow in this country—there could well be panic here, because our people have not been prepared."

Backdrop
The winter of 1978/79 in Britain was a time of strikes and unrest. It became known as the "winter of discontent". Yet it seems that the House of Lords had other more important things to discuss.

The Book
The book is the transcript of a debate in the House of Lords which took place in February 1979. Their Lordships debated the need for an international initiative in response to the problem of Unidentified Flying Objects. There were several notable speeches from noble lords and distinguished prelates.

ISBN 0 11 702413 9   Price £6.99

The Irish Uprising, 1914–21: Papers from the British Parliamentary Archive

"Captain Bowen-Colthurst adopted the extraordinary, and indeed almost meaningless, course of taking Mr Sheehy Skeffington with him as a 'hostage'. He had no right to take Mr Sheehy Skeffington out of the custody of the guard for this or any other purpose, and he asked no one's leave to do so. . . . Before they left the barracks Mr Sheehy Skeffington's hands were tied behind his back and Captain Bowen-Colthurst called upon him to say his prayers. Upon Mr Sheehy Skeffington refusing to do so Captain Bowen-Colthurst ordered the men of his party to take their hats off and himself uttered a prayer, the words of it being: 'O Lord God, if it shall please thee to take away the life of this man, forgive him for Christ's sake.' "

Backdrop

In 1914 it was still the case that the whole of Ireland was part of Great Britain, under the dominion of the King, and Irish constituencies were represented in the British Parliament.

The Book

This book contains five remarkable documents published by the British Government between 1914 and 1921, relating to the events leading up to the partition of Ireland in 1921. In the first, a report is made into the shooting of civilians following a landing of arms at Howth outside Dublin. The second is of the papers discovered relating to the activities of Sinn Fein and particularly of Sir Roger Casement. The third is the government inquiry into the Easter Rising of 1916. The fourth describes the treatment of three journalists by the British Army shortly after the uprising, and the last is an exchange of correspondence between Eamon de Valera and David Lloyd George prior to the Anglo–Irish Treaty of 1921.

ISBN 0 11 702415 5   Price £6.99

The Siege of the Peking Embassy, 1900

"I cannot conclude this despatch without saying a word of praise respecting the ladies of all nationalities who so ably and devotedly assisted the defence, notwithstanding the terrible shadow which at all times hung over the legation—a shadow which the never-ceasing rattle of musketry and crash of round shot and shell and the diminishing number of defenders rendered ever present. They behaved with infinite patience and cheerfulness, helping personally in the hospital or, in making sandbags and bandages, and in assisting in every possible way the work of defence. Especially commended are two young ladies—Miss Myers and Miss Daisy Brazier—who daily filtered the water for the hospital, in tropical heat, and carried it with bullets whistling and shells bursting in the trees overhead." Sir Claude MacDonald

Backdrop

The Boxer movement in China was a secret society which preached hatred of foreigners. By the spring of 1900, this movement was out of control. On 9 June, the Boxers launched their first attack against foreign property in Peking by burning down the racecourse. On 19 June, all foreigners were order to evacuate Peking within 24 hours. The order was not complied with.

The Book

As events worsened for the diplomats and their families in Peking, Sir Claude MacDonald, the British ambassador, wired the Admiralty in Taku to request the immediate despatch of a relief force. Just how that relief force fared, and how the hundreds of diplomats and their families who were stranded inside the Legation buildings coped with the rigours of the siege, are the subject of the diplomatic papers presented in this book. The central part of the story is the gripping diary of events kept by Sir Claude MacDonald.

ISBN 0 11 702456 2   Price £6.99

The Siege of Kars, 1855

"We had, up to that date, suffered from cold, want of sufficient clothing, and starvation, without a murmur escaping from the troops. They fell dead at their posts, in their tents, and throughout the camp as brave men should who cling to their duty through the slightest glimmering of hope of saving a place entrusted to their custody. From the day of their glorious victory on 29th September, they had not tasted animal food, and their nourishment consisted of two-fifths of a ration of bread and the roots of grass, which they scarcely had the strength to dig for; yet night and day they stood to their arms, their wasted frames showing the fearful effects of starvation, but their sparkling eye telling me what they would do were the enemy to attack them again." W. F. Williams

Backdrop
In 1855, while the British Army was fighting alongside the French and the Turkish armies in the Crimean War, a little-known but serious siege was taking place in the city of Kars in eastern Turkey. Set within mountains and overlooking a gorge, Kars is a natural fortress, but its possession by the Turks was threatened by the Russians.

The Book
During the Crimean War, the British were giving aid to the Turkish army by lending them generals to help organise and strengthen their garrisons. General Williams had arrived in Kars in September 1854, having been appointed British Military Commissioner with the Turkish Army in Asia. He soon began organising the troops there, although his repeated requests for supplies and reinforcements were met with delay and obfuscation. These despatches concerning the siege of Kars date from May 1855. Their unfolding tells a sorry tale of heroism and frustrated hope.

ISBN 0 11 702454 6   Price £6.99

Defeat at Gallipoli: The Dardanelles Commission
Part II, 1915–16

"It has been represented ... that from a military point of view, the Dardanelles Expedition, even if unsuccessful, was justified by the fact that it neutralised or contained a large number of Turkish troops who otherwise would have been free to operate elsewhere. Lord Kitchener estimated this number as being nearly 300,000. But in containing the Turkish force, we employed ... a total of at least 400,000. Our casualties amounted to 31,389 killed, 78,749 wounded and 9,708 missing, making a total of 119,846. The expedition also involved heavy financial expenditure and the employment of a considerable naval force."

Backdrop

The naval attempt by the British to force the Dardanelles was abandoned in March 1915. Rather than losing face, the military commanders decided to send a large army to the area.

The Book

Picking up the story from where the earlier volume, *Lord Kitchener and Winston Churchill*, left off, this second part of the Dardanelles Commission's report deals with the disastrous military campaign to capture the Gallipoli Peninsula using ground forces. As the story unfolds, we learn how the Allies were unable to make any headway against an enemy who was well prepared and well positioned. Within a few months the Allies had suffered a humiliating defeat, and thousands of men had lost their lives. The realisation of the government's incompetence in handling this affair was instrumental in the removal of Herbert Asquith as Prime Minister in December 1916.

ISBN 0 11 702455 4   Price £6.99

The Judgement of Nuremberg, 1946

"Efficient and enduring intimidation can only be achieved either by Capital Punishment or by measures by which the relatives of the criminal and the population do not know the fate of the criminal. This aim is achieved when the criminal is transferred to Germany."

Backdrop
World War II is over, there is a climate of jubilation and optimism as the Allies look to rebuilding Europe for the future but the perpetrators of Nazi war crimes have still to be reckoned with, and the full extent of their atrocities is as yet widely unknown.

The Book
Today, we have lived with the full knowledge of the extent of Nazi atrocities for over half a century and yet they still retain their power to shock. Imagine what it was like as they were being revealed in the full extent of their horror for the first time. In this book the judges at the Nuremberg Trials take it in turn to describe the indictments handed down to the defendants and their crimes. The entire history, purpose and method of the Nazi party since its foundation in 1918 are revealed and described in chilling detail.

ISBN 0 11 702406 6   Price £6.99